Chekhov and Russian Religious Culture

Chekhov and Russian Religious Culture

The Poetics of the Marian Paradigm

Julie W. de Sherbinin

NORTHWESTERN UNIVERSITY PRESS / EVANSTON, ILLINOIS

Northwestern University Press
Evanston, Illinois 60208-4210

Copyright © 1997 by Northwestern University Press. Published 1997.
All rights reserved.
Printed in the United States of America

ISBN 0-8101-1404-6

Library of Congress Cataloging-in-Publication Data

De Sherbinin, Julie W.
 Chekhov and Russian religious culture : the poetics of the Marian
paradigm / Julie W. de Sherbinin.
  p. cm. — (Studies in Russian literature and theory)
 Includes bibliographical references and index.
 ISBN 0–8101-1404–6 (cloth : alk. paper)
  1. Chekhov, Anton Pavlovich, 1860–1904—Knowledge— Christianity.
2. Christianity in literature. 3. Mary, Blessed Virgin, Saint—In
literature. 4. Mary Magdalene, Saint—In literature. 5. Mary, of
Egypt, Saint—In literature. I. Title. II. Series.
PG3458.Z9C454 1997
891.73'3—dc21   97–19248
                                                              CIP

The paper used in this publication meets the minimum requirements of the
American National Standard for Information Sciences—Permanence of Paper
for Printed Library Materials, ANSI Z39.48–1984.

For my parents, Polly R. and Michael J. de Sherbinin

Contents

Acknowledgments   ix

Note on Transliteration, Translation, and Citation   xi

List of Illustrations   xiii

Introduction   1

Chapter One: Two Marys: Chekhov's Religious and Literary Heritage   13

Chapter Two: Early Prose: Genesis of the Marian Context   45

Chapter Three: The Two Marys in Four Stories   67

Chapter Four: Distortion of Text in "Peasant Women"   89

Chapter Five: The Nature of Illusion in "The Teacher of Literature"   107

Chapter Six: The Nature of Conviction in "My Life"   125

Final Remarks   143

Appendix   151

Notes   153

Selected Bibliography   177

Index   185

Acknowledgments

I have benefited from the generosity of many scholars and friends. Several colleagues kindly read the entire manuscript. Patricia Carden supplied unerringly helpful advice on content and style with unerring good humor. Michael Finke offered countless welcome suggestions that have greatly enriched this book. Katherine Tiernan O'Connor shared her invariably stimulating reflections on Chekhov. I gained a great deal from discussions with Jane Costlow, Cathy Popkin, Nancy Ries, Laurel Schneider, and Wallace Sherlock. For their responses to an early draft of Chapter 6, I am indebted to A. P. Chudakov, V. B. Kataev, and I. N. Sukhikh. A. P. Kuzicheva and E. A. Polotskaia deserve special note for their helpfulness and hospitality. To Susan Haskins goes my immense appreciation for reviewing the discussion of the "sinful" Marys. Willa Chamberlain Axelrod's dissertation led me to sources on Chekhov and Christianity that I might otherwise not have found, and George Pahomov helped identify several lines from Orthodox prayers. N. I. Rudakova of the Russian National Library in Saint Petersburg assisted in the location of *lubok* prints of Saint Mary of Egypt. L. A. Voronova of the Tretiakov Gallery in Moscow expeditiously accommodated my requests for photoreproductions of two icons. Olga Smirnova and Ramiz Akhundov assisted me in Moscow; in Saint Petersburg, Masha Soloveichik tracked down a number of important books and translated parts of the manuscript into Russian.

Three scholars have shaped my thinking on Chekhov and have offered sustained support to this effort. Robert Louis Jackson first tuned my ear to the inner stuff of literature; I followed his tracks from Dostoevsky to Chekhov and thank him many times over for all he has given me. Marena Senderovich laid the foundation for my understanding of Chekhov; her premature death in 1996 has impoverished the scholarly world and has left me personally bereaved. I would like to express my profound gratitude to Savely Senderovich, who blazed the trail to the Chekhov in this book. He has been unstintingly generous with time and has commented on my work with breathtaking precision and depth of thought. Needless to say, all infelicities in argumentation and presentation are my own.

I am grateful to Caryl Emerson for her support of this project and to Susan Harris, editor-in-chief at Northwestern University Press, with whom it has been a unqualified pleasure to work. Ellen Feldman and Betty Waterhouse did a marvelous job with manuscript production. Tanya Churilina can be credited with a meticulously compiled index.

Thanks, finally, to family members and friends who took an active interest in this project. First among them are my parents, my treasured siblings, and their families. Supportive from the outset were several dear friends: Philip Bennett, Wendy Kohli, Nancy Ries, and Jon and Anna Rosen. My thanks for steady words of encouragement go as well to Elsa Aegerter, Catherine Besteman, Sheila Cooley and Mark Fagan, Victor Donnai, the Hall family, Patricia Kane, Robin and Dan Moriarty, Peter Rice, and Alison and Jim Webb.

An earlier version of Chapter 5 appeared in *Reading Chekhov's Text* (Evanston: Northwestern University Press, 1993). My article on "Peasants" in *Anton P. Chekhov: Philosophische und religioese Dimensionen im Leben und im Werk* (Munich: Otto Sagner, 1997) replicates a portion of Chapter 4. Several passages in the Introduction and Chapter 3 first appeared in "Chekhov and Christianity: The Critical Evolution," in *Chekhov Then and Now* (New York: Peter Lang, 1997). Research on this book was facilitated significantly by an A. D. White Fellowship at Cornell University, by the International Research and Exchanges Board, and by Colby College Humanities Grants. I thank the Office of the Dean of the Faculty at Colby College for funding compilation of the index and for providing a generous subvention to defray the cost of illustrations.

Note on Transliteration, Translation, and Citation

The Library of Congress transliteration system is used throughout. Names commonly anglicized, such as Dostoevsky and Tolstoy, have been so rendered here. The Russian "Mariia" and "Mar'ia" become "Maria" when there is a concrete referent, but "Mary" in reference to the Virgin and the Christian saints.

All translations are my own unless otherwise noted. Titles of Chekhov stories are cited in English and are accompanied by a transliteration of the Russian title and publication date (1) when first mentioned in the text, and (2) at the outset of an analysis of the work. In footnotes, stories are cited in English only and the date of publication is provided.

Citations from Chekhov's prose come from A. P. Chekhov, *Polnoe sobranie sochinenii i pisem v tridtsati tomakh* (Moscow: "Nauka," 1974–83). The volume and page number following each citation refer to Part 1 (vols. 1–18) of the Complete Works. Citations from the letters (Part 2 of the Complete Works) are indicated in endnotes.

List of Illustrations

Figure 1. Icon of the Crucifixion.

Figure 2. Acathist to the Most Holy Mother of God. First two kontakion and ikos verses.

Figure 3. Icon of Saint Mary of Egypt with Scenes from Her Life.

Figure 4. *Lubok* print of Saint Mary of Egypt with Scenes from Her Life.

Figure 5. Icon of the Mother of God, Uncut Mountain.

Figure 6. Icon of the Annunciation.

Когда великое свершалось торжество
И в муках на кресте кончалось вожество,
Тогда по сторонам животворяща древа
Мария-грешниса и пресвятая дева
Стояли, вледные, две славые жены,
В неизмеримую печаль погружены.

(When the great triumph took place
And in torment on the cross the divine being died,
On each side of the life-giving cross
Maria the Sinful Woman and the Most Holy Virgin
Stood, two pallid and frail women,
Engrossed in immeasurable grief.)

A. S. Pushkin, "Earthly Authority" (1836)

Introduction

IN HIS POEM of 1836 describing Christ's crucifixion, Pushkin wrote, "On each side of the life-giving cross / Maria the Sinful Woman and the Most Holy Virgin/Stood, two pallid and frail women, / Engrossed in immeasurable grief." This image of the two Marys was frequently depicted on Orthodox icons of the Crucifixion (see Fig. 1) and "Chairete," or Christ's appearance to the Virgin Mary and Mary Magdalene. It represents a pairing central to Christian thinking about female identity, the familiar paradigm of the virgin and the whore. The paradigmatic nature of the relationship is conveyed by the common name. In Russian Orthodoxy Saint Mary of Egypt bears the stamp of the harlot assigned (mistakenly) to Saint Mary Magdalene in the West. These two figures form a symbolic nexus, sometimes intimated, sometimes explicit, in the prose of Anton Pavlovich Chekhov.

Chekhov was the Russian writer most conversant with the rites and texts of Orthodoxy, as jarring as such a claim might seem given the centrality of Christian thought to the giants of nineteenth-century Russian letters. He received a strict religious upbringing in provincial Taganrog, where he sang in the church choir and endured the rigors of his father's enforced domestic prayer regime. The reminiscences of Chekhov's two brothers, Aleksandr and Mikhail, document a boyhood filled with long hours of choir practice, performance of weekly services, lengthy holiday liturgies, and the compulsory home readings of Scripture aloud, all orchestrated by the family patriarch, Pavel Egorovich Chekhov.[1] Mikhail, commenting on Chekhov's parodic treatment of the Orthodox marriage ceremony in *Tatiana Repina* (a play based entirely on church liturgy), reports that his brother maintained a library of service books to consult as he was writing (12:365).[2] Chekhov exhibited a verbatim memory of liturgy as well, evidence of an exacting religious training. In a letter to a fellow writer, he confidently rectifies an error in ecclesiastical usage: "At the end of the story the sacristan (this is very nice and apropos) sings: 'Bless, O my soul, O Lord, and be joyful.' . . . There is no such prayer. There is one

1

that goes like this: 'Bless the Lord, O my soul and all that is within me bless His Holy Name.' "[3]

I argue in this book that Chekhov fully grasped the authority that the Christian paradigm of the two Marys wielded in Russian culture. Chekhov would have become thoroughly familiar in his youth with the qualities of the Virgin Mary, Mother of God, and Saint Mary of Egypt as they are conveyed by the Orthodox service and iconography. Throughout his career, these figures are recalled in his prose explicitly and as background or shadow prototypes, evoked by the language characters use or by narrative configurations. Cognizant of the significance assumed by the meaning of names in the Orthodox tradition (a phenomenon stemming from Hebrew custom and reflected in the Russian practice of celebrating the nameday of the saint for whom one was named instead of observing birthdays), Chekhov would not have assigned the name "Maria" to characters in stories that refer as well to Marian holidays, Scripture, icons, acathists (doxological prayers sung in honor of the Mother of God), the life of Saint Mary of Egypt, and "sinful women" without at least some awareness of the symbolic repercussions. (The vexing question of intention will be addressed below.) But Chekhov indisputably breaks with literary convention in at least two respects: he does not portray virginal or seductive heroines as offshoots of their religious prototypes, nor does he attach any consistent set of metaphorical significations to the figures.[4]

A writer attracted to paradoxes, Chekhov understood the irony of an idealized Mother of God who stands inaccessibly "Alone of All Her Sex" and who represents what Julia Kristeva calls "one of the most powerful imaginary constructs known in the history of civilizations."[5] He recognized as paradoxical, too, the persistent synonymy in the popular mind of Saint Mary Magdalene and Saint Mary of Egypt with "fallen women" and prostitution despite their religious status as exalted saints. Contradictory sexual identities mark both poles of the paradigm, neither of which accommodates biological reproduction: the "Virgin Bride" remains sexually untainted even as she bears a child, while the lustful Saint Mary of Egypt remains barren. These many paradoxes provide fertile ground for Chekhov's unique approach to the Marian theme.

In his study of the mytheme of Saint George the Dragonslayer in Chekhov's life and work, Savely Senderovich demonstrates that Christian legends and iconography do not function in a straightforward manner in Chekhov's prose. Rather, they appear in a variety of transposed forms, subject to reversals, inversions, and displacements.[6] Transposition is key, too, in Chekhov's treatment of the two Marys. His "Maria" characters, and sometimes those adjacent to them, are subversively linked to the prototypal Marian roles through ingenious detours around the Christian projections of virtue and sin.

Chekhov interrogates the Marian cultural prism, through which women are so readily perceived and/or perceive themselves, and exposes a host of diverse interpretations—sometimes at complete odds with religious norms—derived by individuals from the Christian dictates about women. In other words, Chekhov charts the erosion of the Orthodox constructs of female identity that intend to offer a viable model for women's comportment. This study, then, investigates the cultural psychology behind the Marian figures when they are translated into the vernacular of quotidian life.

Religious traditions and cultural values are transmitted through language and texts. Consequently, Chekhov's emphasis on the way that texts are received by characters within his works garners special attention in my analyses. In general, the wealth of intertextual allusions, literary references, inserted texts, and rich use of language in Chekhov's prose has only recently begun to receive the concentrated attention it is due. Chekhov plays extensively with popular configurations of Christian discourse, addressing both the comic possibilities of religious linguistic formulas gone awry in the speech of the common person and the tragic consequences of an inflexible church language that discounts the need for individual self-expression. Underlying these observations is a profound awareness of what Bakhtin identifies as the authoritarian discourse of the biblical idiom, a monologic language that does not invite interlocution.[7] Bakhtin, in speaking of the uses to which the authoritative word of the Bible was put in the Middle Ages, locates at one end of a spectrum of meanings "the pious and inert quotation that is isolated and set off like an icon."[8] For Chekhov, conscious or unconscious allegiance to any textual system of fixed meaning, be it Scripture or icon, operates as an impediment to self-awareness, a force most often destructive to self and others. In this sense, this book is not only about Chekhov and the Russian Orthodox religious tradition, but also about Chekhov's skeptical view of *orthodoxies* in Russian life.

Quite often Chekhov's characters misconstrue or ignore the prescribed meanings of religious discourse and iconography. These languages may figure as reference points for plot configurations and character; subjected to interpretation, however, they yield unexpected results. What interests Chekhov is how, as Roland Barthes puts it, "the number of readings of the same lexical unit or *lexia* (of the same image) varies according to individuals."[9] In a (post)modern spirit of semiotics, Chekhov shows how the boundaries of meaning expand as individuals budge "unequivocal" texts in directions that suit personal exigency or tend to psychological needs. Needless to say, this is a highly un-Orthodox position.

The critical eye Chekhov brings to Christianity by no means makes of him its sworn detractor. Certainly the oft-cited lines from his letters— "I no longer have religion," "when you perform an autopsy, even the most inveterate spiritualist has to wonder where the soul is"[10]—establish an absence of formal church allegiance. They provide, however, slim grounds upon which to prove that Chekhov was an atheist, or, in any event, that he was antagonistic toward religion.[11] Commentary in his correspondence overall must be handled contextually: his letters are not only characterized by complex tonalities (respect, scorn, irony, lightheartedness, false humility, and so forth), but were composed for an audience of one and are visited in toto by many inconsistencies and contradictions.[12]

On the other hand, those who would sculpt Chekhov as a believer have also to fumble in order to reconcile the ambivalent yield of his work. Turn-of-the-century Orthodox critics solved this problem by selectively attributing to Chekhov the words of "spiritual" characters (Ivan Velikopolsky, Lipa, the Bishop).[13] Another strategy is voiced by A. Izmailov, who comes to the awkward conclusion that "Chekhov wished for faith with his heart, while judging it with his intellect, and envied the faithful."[14] Any number of scholars subsequently bridge the gap between Chekhov's obvious lack of conventional religious convictions and his commitment to humanitarian activity (a commitment that looks very much like Christian philanthropy) by assigning him faith of one sort or another: "faith in progress," "faith in science," "faith in man," "faith in art." The position of D. S. Merezhkovsky adds further grist to the mill. Merezhkovsky berates Chekhov for seeing in Christianity only a humanitarian subject, acridly accusing him of "walking past Christ without looking back."[15]

Chekhov rather aptly captures the essence of this critical debate about his religiosity in a notebook fragment: "An enormously vast field lies between 'God exists' and 'there is no God,'" he writes, "one that the true wise man traverses with great difficulty. A Russian knows one or the other of these two extremes, but is not interested in the middle ground" (17:33–34). Chekhov had an almost baffling talent for depicting with equal sensitivity spiritual epiphanies and nihilist cynicism. Simon Karlinsky comments about Chekhov that "in a literature that had produced Gogol, Tolstoy, Dostoyevsky and Leskov, the view that Christianity and religion in general are morally neutral is startling enough."[16] A "morally neutral" positioning on "middle ground" equips Chekhov with what might be called an ethnographic perspective on his own culture. By "ethnographic" I mean a concern for observing the ways in which people construct meaning through their language and from their surroundings, a concern Chekhov shares with the anthropologist.

Chekhov appreciated the extent to which the symbolic forms of Russian Orthodoxy permeated Russia's cultural mindset. He shares with his contemporary, Max Weber, who linked Calvinist doctrine to the flourishing of capitalism, the insight that the precepts of a religious culture can serve as a defining factor in the secular activity and thinking of a people. In fact,

4

Chekhov himself defines religious identity as a cultural construct: "Can such words as Orthodox, Jew, and Catholic really express some sort of exclusive personal virtues or merits? In my opinion, whether willingly or unwillingly, everyone should consider himself Orthodox who has that word written in his passport. Whether you are a believer or not, whether you are the prince of the world or an exiled convict, according to custom you are still Orthodox."[17]

These readings of the Christian context in Chekhov's prose, then, leave behind the question of the author's personal beliefs and address instead his understanding of Russian religious culture. But it is not the case that the "biblical images and citations, spiritual verse, descriptions of church rituals and religious holidays create a substantial 'cultural stratum' in the works of the writer [that] easily submits to scholarly analysis."[18] Rather, this cultural layer in Chekhov's writing represents one of the most interesting problems for interpretation. Recent scholarship has opened up new and thought-provoking vistas, deciphering symbolic meanings and semantic depths in the Christian imagery that for a hundred years was thought to reflect no more than the realia of nineteenth-century Russian life described by the quintessential realist.

Robert Louis Jackson has pioneered work on the symbolic ramifications of Chekhov's allusions to Christian texts. From his earliest reflections on the subject, Jackson has championed a deeply humanistic view of Chekhov, insisting that "to conceive of the tragedy of the Chekhovian hero in a Christian perspective violates both the maturity and the integrity of Chekhov's human-istic outlook."[19] In his analyses of a number of stories, most of which do not appear to have any obvious points of contact with the biblical world, Jackson uncovers scriptural reminiscences that illuminate the moral dilemmas and choices set before Chekhov's characters.[20] My study owes a great deal to the sensitivity Jackson displays in understanding the subtlety of Chekhov's art.

Savely Senderovich's work on the Christian context in Chekhov, from which this inquiry draws extensively, focuses on the manifestations of the religious mind in Russian popular culture. Senderovich first realized that a name in Chekhov that recurs in a number of texts throughout the writer's career can be symbolically charged, and that its elevated semantic status may be related to a broad religio-cultural complex of meaning. His innovative study of the Saint George mytheme in Chekhov's life and works motivated my investigation. The name "George" (and its many variations in Russian) enjoys a singular status in this respect; it signals a symbolic component of Chekhov's biography and his literary works.[21] Elements of the Saint George legend, how-ever, never appear in unaltered form in Chekhov's prose; they are consistently disguised through inversion, a device that "represents a means of penetrating into the other, unapparent side of things."[22] Senderovich's discoveries and insights concerning the functions of Christian texts in Chekhov's prose have served as an indispensable requisite to this exploration of the Marian theme.[23]

The work of Jackson and Senderovich promotes symbolic interpretations of Chekhov's prose, an approach freely granted other realists, but often withheld from Chekhov because of the naturalistic fallacy that has dominated the critical tradition. While these scholars differ in their vision of Chekhov, they both agree that the discovery of deeper strata of meaning in Chekhov depends on reading his texts with the attention accorded poetry.[24] Such a reading necessarily supposes the importance of close attention to the texture of language. Senderovich has formulated a semiotic theory of poetic prose that privileges the seemingly incidental as key to the meaning of the Chekhovian text. Recurrent semantic units on the lexical level form semantic series, and at the intersection of these series one discovers points of semantic condensation.[25] The structuralist grounding of this approach (in conjunction with a degree of scholarly intuition) commands a unique capacity to uncover intricate verbal associations that illuminate the symbolic planes behind the immediate narrative. As a heuristic strategy, this approach alerts the reader to the rich weave of the Chekhovian text that otherwise might not see the light of day. It requires that we adjust our eyes to the uncommon subtlety of the writer.

Another feature of poetry marks Chekhov's oeuvre as a whole. Much as in a cycle of poems, meaning associated with certain words, phrases, and images migrates from work to work. Marena Senderovich first demonstrated the "implicit semantic unities" that can connect stories exhibiting no readily apparent kinship.[26] Verbal migration patterns hold true, as well, not only for the Saint George mytheme, but, as Laurence Senelick has shown, for Chekhov's references to Offenbach's *La Belle Hélène,* as Michael Finke has demonstrated, for the motif of the katabatic journey, and, as Caryl Emerson has suggested, for the Tolstoyan "Anna" plot.[27] Each of these studies probes the ways in which a Chekhov text can be illuminated by attention to the cumulative meanings effected by a theme that surfaces repeatedly, each time in a unique form, in stories and dramatic works throughout the writer's career. In this consideration of Marian imagery, too, the totality is greater than the individual parts. Chekhov consistently reproduces configurations (frequently accompanied by reiterated verbal associations) in which signs of the Christian Marys appear adjacent to a fictional namesake.[28] Clearly a story's internal system of reference must provide the basis for a plausible analysis, yet cross-references to identical semantic groupings in other texts can at times impressively endorse an interpretation.

This brings us to the thorny issue of intention. Did Chekhov consciously incorporate these networks of images, or did involuntary cultural associations creep into his prose subliminally? While in many instances I am inclined toward the former view, the answer is by no means straightforward. Chekhov was notoriously close-mouthed about his understandings of his own work. His scanty notebooks, filled with miscellaneous anecdotes, pale beside the voluminous self-revelatory notebooks and diaries of many writers. Virtually no drafts exist that might map the thought processes of his work in progress. Chekhov regularly destroyed the drafts of his work, and extant corrections on galley-proofs consist largely of minor stylistic adjustments. In his letters, Chekhov is more likely to manufacture vivid disclaimers concerning the miserable flaws of his latest story than to pilot us toward its hidden reaches. Intention, then, remains a puzzle ultimately impossible to resolve authoritatively.

Sorting out the degree of calculation in Chekhov's references to Christianity depends, in large part, upon how the depth of those references is measured. If Chekhov's citation of Christian Scripture and allusions to Christian images are taken for something akin to the "real coin," as they have been in several recent studies, then the question of intention is resolved by stating or intimating that these references reveal authorial sympathies in accord with the values of the sacred, of moral betterment, redemption, and/or salvation.[29] If, however, as in the present study, an overall context is extrapolated from a few sparing details that point to inverted and redefined functions of those references, then a more enigmatic situation obtains in gauging intent. At stake is the plausibility of interpretations of Chekhov's use of language.

Roman Jakobson observes, "whether it concerns the unbeliever Pushkin, the heretic Blok or the anti-religious writings of Maiakovskii, Russian poets have grown up in a world of Orthodox customs, and their work is unwittingly saturated with the symbolism of the Eastern Church."[30] The work of the "poet" Chekhov, too, undoubtedly reflects the Orthodox world "unwittingly" at times. Senderovich identifies this modality—the author's unconscious use of the language of the culture—as one of four narrative modalities in which the Christian idiom appears in Chekhov. In the other cases (1) Chekhov may have the protagonist consciously manipulate religious language to serve his own ends; (2) the hero's unconscious usage of language may manipulate him; or (3) Chekhov may call upon religious language that belongs to idiomatic usage, the special (intended) significance of which is marked by an explicitly Christian motif artfully worked into the text.[31] The nuances of Chekhov's language, then, should be relied upon to steer interpretation.

The status of the Marian motif in Chekhov ranges broadly from conscious and deliberate beacons (the procession of the icon of the Life-Bearing Mother of God in "Peasants," for instance) to potentially quite unconscious associations (for example, the female pictorial image in "Maria Ivanovna"). Since, for reasons that can only be surmised, Chekhov's mind and pen preferred camouflage, the lighthandedness with which he more often handles the motif rarely produces concrete "proof" of his intentions. Because of this cryptic bent, I tend to think that many of the Marian associations are implied

7

by the author with some degree of conscious design. Nonetheless, I shall make every effort to distinguish those about which no certain claims can be made.

The topic of this book invites some remarks on the question of gender. Since the early twentieth century, critics have tried their hand at defining Chekhov's relationship to women and the nature of his depiction of women.[32] A contemporary critical literature has grown up in the wake of Sophie Lafitte's 1963 biography, in which she brands Chekhov a misogynist.[33] Virginia Llewellyn Smith bears this torch a decade later, rather viciously critiquing Chekhov on all fronts.[34] Counterarguments ensue: Chekhov portrays women very sensitively, writes Beverly Hahn, while Caroline de Maegd-Soëp contends that his contradictory remarks about females over the years, and the variety of relations that he had with women, make it difficult to pigeonhole Chekhov at all.[35] Without apologizing for Chekhov's share of pronouncements blatantly demeaning to women, I urge judgment of this question based on balanced studies of the hundreds of fictional portraits of women in his works. Because of Chekhov's psychological insightfulness, we should not point to a handful of works and then damn him globally as insensitive to gender. We do well, too, to keep in mind that Chekhov aimed critical and satirical salvos at both genders and at all classes. Nonetheless, gender bias was his unfortunate cultural heritage.

Barbara Heldt's generous assessment of Chekhov indicates that his gender depictions do not necessarily run afoul of contemporary feminist sensitivities. Her push for Chekhov's ample range of heroines to receive individual readings represents a solid advancement over the sociological typologies of women that mark many studies.[36] Among other things, attentive readings of his letters and fiction account credibly for his elusiveness and arrogance around strong women, and his outright repugnance for aggressive women, perhaps grounded in psychosexual fears.[37] My readings attempt to take into consideration the multifarious dimensions of Chekhov's fictional depictions of women. While I do not actively engage feminist theory, I do intend that this study demonstrate Chekhov's recovery of a weighty feature of women's oppression: the manner in which an authoritarian Christian discourse attempted to shape female identity and to dictate women's options through qualification, limitation, and prohibition. Chekhov's "take," however, eschews the simplistic utopianism of a Chernyshevsky.

The lack of identification between Chekhov's female characters and the saintly and sinful religious prototypes announces not women's liberation, but a whole array of problematized relations to the paradigm on the part of women and men. In some instances, female characters unconsciously collude with, or manipulate, features assigned to the saintly Marys. In others, as in the case of Maria of "Peasant Women," a refusal to submit to the prefabricated Christian roles leads to death. Elsewhere, it is a male character who overcomes the constraints of the Christian projections (Nikitin in "The Teacher of Literature"). Female characters sometimes find the paradigm irrelevant and go their own way (for instance, Maria in "The Uproar" and Kleopatra in "My Life"). In this Chekhov was a realist, not an idealist. More significant, as Marena Senderovich was the first to show, Chekhov, perennially hostile to packaged ideologies, was a phenomenologist.[38] He does not merely depict "things as they were" for women, or between women and men: he shows in full measure the pitfalls of an underlying religious belief about women when it descends from the icon to enter life.

Chapter 1 provides background material for consideration of Marian imagery in Chekhov's stories through a discussion of religious traditions and by rehearsing literary conventions attached to the imagery in literature prior to Chekhov. I locate the Mother of God and Saint Mary of Egypt in relationship to their Catholic correlates and in nineteenth-century Russian popular religious culture as manifest in the Orthodox creed and liturgy, iconography, legend, and folk verse. The term "Marian paradigm" is proposed to describe the relationship between Mary of Egypt and Mary Magdalene, and their sexual antithesis, the Virgin Mary. Next, in order to establish a baseline of literary convention from which Chekhov departs, I discuss references to both Marys in Pushkin and the poetry of Romanticism, in popular narrative poetry about Mary of Egypt, and in selected prose works of Gogol, Turgenev, Dostoevsky, and Tolstoy. Works by all of these authors harbor a common disposition toward equating female characters named Maria with their religious prototypes, but rarely challenge the religious code that would so construct them.

Analysis of Chekhov's stories begins in Chapter 2. I point to indications of the genesis of the Marian associations in a dozen or so early stories written between 1881 and 1886. Here the notion of "translation" comes into play as a serviceable means to approach the discourse of Chekhov's characters: the authoritarian texts of the Orthodox liturgy find themselves displaced time and again as individuals adapt religious language and concepts to personal needs and private circumstances. Chekhov's very modern (and Bakhtinian) insight is that an individual commands many different languages and rhetorical strategies that do not remain compartmentalized under the headings "the religious," "the political," "the social," "the personal," and so forth, but interpenetrate one another in unpredictable, and sometimes startling, ways. These early intimations of the Marian context set the stage for the more complex treatment observed in subsequent chapters.

If Chekhov acts as a sort of cultural psychologist in all of the stories that seem to draw on the Marian polarities, in four stories he executes a rather more pointed investigation into the status of images of these prototypes in the Russian religious mind. These texts are discussed in Chapter 3. I read

"The Lady" ("Barynia," 1882) as Chekhov's response to a didactic tale by a second-rate writer who applauds the moral righteousness of the Mother of God. Chekhov's story dismisses facile moral verdicts by disclosing the flaws in a Christian discourse that claims to unite its practitioners, but in fact tragically estranges them. "Peasants" ("Muzhiki," 1897), a story in which the Marian context is, perhaps, most clearly articulated, I see as an investigation into the topography of motherhood in peasant culture: an icon of the Mother of God refracts the identity of each female character. The Virgin's counterpart becomes the referent point for women in "The Requiem" ("Panikhida," 1886), where the deceased actress Maria Andreevna is mourned by her father as a "whore" akin to Saint Mary of Egypt. The hero of "An Attack of Nerves" ("Pripadok," 1888) fantasizes the rescue of prostitutes from a brothel based on Saint Mary of Egypt's life. Throughout, Chekhov is interested in how Russians "act out" their religio-cultural heritage, in how the premises of a religious creed become translated into individualized, idiosyncratic, and sometimes highly profane understandings.

The last three chapters of the book each consider one story in depth. All of these stories, while frequently translated and anthologized, have received limited critical attention, most of which consists of brief commentaries in the dozens of critical surveys that form the corpus of Chekhov scholarship.

Chekhov wrote "Peasant Women" ("Baby") in 1891 after his return from Sakhalin, a trip during which he was exposed to folk narrations. The story studies modes of discourse as the source of distorted Russian understanding of Christianity. In Matvei Savvich and Diudia, Chekhov travesties the misogyny of a perverted Christian ethos by showing how petrified linguistic formulas (aphorisms, scriptural citations, Church Slavonicisms) and blasphemous claims to male dominance in fact distort the ordered gender relations of the Judeo-Christian tradition. The peasant women bear three prominent female names of Orthodoxy: Varvara (the Great Martyr), Sofia (Divine Wisdom), and Maria. I read each as a dislocation of her saintly prototype. Central is the story of Mashenka (Maria), crafted as the tale of a fornicatress by Matvei Savvich, but informed by contours reminiscent of the martyr's life. Chekhov's story moves away from the widespread assumption that the oppression of women in patriarchal peasant society derives from Christian belief to examine how texts of Christianity function, especially when falsified and used to manipulate others.

The question of discourse and textuality finds further articulation in Chapter 5, devoted to "The Teacher of Literature" ("Uchitel' slovesnosti," 1894). Nikitin, a presumed specialist in literature, is initially blinded by the "texts" surrounding him. He models his fantasies on Pushkin's *Count Nulin* and imagines his life in terms of literary genres; he views his future wife, Maria Shelestova, in terms of Marian veneration, and projects onto her unwed sister Varia the text of A. K. Tolstoy's poem "The Sinful Woman." Nikitin eventually recognizes in Maria a woman of spiritless sensuality associated in Christian doctrine with the whore. Nikitin constructs his life on all manner of texts, only to discover the limitations they impose on imagination and freedom. His move toward self-liberation at the story's end has to do with rejecting the predetermined meaning inscribed in the literary and religio-cultural textual canons.

The final chapter treats "My Life" ("Moia zhizn'," 1896), a story in which the two poles of the Marian paradigm are developed the most fully. I argue that the many forms of conviction held by characters in the story—the "Tolstoyan" Misail Poloznev, the "agronomist" Maria Viktorovna, the "Darwinist" Dr. Blagovo, and the "traditionalist" Kleopatra—are fed by underlying Christian modes of conceptualization drawn from texts of the Book of Daniel and the (related) paradigm of the Virgin and the harlot. What individuals *do* with these Christian texts again occupies Chekhov in the story. Maria Viktorovna is held up to Marian iconography, Blagovo's philosophy is held up to Christian eschatology, and Kleopatra is held up to the figure of the "sinful woman." Misail grounds his behavior in Christian texts, and it is the consciousness of his realization that we cannot dodge our cultural heritage that sets him apart from the others.

This book ends with some final remarks on the post-Chekhovian development of the Marian images in Russian twentieth-century literature. Whereas Chekhov explodes the cultural myths about women grounded in the Christian model of the two Marys, his successors were mostly to preserve the bifurcated paradigm when they called upon Christian images of the feminine. I gesture toward the paradigm in twentieth-century writings not to cast judgment, but to highlight the remarkable innovation of Chekhov's vision.

Attentiveness to the Christian context in Chekhov's prose, held at bay in the past by Soviet ideology and by a reticence to see Chekhov outside the matrix of a narrowly defined realism, has recently spiraled. A recent conference and a surge of publications devoted to the question make the vigor of the enterprise and the diversity of its scholarship clear.[39] I intend here to offer fresh readings of Chekhov's texts with the aim of stimulating further dialogue on this question.

Chapter One

Two Marys:
Chekhov's Religious and Literary Heritage

> O, Most Holy Virgin! We offer our humble prayers
> to Thee and regard Thine icon as if Thou were
> living among us, for we have no other succor, no
> other protector, save for Thee.
> —*Eastern Orthodox prayer*

> For seventeen years or more I indulged in lechery
> with all comers, not for gifts or clothing, since
> I didn't want to accept anything from anyone; I
> thought that without payment they would come
> more frequently and satisfy my lust.
> —Saint Mary of Egypt, *Vita*

> "I've neither fantasized nor dreamt
> Of pyramid, palace, gold, brocade;
> Mine's a mirthful life of play,
> And I love him whom I elect!"
> —I. S. Aksakov, "Mary of Egypt's Song" (1845)

THE PANTHEON of broadly known, highly venerated fe-
male saints in Russian Orthodox Christianity is fairly sparse. A number of
female grand martyrs distinguish themselves by their own icons, churches,
and followings (for example, Varvara, Paraskeva Piatnitsa, Irina, and Tatiana).
For the Orthodox, Sophia embodies Divine Wisdom. Unlike other Christian
female saints, however, Mary, Mother of God, and the "sinful" Mary of
Egypt—along with her Catholic counterpart, Mary Magdalene—are strongly
defined by their relationship to female sexuality. This chapter will take up the
question of the two Marys and their respective sexual identities in Russian
religious culture and Russian letters. The discussion of religion first situates
Orthodox beliefs relative to the Catholic creed, then addresses the media
through which Russian Orthodoxy presented the Marian stories to its con-
stituency, periodically commenting on the advent of these texts in Chekhov's
life and work. The second half of the chapter considers images of the Mother

13

of God and Mary of Egypt (and their fictional namesakes) in the literature that preceded Chekhov with the intention of providing a backdrop against which the uniqueness of his perceptions can be measured. It should become clear that the Marian figures were frequently understood in paradigmatic relationship, a phenomenon latent in the nature of their stories and manifest in legend and literary text. Central always is the bond of their common name.

Mariology in the West, as the word suggests, comprises a vast body of commentary on the dogma, beliefs, and cult of the Virgin in the domain of Catholicism. Nothing quite comparable exists in the Orthodox world. To the Western eye, accustomed as it is to outright exaltation of the Virgin, reverence for the Mother of God in the Eastern Church can, in fact, look quite reserved. In his study of the Catholic Mary cult, Michael Carroll posits a scale of Marian veneration, assigning "the Orthodox tradition a position on this continuum that falls somewhere between the Roman Catholic and the Protestant tradition."[1] Carroll credibly argues that the Roman Catholic Mary is more readily seen as a goddess or independent deity than is the Orthodox Mary—something documented quite thoroughly by studies of Marian statuary, relics, shrines, apparitions, legends, communities, and legions in Europe and the Americas.[2] Yet the two major points with which Carroll bolsters his contention about the greater prominence of Catholic Marianism speak rather of important cultural differences in the nature of veneration between the East and West than of a less potent Orthodox tradition.

Because Orthodoxy rejected the doctrines of the Immaculate Conception and the Assumption (the first holds that Mary was free from the taint of original sin; the second, that Mary ascended to Heaven bodily upon her death), Carroll suggests that "Mary does not enjoy in the Orthodox tradition the same exalted status that she does in Roman Catholicism."[3] It is true that official doctrine concerning the Mother of God was conspicuously underdeveloped in nineteenth-century Russian Orthodox theology. Doctrine, such as it was, tended to advance modest claims. As the prominent twentieth-century theologian Sergei N. Bulgakov explains when challenging the Catholic denial of the Virgin's original sin, as a human being the Mother of God was necessarily implicated in the fall from grace represented by Adam and Eve, but she was free of all personal sin as a result of God's grace.[4] Orthodoxy consistently upholds the notion of the Mother of God's human nature (parallel, of course, to its position on Christ). Rather than constituting a weak theological link that might dissuade believers from honoring Mary, however, this dogma accomplishes quite the opposite. A highly personalized view of the Virgin becomes the cornerstone for popular worship of a divine being who, because of her human compassion and capacity for forgiveness, holds out the hope of redemption for each individual believer: "We . . . regard Thine icon *as if Thou were living among us,* for we have *no other succor, no other protector,* save for Thee."

Second, it is often noted that the Orthodox emphasis on motherhood, as reflected in the appellation *Theotokos*, or Mother of God, downplays the Immaculate Conception and seemingly diminishes the status of Mary as Virgin. According to this logic, Marian veneration remains ancillary to an essentially Christological faith. Certainly Mary's act of giving birth to Christ distinguishes her above all for the Orthodox. Yet eminent commentators have said of the Orthodox Mother of God in the Russian tradition that "her significance is incomparably more real than that of Christ," that "Russian religious sentiment is not so much the religion of Christ as the religion of the Mother of God," and that "love and veneration of the Virgin are the core of Orthodox piety, its heart, that which restores and rejuvenates the entire body."[5] It has been noted, too, that "the icon of the Virgin is undoubtedly the most highly venerated icon, more so than the icons of other saints, and more even than that of Christ."[6] The types of icons on which the Mother of God appears without child (icons of the Intercession, the Bogolubsky Virgin) have been viewed as further evidence of the Virgin's prime stature in Orthodox Christianity. Spurious, indeed, is any attempt to establish superiority of either Christ or Mary in a religion that advocated (and depended upon) the worship of both. The point, rather, is that "the cult of the Mother of God was highly developed in both the Orthodox and Catholic churches."[7]

The name Mary—key to this study of Chekhov—may seem to resonate more naturally with the Catholic Madonna than with Russia's Holy Mother. This is a prejudice of those not conversant with Orthodox liturgy and prayer. A look at any of the assorted prayer books that consitute the frontline exposure of the believer to the faith immediately dispels such an assumption. In prayers and hymns, addresses to the Mother of God (*Bogoroditsa, Bogomater', Bozhiia mater'*), the Virgin (*Deva, Prisnodeva*), and the Virgin Mary (*Deva Mariia, Prisnodeva Mariia*) are virtually interchangeable. In fact, they appear with great frequency in unexpected hybrids such as "Mary Mother of God" and "Virgin Mary Mother of God" (*Bogoroditsa Mariia, Mariia Bogomater', Deva Mariia Bogoroditsa*).[8] The closer one gets to folk sources, the more often the name Mary stands on its own. An apocryphal account of the Dormition refers to the Virgin throughout solely by the name "Maria."[9] Lines of one popular verse read, "Dear mother Mary walked out / From the city of [Je]Rusalem," while in the broadly known "Dream of the Mother of God" Jesus says to his mother, "Don't weep, my dear mother Mary."[10] It should be added, conversely, that the Catholic devout regularly worship the Mother of God, especially in folk traditions. In other words, attempts to draw artificial lines between popular practices of Western and Eastern Christianity—practices that experienced a vast amount of cross-fertilization over the centuries—must be tempered by the realization that Marian veneration everywhere had far more in common than not.

Yet given that the enterprise here is to establish the particularities of Marian veneration in Russian Orthodox society—insofar as these are the traditions upon which Chekhov draws—let me suggest in broad outline ways in which popular reception of the Virgin in Russia may be distinguished. Despite a common church history that saw the *Theotokos* emerge triumphant as an object of devotion from the fifth-century Council of Ephesus, and saw Rome actively embracing the fervently Marian "iconodules" from Byzantium during the Iconoclast controversy of the eighth and ninth centuries, the eventual split between the Greek and Latin churches led to more than just theological distance. Different routes of social and political development in Europe and Russia, and the evolution of distinct kinds of cultural imagination, shaped Marian veneration in different ways.

The Orthodox insistence on, and celebration of, the Virgin's humanity manifests itself in the specific nature of texts produced to laud her. In general terms, it is worth noting the fact that Russian Orthodox liturgy has always been read in Church Slavic, a vernacular comprehensible to all believers and therefore more accessible than was Latin in the Western church. But while one might anticipate that such access would yield more personalized or innovative understandings, because Russia isolated itself for centuries from Europe, the body of texts it fed upon was extremely limited and had "an overwhelmingly practical and didactic character."[11] The Eastern church willingly embraced imaginative apocrypha that were rejected by the skeptical West, yet the elastic perimeters of the legendary by no means encouraged a culture of creative thought. We encounter the paradox, then, of a Russian religious textual tradition at once more accessible and accommodating than that of the West, and more conservative in its impulses toward rigidity and the preservation of form.

Apocrypha were central to Russian constructs of Mary. The actual substance of all Marian celebrations depended almost entirely on a large body of apocryphal and exegetical writings generated to fill in the glaring gaps left by meager biblical data on the Virgin's life. Marian Apocrypha, highly spirited in the East, originated in the fourth or fifth century and were reproduced over the ages in ever more embellished versions. The fact that an account of the Virgin's life that fills roughly ten pages in Scripture can fill many hundreds of pages in legend attests to the free hand with which additions were made.[12] Apocryphal writings elaborately embellish the events of Mary's girlhood, betrothal, conception of Christ, birth-giving, flight to Egypt, and motherhood, detailing in particular her grief and suffering as a mother. Saint Dmitry of Rostov and church fathers such as John of Damascus and Andrew of Crete borrowed heavily from apocrypha in their sermons, creating imaginative details of the Virgin's words and activities in order to inspire the faithful.[13] Apocrypha concerning Mary's life were thoroughly incorporated into Orthodox liturgies.

By the nineteenth century they were taught in the catechism studied by all children. This Mother of God was constructed in a highly personalized manner that could not but appeal to a largely unsophisticated, illiterate populace.

The paramount text of the Mother of God in Russia has always been the icon. The peerless role of iconography in Eastern Orthodoxy strikes at the heart of the cultural differences between Marian veneration in the East and the West. Icons of the Mother of God, "written" for the most part by anonymous masters or collectives, stand in sharp contrast to the individualistic, personalized portraits of the Madonna adorning European churches, chapels, and homes. The basic cast of Russian icon painting was inherited from Byzantium. Regulations for depicting the Mother of God were spelled out in manuals (*podlinniki*) composed expressly to forestall any innovation in content. Manuals strictly prescribed facial features, gestures, position, background, and color. Icons of the Virgin and Child can be classified as one of four types: *Orans* (*Znamenie*), or icon of the Sign; *Hodigitria* (*Putevoditel'nitsa*), or the Guide; *Glikofilussa* (*Umilenie*), or icon of Tenderness; and *Nikopeia*, or Enthroned (in Russia, the crowned and enthroned Queen of Heaven appears on several thematic icons). Icons of Marian holidays are governed by their own representational dictates, as are icons celebrating a local prophecy, vision, or prayer. Thus there are literally hundreds of types of miracle-working icons of the Virgin, but, with small variations, each depicts an essentially familiar figure. For the religious Russian, Marian icons were "exact portraits" of the Mother of God, "patches of light" sent to earth with the Virgin Mother's own personal approval.[14] It was considered blasphemous to distort this eternal image by rendering her a blond or brunette, young or old, or the likeness of a wife or a friend.[15]

Of course very different standards obtained in Europe, where the artist aspired to create as uniquely beautiful a representation of the Virgin as possible. Frescoes, illuminated manuscripts, triptychs, stained-glass windows, individual paintings—the media alone speak of variety and variance. From Botticelli's expressive faces and Raphael's delicate Madonnas, to the white-skinned noblewomen of the Flemish school, to the obedient and meek young girl of Rossetti's "Girlhood of Mary Virgin," these visual texts parade the Virgin in an endless display of original appearances, garb, colors, postures, expressions, and settings. The psychology behind this variety of portraiture speaks of an appreciation of novelty and autonomy, of imaginative projections (at times with erotic overtones), and above all, of individualism. In contrast, the psychology behind the fixed image of the icon speaks of an emphasis on a collective cultural identity, of the "we" that has tended to prevail over the "I" in Russian religious, social, and political thought.

If apparitions of the Virgin became the stock-in-trade of Marian worship in the West, miraculous appearances and deeds of icons of the Mother of God fulfilled a similar function in the East. If the rosary represented the primary focus of Marian prayers in the West, the icon fulfilled that function in the East. Marian icons adorned homes, were worn around the necks of the faithful, led men into battle, and were used to officiate over both major and minor rituals of Russian life. This phenomenon of a "fixed" image of the Mother of God, whose depictions and qualities became embedded in the psyche of a Russian from an early age, will play an important role in this investigation.

In a sense, then, we encounter more paradoxes than sound explanations in this brief comparative consideration. I have suggested that, overall, Marian veneration in the East and West had a great deal in common. Yet the ways in which they diverge reveal telling cultural differences. Ironically, the Western Virgin was located theologically quite remotely from the believer because of the doctrines of the Immaculate Conception and the Assumption, but she appeared in visual art and apparitions as an individual. Conversely, the Russian Virgin was far more human in her theological and apocryphal roles, yet her image was moored in a rigid set of artistic conventions that placed her at a remove from the worshiper. Both traditions, however, support sets of associations with the Virgin that would have been recognizable by any member of a national culture. The particular contours of Marian veneration in the Russian Orthodox world, familiar to Chekhov, to his readers, and to many of his characters, can be found in ecclesiastical and folkloric sources.

MORE ON THE ORTHODOX MOTHER OF GOD

The Orthodox calendar begins in September and includes holidays of varying degrees of importance. In Chekhov's "Murder" ("Ubiistvo," 1895) Matvei Terekhov recalls the chapel he founded according to the liturgical canon of Mount Athos: "every day my matins unfailingly began at midnight and the all-night service on the eve of the highly venerated twelve great feasts lasted ten, and sometimes twelve, hours" (9:139). Of the twelve great feasts (*dvu-nadesiatye prazdniki*), five celebrate the Mother of God specifically; she is closely associated as well with the Christ-centered holidays of the Nativity and the Ascension. The Virgin's own great feasts include the Birth of the Mother of God (8 September, Old Style), the Feast of the Purification (2 February), Entry into the Temple (21 November), the Annunciation (25 March), and the Dormition (15 August). Of these, Chekhov abides by cultural priorities in his repeated references to the Annunciation and Dormition, both especially prominent in popular observance. The Annunciation (*Blagoveshchenie*), the Angel Gabriel's delivery of the Good News (*Blagaia vest'*) to the Virgin Mary (Luke 1:26–35), occupied a special place in the folk mind. It has been rated the second most important holiday, after Easter, for the Russian believer; a proverb proclaims, "The Annunciation is God's greatest holiday."[16] The

Dormition (*Uspenie*), known as the Assumption in the West, commemorates the death of the Virgin and the ascension of her soul to heaven.

Numerous holidays of lesser stature honor the Mother of God as well, most of them entirely unknown to Roman Catholicism. For one thing, hundreds of Marian icons served individual churches (churches that often bore the icon's name) and enjoyed their own feast days. In Chekhov's story "A Meeting" ("Vstrecha," 1887) a peasant travels from village to village with an icon of the Kazan Mother of God in a cart to raise funds for rebuilding a church of the Virgin that had been demolished by fire. "In the Ravine" ("V ovrage," 1900) recounts the meek and pious Lipa's pilgrimage on 8 July to the village of Kazanskoe, "in honor of the church feast day of the Kazan Mother of God" (10:160). A most prominent holiday/icon/church was that of the Intercession or the Veil (*Pokrov*), celebrating a tenth-century vision in a Constantinople cathedral where Saint Andrei beheld the Virgin holding a protective veil over the faithful. The holiday later fell into oblivion in the Greek church, but was enthusiastically amplified in Russia.[17] A village church of the Intercession plays a role in Chekhov's story "Peasants" ("Muzhiki," 1897).

The Orthodox Church calendar, so complex that priests required the special *Reference Book for Clergymen* (*Nastol'naia kniga dlia sviashchenno-tserkovno-sluzhitelei*) to negotiate their way through its maze of fixed and movable feast days, liturgies, and prayer books, reflected the (complicated) normative timetable of life for most of Russia's population in the nineteenth century. The rhythm of the Orthodox year was organic to Chekhov's own life. In a diary kept during the Melikhovo years (1892–98), his father plotted many family routines according to church feast days: "Annunciation. Attended the All-night Vigil and Mass at the Church of Peter and Paul"; "Kazan Icon Feast. We had Mass at Melikhovo and the priest stayed for dinner"; "Dormition of Our Most Holy Lady Mary. Went to Vaskino for Mass. The priest gave Masha communion."[18] In Chekhov's correspondence, one also encounters a schedule measured by holidays: "I'll leave during St. Thomas' week or a little thereafter" or "When are you coming to visit? By sleigh before Annunciation, or after it by carriage?"[19] It is little wonder that the omnipresent references to Christian feast days in Chekhov's work should have been understood for so long as a simple reflection of cultural custom. These references, as we shall see, fulfill other, more interesting, functions as well.

Fedotov writes that "to introduce the name of Mary and hymns to Mary into all possible pieces of ancient liturgical treasure was one of the predominant concerns of the Byzantine liturgists."[20] An important source of immutable images of the Virgin comes from acathists (doxological prayers sung in honor of the Mother of God, Christ, and popular saints). Acathists are based on sacred Hebrew poetry and engage many of the same verbal devices: alliteration, assonance, rhymes, paronomasia, and acrostics. In all acathists the priest and choir melodically alternate readings of thirteen kontakion (Russian, *kondak*) and twelve ikos (Russian, *ikos*) verses. Together, the twenty-five verses praise the subject's virtues and recount pertinent biographical episodes. Marian acathists were never circumscribed in number and have been actively composed throughout the history of Orthodoxy. In the nineteenth century at least twenty new acathists were sanctified by the Holy Synod.[21] Nevertheless, the original Marian acathist has always by far outstripped all others as the central anthem of Marian praise. Services on Saturday of the fifth week of Lent celebrate the acathist and it is frequently recited in conjunction with other prayer.[22] Acathist phrases would have become second nature to Chekhov as a member of the church choir.

The major Marian acathist portrays in rich metaphors Old Testament prefigurations of the Mother of God. She is called the Burning Bush (Moses' vision in Exodus), Aaron's rod (Numbers 17:8), the dew on Gideon's fleece (Judges 6:38), Tongs that hold the Burning Coal (Isaiah's prophecy), the Heavenly Ladder (Jacob's vision), the Locked Gates (Ezekiel 44:2), and the Uncut Mountain (Daniel's prophecy). Several other examples (drawn from scores of appellations) include "the Fiery Pillar," "the Door of Salvation," "the Well of Living Water," "the Unsetting Star," "the Indestructible Wall," "the Key to the Kingdom of Christ," "the Sealed Book," and, above all, the epithet that ends each ikos, "Virgin Bride!" (*Nevesto nenevestnaia*) (see Fig. 2). The metaphorical nature of these titles makes them ready material for the literary pen, for commonplace objects assume elevated value in the acathist. Such multivalences characterize certain otherwise "realistic" details that reverberate with acathist phraseology in Chekhov's language.

That Chekhov was well aware of these epithets is clear from his own writing. The story "On Holy Night" ("Sviatoiu noch'iu," 1886) tells of the passionate admiration on the part of the monk Ieronim for his deceased friend Nikolai, the author of acathists. In the course of a lengthy discourse on the poetics of acathists ("the first kontakion always opens with 'O, chosen one.' . . . The first ikos with an angel;" "it must be written so that the heart of the supplicant rejoices and weeps, and his intellect quakes and trembles"), Ieronim quotes to the narrator from the first and seventh ikos of the Marian acathist:

> Here are words from the acathist to the Mother of God: "Hail, Height, unapproachable to human thoughts. Hail, Depth unfathomable to angelic eyes!" Then in another place in the same acathist: "Hail, wonderfully fruitful tree, from which the faithful are nourished; Hail, good shady and leafy tree under which many find shelter!"
>
> Ieronim, as if frightened of something or suddenly ashamed, covered his face with his palms and rocked his head. "Wonderfully fruitful tree . . . good shady and leafy tree . . ." he muttered. "Who could find such words! To whom would the Lord grant such an ability!" (5:97–98)

20

Louis Bouyer distinguishes the Eastern liturgy from that of Catholicism by its poetic nature, suggesting that poetically contemplative hymns substitute for the more intellectual content of Western liturgy.[23] Chekhov exhibits a profound appreciation of the poetic structure and artistic grace of the acathist (something more obvious in the Church Slavic of the original). In fact, Ieronim's insistence that "everything must be well-proportioned, brief, and detailed" approximates Chekhov's own injunctions about the necessity of writing laconically and concisely. This passage underscores Chekhov's understanding of the enormous power of the liturgical images in the Russian Orthodox consciousness. More precisely, it highlights the way in which inanimate objects convey the marvelous symbolic significance of the Mother of God to the believer.

In addition to Scripture, iconography, holidays, and acathists, the Orthodox Mary was known to the faithful over the centuries through many popular texts, including spiritual verse, folk songs, and legends. Scholarly interest in all of the phenomena of folk life mushroomed in the last several decades of the nineteenth century. Books and articles in the "thick journals" took up analysis of Slavic legend. Quite a number of publications addressed the role of the Mother of God in religious and folk belief. Particulary prolific on the subject are works by A. I. Kirpichnikov, N. Pokrovskii, and N. P. Kondakov, the latter of whom Chekhov knew personally.[24] Chekhov himself participated in this trend when he began a dissertation (in 1884–85) on the history of medical practice in Russia ("Vrachebnoe delo v Rossii," 16:277–356), a project that had much to do with folk remedies (spells, herbal brews) and that documents his exposure to work by many of the best folklorists of the century. Following is an overview of the kinds of folk texts that feature the Virgin.

Spiritual verses—oral songs recited by traveling pilgrims—conceive of the Mother of God largely in her key role as patroness. In a popular Russian spiritual verse about the Last Judgment the performer sings, "The Most Holy Mother of God prays for us, / The Lord listens to her pleas, / And forgives our great sinfulness."[25] This is the role of the *zastupnitsa* or intercessor, the critical link between earth and heaven, who consoles her supplicants, calms their fears, nurtures them spiritually, and intercedes on their behalf with the Heavenly Powers. Calling on these qualities, a peasant woman relocated to the city in Chekhov's "At Chrismastide" ("Na sviatkakh," 1900) summons the "Heavenly Queen, Intercessor-Mother!" to deliver her family back to the village (10:185).

At the same time, the Virgin of spiritual verses can be an irascible judge meting punishment out to sinners. She demonstrates both of these capacities in the ancient Russian apocrypha, "The Virgin's Travels Through the Torments." Here the Mother of God is guided through Hell, where she is shown a gruesome array of tortures meted out to sinners of every ilk. The feisty

Virgin revokes all hope of redemption from those who did not pray for Her. But she also spars with the Lord in defense of fallen Christians and intercedes on their behalf, although neither Christ nor any of the patriarchs had hitherto shown any concern for them. This highly influential text emblematizes the contrast between the cultural constructs of, on the one hand, male authority and judgment, and, on the other, the female capacity for mediation and compassion.

The medieval texts that abound in visions of the Virgin, supplications to the Virgin, and the miraculous appearance of Marian icons tend to fall under the rubric of legend and apocrypha.[26] One widespread explanation for the predominance of the Mother of God in folk texts (and her relative absence in the texts of the church fathers) is the notion that veneration of Mary replaced popular allegiance to pagan earth goddesses.[27] She fulfilled ambitions of the state as well. In texts through the seventeenth century, icons of the Mother of God protect the Russian nation from foes, turn the tide of battle, and watch over the country's rulers. Throughout early Russian history we find "this tendency to link Mary with all major national events and to see therein the effects of her mediation."[28]

In a final folk source, village songs, the Mother of God appears as the patroness of weddings. Typically, young women appealed to the Virgin for assistance in procuring a suitable husband. In these wedding songs "Maria" far and away prevails as the name assigned to fiancées. A proliferation of Marias studs early collections of wedding lyrics; the name is often repeated in whole cycles of songs: Maria Ivanovna, Mashenka Efimova, Maria Andrianovna, Maria Gavrilovna, "The beautiful maiden Mashenka / Mashenka, darling Ivanovna," "The darling light Maria Mikhailovna," and so forth.[29]

The composite picture that emerges from these texts—Scripture, apocrypha, iconography, liturgy, and folk verse—is one of a Mother of God who at once towers above believers in her lofty, sinless state of Virgin, patroness, and protectress, and simultaneously ministers to their earthly needs in an intimately human manner, tenderly consoling and nurturing them, and interceding with the less benevolent male powers on their behalf. That this might also describe the Roman Catholic Virgin is no coincidence. It would be odd, indeed, if the overall outlines of Marian veneration in the two ritual-oriented branches of Christianity were at drastic variance. Nonetheless, I have suggested that the specific cultural shape of Russian attachment to the Mother of God differs from Western practice through the set images of icons and acathists, and from the Orthodox theological insistence on the Virgin's human nature. (Interestingly, one of the major sticking points over reconciliation between the Eastern and Western churches in recent history has been Marian dogma.) For the Russian Orthodox believer, Mary's humanity defines her trustworthiness as a guide to human life. Fixed in the Russian imagination as the major locus of tenderness, pity, and clemency, it is to be expected that the Mother of God would exert an influence far beyond the walls of the church.

Indeed, the Virgin's image was not a stranger in the Chekhov home. A popular custom saw the commissioning of domestic icons that illustrated the saints after whom family members had been named. Such was the icon of "The Lord Almighty" that Pavel Egorovich Chekhov ordered for his family in 1864. It pictures Christ surrounded by the guardian saints of Pavel, his wife Evgeniia, sons Alexander, Nikolai, Anton, and Ivan, and daughter Maria: namely, the Holy Apostle Paul, Saint Evgeniia, the sainted prince Alexander Nevsky, Saint Nicholas, Saint Anthony, Saint John, and the Virgin Mary.[30]

The entire complex of mythical meanings associated with the Mother of God entered Chekhov's life even earlier. According to a family story, Pavel Egorovich acquired an icon of the "Shuia-Smolensk Most Holy Mother of God" in 1862, motivated by a longing for a baby girl (the Chekhovs already had four sons). Shuia was a town in which Chekhov's mother, Evgeniia Iakovlevna, had lived as a child. The birth of a daughter on 31 July 1863 was attributed to the ardent prayers offered the Shuia icon by Chekhov's parents.[31] His (only) sister received the name Maria in honor of the Mother of God. Her nameday was celebrated by family and friends each year on the Feast of the Dormition (15 August).[32] Chekhov writes to Liza Mizinova in 1892, "I'll expect you on August 15 for Masha's nameday."[33] Thus a personal circumstance helped to clue Chekhov in to the possible ramifications of the name Maria in quotidian Russian middle-class life. He may have had occasion to reflect on the built-in dissonance between a religious ideal and human behavior in the person of his own sister, Maria Pavlovna.

THE "SINFUL" MARYS

Christianity West and East assigned to its exemplars of repentant harlotry the name Mary. In both Catholicism and Orthodoxy reverence for this type of saint was great, for she held out a concrete promise that the erring human might atone for his or her transgressions, receive forgiveness, and secure admission to heaven after death. Saint Mary Magdalene and Saint Mary of Egypt represent distinct figures with distinctly different textual histories, yet they came to serve nearly identical functions in their respective territories. To each is imputed a history of wild sexual indulgence; each sees the light of Christianity through contact with its foremost sacred figures (Christ and the Mother of God); each retreats to live in remote isolation from the world in expiation of her sins; and, most significant, to each tenaciously clings the reputation of impermissible female sensuality, of prostitution and whoredom, even as she assumes the mantle of revered sainthood. I draw Magadalene into this discussion both because Chekhov alludes to her legend and because the shared name often leads to conflation of the "sinful" Marys. Boris Pasternak once re-called being brought to task for "mixing up the two Marys" in *Doctor Zhivago*: a knowledgeable acquaintance pointed out to him that Sima's commentary in the novel about Mary Magdalene "in fact concerns Mary of Egypt."[34]

Recent revisionist work on the life of Mary Magdalene articulates with especial force how a sinful woman was mythically fabricated from New Testament accounts that never mention sexual promiscuity in connection with her.[35] A large Christian literature exists on this question. Briefly, the momentous confusion emerges from the decision by Western Christian ex-egetes to interpret the scant scriptural divulgence that Christ drove from Magdalene "seven devils" as a reference to earlier sexual improprieties and to merge Magdalene with several unrelated female figures: the contemplative Mary of Bethany (Luke 10:38–42; John 11:1), the harlot whom Christ saves from stoning and who washes his feet (Luke 7:39–47), and, more remotely, two other "sinful" women (John 4:6–42 and 8:3–11).[36] The Western consciousness became completely attached to this artificially constructed Mary Magdalene, producing masses of visual renditions that depict a repentant sinner still satisfyingly provocative, with her long golden red hair often failing to conceal a heaving white bosom.[37] (Such, among many, are Titian's penitent Magdalene, well known through reproductions, and Giampietrino's "The Penitent Mary Magdalene," on exhibit in Saint Petersburg's Hermitage Museum.)

Eastern Orthodox theology remains true to Matthew's Gospel: Mary Magdalene is not conflated with "sexualized" female figures, but is featured as the leader of the myrrh-bearing women in the Christ cycle.[38] The image of Mary Magdalene very rarely stands alone in Byzantine iconography; she is commonly present at the foot of the Cross (with the Mother of God and Saint John) or at the tomb with the myrrhophores (see Fig. 1). It is curious that the Eastern and Western accounts should diverge so completely on this score: one might conjecture that Orthodoxy had no need to recast Magdalene as a repen-tant whore when Mary of Egypt already occupied the position. But if Orthodox exegetes carefully shielded Magdalene from the stigma of sexuality, by the nineteenth century popular Western prejudices were fully operative in Russia and were even sustained by synodal sources. A turn-of-the-century Russian theological encyclopedia reports that Magdalene "led a dissolute life."[39]

Saint Mary of Egypt was relatively unknown in the West.[40] Asceticism is a principal hallmark of the Orthodox religious ideal. The harsh deprivations to which Mary of Egypt subjected herself after repentance may have run contrary to the European medieval and Renaissance (male) taste for female voluptuousness. Be that as it may, the stories of the two "sinful" Marys do intersect. Until the ninth century Mary of Egypt's fifth-century hagiography remains autonomous from the Magdalene legend (which takes root in the West by the end of the sixth century), but thereafter elements of Mary of

Egypt's hermitic life accrue to Magdalene. (Catholic exegetes looked to the East to bolster her profile as a penitent at a time when austerity was much in demand.) As Haskins writes, "it was no doubt the similarity of their names, and their early lives of sin which led hagiographers to assume that the expiation of their dissoluteness would also be analogous."[41] Warner sees Mary of Egypt and Mary Magdalene as "two harlots fused into a single symbol."[42] In tandem, they were the Western and Eastern players designated to fulfill Christianity's need to rein in and condemn female sexuality.

Mary of Egypt enjoyed tremendous popularity in Russia, perhaps because her story offered a degree of titillation absent in more staid *vitae.* As a girl of twelve she goes to Alexandria and for seventeen years indulges in fornication indiscriminately, reveling in her lust. One day the future saint sees pilgrims embarking for Jerusalem and boards the ship. During the journey she corrupts the passengers, seducing many against their will. In Jerusalem, Mary of Egypt continues this activity until, one day, as she tries to follow a crowd into a Christian cathedral for the service of the Ascension, she is stopped by an invisible power. She sees an icon of the Mother of God near the entrance, and, overcome with remorse, pleads with the Virgin for mercy. Leaving behind her life of sin, the saint is baptized and departs to wander in the desert for forty-seven years. There the pious elder Zosima·finds her and convinces her to share her story. Saint Mary of Egypt admits in the course of her account that during the first seventeen years in the desert she fought off urges to sing lascivious songs and evoked the Mother of God to overcome desires of the flesh. But her present state of holiness is evidenced by many miraculous signs. On his third visit, Zosima finds a note in the sand reporting her death on the first of April (subsequently designated Saint Mary of Egypt's Day) and (with the help of a lion) he buries her nude body (see Fig. 3).[43]

Exposure to Saint Mary of Egypt's story in Russian life would have come from the volumes of *The Lives of Saints* (the Menologies, or *Chet'i menei*) present in many homes, from the liturgical texts sung on her immovable feast day and on the Thursday of the fifth week of Lent, and from the spiritual verses, popular prints, and folk sayings that grew up around the most favored saints. Orthodoxy strategically schedules both holidays toward the end of the Lenten fast, for Mary of Egypt models the self-denial, abstinence, and repentance required of the successful Christian. The troparian to the feast congratulates her on overcoming all-out lechery and conquering her demons by emulating the angels. The proverbs that characterize Mary of Egypt's feast day are connected with the spring: "Maria, melt the snow and empty out the ravines, our cabbage soup is wanting"; "If there's a flood on Mary of Egypt's day, grass will grow aplenty"; "Maria opens up the flood waters."[44] Notably, she is poised in these sayings on the border between barrenness and fertility.

Indeed, Mary of Egypt's sexuality does seem the subject of far greater fascination than that accorded the bodies of male ascetics. The spiritual verse "About Mary of Egypt" documents the transformation of her sensuous youthful female body into the androgynous body of an ascetic. When the elder comes across Mary of Egypt in the desert, he wonders if she is swine or wild animal: "Her hair falls down to the damp earth, / Her body is like oak bark, / Her face like the bottom of a cauldron."[45] She prays in the desert for absolution of her "highly lecherous [*velikobludnye*] sins," broadcasting an unambiguous message about the evils of female desire and the vileness of the female body.

In a series of *lubok* (woodcut) prints, too (and on some late icons of Mary of Egypt), the hermit saint can only be distinguished from male martyrs with some difficulty. Let us note, first, that the large print runs and apparently frequent reproductions of this *lubok* theme (into the early twentieth century) confirm Saint Mary of Egypt's popularity in Russia.[46] The standard rendition shows Saint Mary surrounded by episodes from her life: in the desert, she appears nude and slightly bearlike, her private parts covered by a tutu of greenery, her breast more that of a corpulent man than a shapely woman (see Fig. 4). True, some prints marketed in Chekhov's lifetime endow Mary of Egypt with long, loose hair and feminine contours. (A color poster of 1912 paints her as a Victorian floozy.) But she wins the adoration of Orthodox worshipers in her androgynized incarnation, where the magnitude of the sin of female sexuality is brought home. The Russian Orthodox ascetic ideal and prudish social norms were not prepared to tolerate a female saint who, after repentance, might still occupy the ample and beautiful body that she possessed as a harlot. Such unthinkable sensuality was ceded to Catholicism's Mary Magdalene.

Saint Mary of Egypt represents complex impulses in the Russian religious mind. In contrast to the esteem she received as a celibate anchoress, the blatant female sexual appetite portrayed in Mary of Egypt's life must have both excited and threatened believers. Thus we find 1 April described as "Maria the shit-lover" in a Siberian saying—an epithet that may be construed at once as a witty reference to muddy spring conditions and a denigrating remark about the saint's sexual activity prior to her conversion.[47] Mary of Egypt was lauded, venerated, and loved even more than other saints precisely because she was felt to illustrate the human capacity for overcoming morally unacceptable weaknesses. Yet her reputation as a sinful woman clung to her above all. The idiomatic Russian expression "Egyptian whore" (*Bludnitsa egipetskaia*) dramatizes this reputation; it derives from the saint's name but baldly eliminates any reference to her holiness.

There can be no doubt that Chekhov knew Saint Mary of Egypt's famous *Vita* well. First, he refers to her life and to popular prejudices about her in several stories. His story "The Requiem" makes abundantly clear Chekhov's awareness of Mary of Egypt as the cultural bearer of both the stigma of the fornicatress and the crown of most exalted sainthood. Second, a close acquaintance of Chekhov's (and one to whom, judging by the frequency and quality of his letters to her, he felt quite warmly) celebrated her nameday on 1 April. Chekhov sends greetings to Maria Kiseleva, the mistress of the Babkino estate, toward the end of March in 1886 and 1888: "Best wishes on your angel's day. I give my word to drink your health on that day."[48]

Maxim Gorky, who grew up nearly contemporaneously with Chekhov, recalls his grandmother's endless tales about the legendary feats of Russia's heroes. She regaled her audience, he writes, with the stories of the Mother of God; Aleksei, Man of God; the sixth-century martyr Ivan; Vasilisa the Beautiful; the Goat Priest; Marfa Posadnitsa; the robber ataman Bab'e Uste; and Maria, the Egyptian sinner.[49] In this amalgamated assembly of saints, fairy-tale favorites, and the superstars of ancient *byliny* (heroic folk tales in blank verse) Gorky appropriately locates both the Mother of God and Mary of Egypt as primary figures belonging to the folk imagination. These two Marian figures beg to be looked at in relationship to one another.

"Christianity has offered, one could say imposed, two alternative feminine symbols, Mary the Virgin and Mary Magdalen, the whore, encapsulating in these two figures a moral code, based on the virginal ideal which has obtained for nearly two thousand years," writes Haskins.[50] Iconography of the Crucifixion pairs the grieving Mother of God with Magdalene at the base of the cross, while the Greek "Chairete" icon depicts Christ's appearance to the Virgin Mary and Mary Magdalene. Margaret Miles writes that "these two figures must be interpreted together, as their iconography consistently represents them together, juxtaposing and sometimes contrasting their lives, their personalities, and their actions."[51] Pushkin's poem "Worldly Authority" proves that the polarized pairing of the Virgin and Magdalene was common currency in nineteenth-century Russia as well ("On each side of the life-giving cross / Maria the Sinful Woman and the Most Holy virgin, / Stood . . ."). This opposition, clearly important to the Russian imagination, was succinctly played out in the religious sphere as an opposition between the Mother of God and Mary of Egypt.

It is no coincidence that the Mother of God plays the role of intercessor in the life of Saint Mary of Egypt. Because of her purity, the Mother of God was the natural mentor for those suffering from the torments of the flesh, something brought home by Mary of Egypt's conversion in front of a Marian icon—the scene depicted centrally on icons recording her saintly life. These two Marys also appear together on an icon of the Sign.[52] The holiday of the Marian acathist follows on the heels of services honoring Mary of Egypt during the fifth week of Lent. These two Marys form a dialectic association in the register of Orthodox saints grounded in their paradoxical representations of female sexuality. The virtue of the sexually untainted Virgin, Christianity's idealized archmother, is highlighted in the presence of the degraded sinner. Saint Mary of Egypt's life, on the other hand, instructs on the literal fruitlessness of promiscuous female sexuality. Her harlotry can be more thoroughly condemned when held up to the motherhood of a woman not tarnished by carnal knowledge. Their bodies tell the tales. The modest and fully robed Virgin's body receives wide veneration as the host of the Word Incarnate, while Mary of Egypt's nude body earns its deplorable barrenness. Each figure depends upon the other to illuminate her respective qualities fully. It seems appropriate to call this interrelationship the Marian paradigm.

The notion of a Marian paradigm is affirmed by the common name. B. A. Uspenskii observes that in Russia for many centuries a strict distinction was maintained between the name Maríia, reserved exclusively for the Mother of God and never assigned to a child, and Már'ia, the name of both the Egyptian Mary (Már'ia Egipetskaia) and of Magdalene.[53] This discrimination in names obviously issued from an inclination to carefully segregate the virginal holiness of the Madonna from the other "promiscuous" Marys. The name and its derivatives—Masha, Mashenka, Mashutka, and so forth—became one of the most common female names in Russia. Despite (or, perhaps, because of) its ordinariness, the name suited well the designs of Russian authors long before Chekhov, who drew on its religious connotations as part of symbolic codes and character portrayals. Correlations between fictional characters and the Marian figures dominate in the literary tradition prior to Chekhov. The thumbnail sketch that follows of the two Marys in Russian letters illustrates the conventions in order to throw into graphic relief Chekhov's innovation.

MARIAN FIGURES IN THE RUSSIAN LITERARY CANON

"In your absence, [mother] blessed you with your angel and the Farsul Mother of God, and me with the Virgin of the Burning Bush," writes N. I. Novikov, in his satirical "Letters to Falalei" (1775). Iconography of the Mother of God claims a consistent place in Russian literature ever since Prince Igor rode "along the Borichev rise / to the Holy Pirogoshch Mother of God" on his return from captivity in the famous twelfth-century *Lay of Igor's Host*. In the seamless world of belief reflected in medieval texts, of course, the image of the Mother of God represented that which she meant to the author and his audience in life. Even in the fifteenth century, however, we find a rudimentary association of "fictional" characters with the Virgin's name. The spiritual biographies of Saint Sergius and Saint Stephen of Perm, composed by Epiphanius the Wise, assign the mother of each of the saints the name

"Maria," a name used to magnify the aura of holiness around the subjects by affiliating them with events of the New Testament. This bud of symbolic characterization anticipates the standing of the name in the modern tradition.

V. A. Zhukovsky's gothic tale "Mary's Grove" (1809) illustrates unambiguously the close fit between the name Mary and its associative field at the outset of the nineteenth century. Fashioned as an "Ancient Legend" (or archetypal cultural narrative), the tale relates the fate of two lovers in medieval Moscow: Uslad and Maria. Maria, momentarily captivated by the wealth of a rival suitor, agrees to marry him; recognizing her mistake, she implores the Mother of God to protect her forsaken and beloved Uslad. She weds joylessly and is soon murdered by her jealous husband. Uslad, inadvertently learning of Maria's devotion, seeks her out in the now abandoned tower where she had dwelt. He finds the icon of the Virgin he had given her and dons it, only to have her apparition appear and lead him to her grave, over which he erects a chapel to the Mother of God. This, explains Zhukovsky, is the legend behind the copse near the Yauza River called "Mary's Grove."

Of course Marian imagery in Russian letters came to mean many things in the nineteenth century, effected by principles of the Romantic canon, parody, irony, and reconfigurations of the realist school. The Marian image, and characters bearing the name, appear in a variety of guises. Reference to the Marys ("lofty" and "lowly") in texts from Pushkin to Tolstoy may advertise the moral bearings of a work or may play satirically with their religio-cultural significations. What the vast majority of these texts have in common, however, is that *association* of one sort or another with the Christian prototypes prevails. In other words, writers use the Marian semantic orbit to dress certain female characters in the garb of virtue or sin, even when their commentary on these associations is facetious. Chekhov breaks with these rough equations by *dissociating* his characters from the Marian female identities, and thereby baring them as cultural constructs.

Here I shall illustrate two phenomena: (1) authorial interest, over time, in the religio-cultural complex associated with the Marian figures; and (2) the heightened status of the name "Maria" in association with literary characters configured as "Virgins" or "sinful women." In treating this pivotal aspect of the so-called madonna/whore syndrome, I suggest that the Marian paradigm provided Russian culture with a convenient symbolic shorthand for discussions of (and judgments about) woman's sexuality. This survey looks first at nineteenth-century poetic figurations of the Virgin, then at edifying popular poetry devoted to Saint Mary of Egypt, and finally at the canon of realist prose, which casts characters in both Marian roles. If authors prior to Chekhov engage predictable associations to frame "Marian" characters, this in no way means that their texts are simplistic or uninteresting. The point,

29

rather, is to identify an unmistakable trend, and one readily identifiable by an astute reader of Chekhov's mettle.

POETIC MADONNAS

In nineteenth-century poetry, images of the Virgin and (virginlike) women stand at a certain remove from their Christian source. Yet it is typical of the Romantic canon that the core associations and linguistic formulas found in depictions of Madonna figures should remain closely linked to the religious prototype. Andrzej Dudek writes that almost every Russian poet of the nineteenth century "wrote at least one poem openly dedicated to the Mother of God or referring to Her indirectly."[54] At the same time, in an age of stringently enforced church and state censorship, caution surely argued against depicting the Most Holy Mother as anything but a sanctioned static emblem. What were the conventions and constraints governing portrayals of poetic Madonnas?

K. N. Batiushkov exploits the Romantic practice of regarding the beloved as Madonna to its logical end in his frolicsome epistle "To Masha" (1810). The poem reads: "Hail, O my friend, the beautiful Maria! / You are full of charms, of love and reason, / Grace is with you, you are Grace itself. / May the Fates forever spin you golden hours! / Eros has blessed you, / And I—have spoken like an angel." This amorous "annunciation" cuts close to the Orthodox bone. A commentator sees how this poem could potentially run afoul of censorship: "the possibility of publishing such a poem clearly demonstrates the temporary relaxation of censorial rigor in the first decade of Alexander I's reign. Several years later it was not only unthinkable to compare your beloved Masha to the Virgin Mary in print; even the epithet 'heavenly' was prohibited in descriptions of an earthly woman's beauty."[55]

Pushkin (who must have known Batiushkov's poem) was the poet of the Romantic era who went the farthest in refusing to let questions of sanctity intimidate him. Pushkin's narrative poem *Gavriiliada* (1821)—a profane portrayal of the young Jewess Maria's sexual initiation—far outstrips Batiushkov's tame version of the Annunciation by dint of its conspicuous erotic imagery. In *Gavriiliada,* Joseph's untouched wife Maria succumbs (in a rather self-assured manner) to three suitors: Satan, the Angel Gabriel, and the Lord. Upon overhearing the Lord confess to Gabriel that he lusts after Maria, Satan rushes in and seduces her; Gabriel then arrives from Heaven to press the Lord's suit, knocks out Satan, and himself enjoys Maria's favors; finally, the Lord assumes the shape of a dove and descends to have his way. An exhausted Maria exclaims at the end of the poem, "I gave myself on one and the same day / To the Evil One, to an archangel, and to God." Robert Sorenson suggests that *Gavriiliada* be read not as a parody of biblical events and language, but as a sophisticated translation of biblical myth into the language of erotic poetry, the inherent possibilities of which exist in liturgy and apocrypha.[56] In this sense Pushkin echoes the aesthetic of Renaissance artists, who depicted "a tension between the spiritual and the sensual which is central to the Mariolotry of the west."[57] The idea of celebrating unrestrained male *and* female sexual desire through reference to the Annunciation, of course, was guaranteed to provoke the harsh reaction that it did from church and state.

Pushkin, too, penned several lyrics in which the object of his devotion is configured as a Madonna. In each the indelible print of Pushkin's inventiveness can be felt. The female addressee in the playful "You are the Mother of God, there is no doubt" (1826) appears far more desirable than the Virgin, who "captivated only the holy spirit." The sonnet "Madonna" (1830) is addressed to Pushkin's fiancée Natalia Goncharova. "A poor knight lived in the world" (1829) farcically grafts ecclesiastical precepts onto the chivalric code: a knight falls in love with the Virgin, only to have the devil claim his soul when he dies on the grounds that he neglected Christ in order to pursue Christ's mother! ("He didn't stay on the Path / He went after Christ's *matushka.*") In the final stanza the Most Pure Mother intercedes on her admirer's behalf and gains him entrance to heaven. Thus Pushkin both honors and debunks the Romantic propensity for expressing male ardor through language of religious adoration.

Frequently Pushkin pairs imagery of virginlike characters with the name Maria, and not only when circumstance so requires (for example, in *Gavriiliada*). Joe Andrews writes of the Polish captive in *The Fountain of Bakchisarai* (1824), "Mariya's very name announces her as the virgin," while Stephanie Sandler notes that "she lives up to the prophecy of her name, a woman whose religious ecstasy is so great that sexual passion seems both small and inappropriate by comparison."[58] Pushkin deliberated over a name for the heroine of *Poltava* (1829), rejecting Natalia, Matryona, and Anna for Maria. He wrote in the margin of an early draft (in English), "I love this sweet name." The poet may not have heeded the religious associations (Lotman has discussed possible dedicatees), but Pushkin's version of the Battle of Poltava does linguistically chart the transition of Kochubei's daughter Maria from "virgin" to "whore" in the eyes of her parents when she opts to forsake them for Mazepa.[59] Recall, as well, that the virgin's counterpart is named by the poet in "Earthly Authority" ("Maria the Sinful Woman"). Pushkin's prose features several Marias, some of whom are symbolically linked to aspects of the Marian paradigm. For reasons perhaps having to do with its multivalence Pushkin appears to have truly loved "this sweet name."

Pushkin's treatment of the virgin-harlot paradigm runs the gamut from highly conventionalized representations of the Romantic canon to the erotically charged tale of sexual initiation that, had it been published, would have stunned a public steeped in puritanical Christian values. While coding his Madonnas to the religious prototype, he experiments creatively with all

31

manner of variation on the Christian myth. This extension of religious imagery into imaginatively reworked text offers a certain precedent for Chekhov's Marian context. Never, however, does Pushkin venture to challenge the associations inherent in the dual model of the Christian Marys.

In the lyrics of Russian nineteenth-century poets, the diction of European Romanticism provided a means of distancing the Virgin motif, a theme that might have been tolerated poorly by the Orthodox Church. Lermontov's "Prayer" (1837) and Fet's poems "Our Lady of Zion, my icon lamp is lit before you in the darkness" (1842) and "Ave Maria" (1842) appeal to the Virgin for intercession in securing the love of young ladies. Fet also wrote some contemplative lyrics based on Catholic motifs. His "Madonna" (1842) and "To the Sistine Madonna" (1864) meditate in sonnet form on the beauty of Raphael's paintings. It is unthinkable to imagine the personalized relationship between mother and child of Fet's "Madonna" (Christ joyfully "inclined toward Maria with a smile") describing an Orthodox icon of the Mother of God.

Recourse to a Western setting can also be found in the plots of lyrics. Baratynsky sets his balladic poem "Madonna" (1832) in Italy, an exotic setting consonant with the Romantic canon—and one that also safeguarded the poem from the Russian censor. Baratynsky puts a spin on the typically sentimental plot of Karamzin's "Poor Liza." An impoverished old woman and her daughter pray to the Holy Madonna to improve their state; a wealthy man seeking shelter from a storm espies a Corregio Madonna in their hut; the old woman declines to sell it ("to do trade with my soul"), but word gets out and the women make a handsome living by charging a fee to view their treasure. The commercial profit that brings the earthly salvation for which the women had prayed to the Madonna would have been nothing short of blasphemous in the world of Orthodox Christianity.

Poetic imagery of the Mother of God worked in other ways as well. A critic suggests that in two Tiutchev poems the motif of the Mother of God subsumes the chthonic image of "Mother Earth" to create analogies between mythic creation and the poetic act.[60] In his poem "The Harvest" of 1835, too, A.V. Koltsov traces the cycle of sowing and reaping with imagery of the religious miracle, and, at the end, substitutes an illuminated icon for the withdrawing sun in a late autumn landscape: "But the villager's candle is lit / Before the icon of the Holy Mother." Occasional flattering addresses to the empresses Maria Fedorovna, Maria Aleksandrovna, and Maria Fedorovna (wives, respectively, of Paul I, Alexander II, and Alexander III) hint at an affinity with the Holy Mother.

Finally, a poem about the Mother of God by the celebrated Ukrainian poet Taras Shevchenko (who lived a good part of his life in Saint Petersburg) attracts attention in particular because of the likelihood that Chekhov knew it.[61] Like Pushkin, in his narrative poem *Maria* (1876) Shevchenko tampers with sacred plots. The poet unveils the party responsible for fathering Jesus and denies Christ a resurrection, championing Mary as the hardheaded heroine who gets Christ's program of social justice off the ground. This poem alone testifies to changing trends in depiction of the sacred throughout the century. Although, once again, the poet does not stray from the essential lines of the Gospel narration (even if overturned), the spirit of his reinventions (especially the inversion of roles) hints at an aesthetic compatible with Chekhov's own. In a more straightforwardly religious manner, another kind of poet paid homage to the Virgin's "lowly" counterpart, Saint Mary of Egypt.

POPULAR NARRATIVE POETRY

If censorship, along with religious inhibitions and social customs, hindered widespread allusion to the Orthodox Mother of God in nineteenth-century poetry, that may help to explain a rather extensive body of works depicting "fallen woman," for whom no such strictures held. Poets and prose writers with many different purposes looked at how brazenly sexual women violated social norms and challenged the boundaries of sanctity. The "fallen woman" who had long served as a cliché in medieval sermons against sin was now, so to speak, fleshed out, becoming a literary character in her own right.

Taxonomic overviews of the female sexual "transgressor" in nineteenth-century Russian letters have been undertaken elsewhere.[62] More essential here are the works devoted to the theme of Saint Mary of Egypt and the ways in which Christian legends of Mary of Egypt / Mary Magdalene help to create the background of the "sinful woman's" tale. Representations of these Marys tend to be put forth in a solemn religious spirit, a sobriety evident in Tiutchev's famous poem, "Oh my prophetic soul!" (1855), which ends with the poet's soul "like Maria, prepared to cling to the feet of Christ." As it happens, the theme of the fallen woman became a fashionable subject in narrative religious poems.

At least three narrative poems based on Saint Mary of Egypt's legend appeared in print during the second half of the century.[63] All of them retain the contours of the hagiography but differ in emphasis. Ivan S. Aksakov wrote "Mary of Egypt" in 1845 (although it was not published until 1888). This poem treats only the first part of the saint's *Vita*, when she lived as a harlot in Alexandria—a partial treatment that itself indicates a fascination with the more lurid, earlier installment of Mary of Egypt's life. Aksakov does not paint this early Mary of Egypt as a wanton whore, but takes care to plant some small seeds of a thirsting soul in the merrymaker who delights in her physical charms and gives herself over to iniquitous behavior. Mary of Egypt openly broadcasts her intentions, anticipating good times with pilgrims on the ship to Jerusalem, and countering the naysayer who would thwart her ocean journey ("you know, Maria, they only take those who can pay in gold") with the confident prediction:

> Why pay?
> At the pier I'll say:
> Take me without gold,
> And I'll lavishly present you
> With all of the wealth a poor woman has!

Thus, despite foreshadowing of better things to come, Aksakov's Mary of Egypt remains in a "corrupted" state—or, as we might say today, she remains in charge of her own sexual pleasure. The poem confirms the supposition that this tantalizing brand of female sin caught the Russian imagination.

B. N. Almazov's *Mary of Egypt*, probably written in 1864, remains more faithful to the *Vita*. The poem mimics the narrative frame of the hagiography with its long prelude documenting the discovery of the saint by the elder Zosima. The most interesting lines in the poem for our purposes relate to Mary's name and to the paradigmatic relationship between harlot and virgin. Mary of Egypt explains to Zosima when he finds her in the desert:

> I was born in Egypt. At christening,
> My father and mother, not knowing my fate,
> Gave me a great name:
> I was called Maria; this name,
> Perhaps, served as a concealed veil,
> And saved me from eternal ruin.

Almazov foregrounds the relationship between the two Marys as his poem progresses. He dwells in detail far beyond anything supplied by the *Vita* on Mary of Egypt's conversion outside the church doors. Here she falls into a faint upon recognizing her depravity, wakens with her gaze on the face of the Most Holy Virgin, but cannot look her in the eye for shame. She cries out:

> O, Holy Lady! Do not repudiate me!
> I understand how terrible for you is
> The sight of a cursed fornicatress, O, Most Pure Virgin,
> And my sins make me unworthy
> Of entering your temple! . . . But you are merciful!

In the ensuing dozen lines, Mary of Egypt wholly repents before the icon. That Almazov chose to spell out so fully the interrelationship between the two Marys speaks to its importance as a cultural paradigm.

This relationship captures the interest of a female writer as well. The poet-nun Elizaveta Shakhova introduces narrative innovations such as an inserted "Sinful Woman's Prayer" into her lengthy poem about Mary of Egypt, *The Power of Repentance (The Story of an Ascetic)*. The fact that this prayer appears early in the poem with no regard for the chronology of the *Vita* marks its significance in Shakhova's narrative scheme. The prayer to the Virgin is mouthed by Mary of Egypt, once again, at the entrance to the cathedral in front of an "Icon of the Virgin Full of Grace, / With the Heavenly Infant in her arms." Shakhova emphasizes the dreadful disgrace of childless female sexuality ("A fornicatress, fallen from her very childhood years / Who has no equal in the world!") by juxtaposing her against an image of the Virgin with Child. This point is reinforced at the end of the prayer by Shakhova's choice of epithets. Mary of Egypt falls again "before the Unwed Bride" who directs her to seek peace beyond the Jordan. One might speculate that Shakhova's preoccupation with the saint's untoward sexual conduct and with the role of the Virgin Mother in her conversion has to do with the monastic vows that the author herself had taken.

All three poems dedicated to Mary of Egypt represent a genre of poetry tailored to popular tastes and intended for widespread consumption. In this sense they represent a vehicle of cultural reproduction, not unlike the Menologies themselves, in an era when oral transmission of religious folk texts had become more rare. Aleksei Konstantinovich Tolstoy also authored several reworked versions of saints' lives (notably a poem about Saint John of Damascus, a church father known for his Marian exegesis) and comes to our attention through a poem to which Chekhov refers several times in his works. The poem *The Sinful Woman,* probably written in 1857, takes as its subject a harlot at a raucous feast who, after wagering that she can seduce Christ, falls at his feet and repents. Typologically this poem clearly relates to the tales of the sinful Marys. I shall have more to say about it in relationship to "The Teacher of Literature" (see Chapter 5).

The similar overall scheme of these narratives suggests that the Christian "master plot" of the sinful woman enjoyed immense popularity in the Russian milieu. They are joined by a plethora of short lyrics that, with sundry truncations, adhere to the essential contours of the story: for example, Polezhaev's "The Sinful Woman" (1837), Fet's "The Fornicatress" (1843), and Pleshcheev's translation of Friedrich Hebbel's "The Sinful Woman." If we look to the fine arts, the renown of Vasily Polenov's enormous canvas *Christ and the Sinful Woman,* painted in 1888, affirms the appeal of the plot.

These narrative poems also attest to the special station occupied by Saint Mary of Egypt in the literary and cultural imagination. Notably, authors who take up this theme lavish attention on the exotic Egyptian origins of the harlot-saint. Aksakov paints the "Egyptian maiden" as a dark-skinned, timbrel-jingling gypsy. Shakhova describes the young Maria as "the pharaoh's handiwork" and "the magnificent cream of the Egyptian lands." Surely this ethnic distancing reassured Russia that the threat of expressive female sexuality resided elsewhere. Just as surely, this exoticism contributed to the "othering" of woman and the perpetuation of Christian myths about her wiles, wickedness, and impurity.

REALIST PROSE

Realism's appetite for variety, its sprawling texts and unofficial license to quarry all spheres of life meant that authors could choose subject matter and tone quite freely. Practices of censorship were relaxed in the wake of Nicholas I's "Kingdom of Darkness," encouraging more casual use of Christian codes in the second half of the century. The religious prototypes of virginity and harlotry come to fashion a number of situations in which realism's female characters are placed. In Gogol, Turgenev, Dostoevsky, and Tolstoy, the Virgin Mary figures prominently as a symbolic locus of a desirable femininity, while female seductiveness and sexuality frequently menace this coveted purity. The discussion that follows will range selectively through stories and novels in which the Marian paradigm has been called upon more or less explicitly to sculpt the character of woman, again with the reminder that this overview is so that Chekhov's handling of the paradigm might be better appreciated. Treatment of the Marian figures in works by Chekhov's realist predecessors can be both serious and parodic, but remains anchored in a reservoir of common cultural understanding.

Nikolai Gogol draws attention to competing cultural constructs of the Virgin in *Taras Bulba* (1842) through iconographic images. Gogol's Cossack-Christian soldiers wage their holy war in the name of a highly feminized Russian Orthodoxy.[64] The rhetoric of sacred Mother Russia is omnipresent. Cossack booty from campaigns in Turkey features rizas (ornate frames) for icons of the Mother of God; Bulba's wife twice bestows Marian icons on her sons and entrusts them to the Mother of God as they leave for the Zaporozhe Cossack camp and thence for battle. But individual human women represent disposable commodities in the Cossack world (Bulba tells his sons to regard the saber as their mother).

Taras Bulba's younger son, Andrii, transgresses the law of allegiance to an abstracted archmother—Holy Mother Russia—by attaching his affections to an individual woman, the Polish beauty in the adversary's camp. His path toward her brings him past a faded image of the Catholic Madonna, and he finds her sitting before the holy image; she in turn repeatedly implores the Most Pure Mother of God to forgive her the transgression of her love for an enemy "knight." Andrii is initially beckoned into the Polish town by the Tartar maidservant with the plea, "For the sake of Christ and Holy Mary," a hint at his beloved's (unstated) name.[65]

When Andrii takes up arms for the Poles against his former comrades, then, he betrays the Russian shape of Christianity. As he abandons his native

36

culture's proto-image of Woman for an alien female individual, he forsakes his own collective identity. Falling for the Polish woman leads to the moral lesson that succumbing to foreignness, splitting off from the organic body of male communality presided over by the Orthodox Holy Mother, can only result in death—and death, for that matter, at the hands of the father. The power of the Virgin's image to the quintessentially "Russian" mentality of the Cossacks may be depicted with a tinge of irony, but it also speaks to Gogol's famous ambivalence about women, or, more strongly put, to his gynephobia. Ensconced in the territory of abstraction—the territory of angelic beings occupied by woman in Gogol's "Woman in the World"—the image of woman averts uncomfortable questions raised by women in the flesh.

Midcentury Russian letters saw the novel in ascent. Novelists evinced a more evenhanded interest in both Marian figures than had their forerunners in poetry. In fact, the paradigmatic relationship between virgin and harlot seemed to engage many writers. Turgenev emblematically represents the fate of at least two of his heroes as an alternative between "virgin" and "loose woman." Lavretsky in *A Nest of Gentry* aspires to union with the chaste and virginal Liza (who enters a nunnery), but is thwarted by his former wife who has cuckolded him. In *Spring Torrents,* Turgenev portrays a femme fatale—Maria Nikolaevna—who seduces (and ruins) his hero Dmitry Sanin. The lustful Maria is described as a snake. She has long red hair (the fabled color of Mary Magdalene's hair) that is let loose from the "snake-like braids" just before her final victory over Sanin. Maria Nikolaevna stands in direct contrast to the Madonna-like Gemma, a sweet and gentle Italian beauty to whom Sanin is betrothed when he meets the temptress. The choice between the two women ultimately exposes Sanin for one of the weak-willed Russian men who inhabit Turgenev's works. Finally, the closing scene of domestic bliss in *Fathers and Children* takes place under the roof of Marino, the Kirsanov estate named after Nikolai Petrovich's deceased wife Masha, namesake of the sheltering Mother.[66]

It will come as no surprise that the question of female saintliness and sinfulness develops most fully in Dostoevsky and Tolstoy, both writers eloquent about the need to orient life on a grid of Christian moral postulates. This field of inquiry is, of course, vast. Degraded virgins, femmes fatales, and saintly whores abound in Dostoevsky's novels. For Tolstoy, Anna Karenina epitomizes the woman who would transgress the boundaries of commonly shared religious/social beliefs to commit adultery (her body, prostrate at Vronsky's feet after their first amorous encounter, announces a literally fallen woman). The brief comments here will focus on the Marian theme.

Mary of Egypt's *Vita* was one of Dostoevsky's favorite readings in the Menologies, a mainstay in the Dostoevsky home.[67] This partiality finds reflection in Dostoevsky's fiction. Arkady in *The Adolescent* fondly recalls the "strange rapture" with which he read Saint Mary's unusual life, and Father Zosima in *The Brothers Karamazov* singles her life out (along with that of Aleksei Man of God) as recommended reading for the monks at the monastery. Such edifying mention of Mary of Egypt, however, is not without more lighthearted articulation.

In Dostoevsky's early story "Polzunkov" (1848), for example, the chatterbox narrator Polzunkov tells a story of personal intrigue (in which he himself is thoroughly hoodwinked) against a backdrop that Dostoevsky cleverly configures as a combination of Saint Mary of Egypt's day (1 April) and April Fools' Day. Throughout the tale, hints of sin and repentance receive ironic and humorous treatment. Polzunkov's corrupt superior, trying to avoid paying him a sum demanded as blackmail, says, "I see you are repentant. . . . You know that tomorrow is . . . ," and Polzunkov rejoins, "Mary of Egypt's day." Of note are the names of the department chief's wife and daughter in the tale: Maria Fominishna and Maria Fedoseevna. Neither woman is painted as sexually suspect, but they both participate in the insincere world of false repentance associated with the April Fools' motif. In other words, the sacred value of the saint's life serves as the (comic) orientation point for their behavior, which has more to do with the pagan and carnivalized trickery of April Fools'. The double naming highlights Dostoevsky's awareness of his play on cultural traditions.

Robert Louis Jackson has written about the importance of the Madonna image in Dostoevsky as a representation of ideal beauty "toward which man turns in reverence and longing," but which also becomes the object of disfigurement by those in the clutches of sensuality and corruption.[68] Polarities mirroring the Marian paradigm function, in one way or another, in all of Dostoevsky's four major novels. The degree to which these polarities are explicitly linked to Marian thematics varies from novel to novel. Within this general field of association Dostoevsky is prone to tamper with the attributes of the Marian figures, to shift them from their foundations, to problematize Madonna and harlot alike.

The religious significations of the Marian models are preserved to the greatest extent, perhaps, in *The Brothers Karamazov* (1880). Characters associated with the Mother of God are those who are pure of heart: Alyosha (whose mother entrusts him to the Virgin's protection), Zosima (whose cell is adorned with icons of the Virgin and who directs pilgrims to Her icons for intercession and repentance), and Lise (who prays to the Mother of God before imparting the secret of her love to Alyosha). Grushenka, of course, is assigned the part of "sinful woman" (Rakitin spitefully goads Alyosha on this score by evoking Magdalene: "Is the harlot back on the righteous path? Have the seven devils been cast out?") As Zosima's fondness for Mary of Egypt's life portends, Grushenka's self-styled penitence can be anticipated. Such schematic observations skirt the substance of an expansive novel, but do attest to Dostoevsky's unflagging interest in the viability of the Virgin and the repentant harlot as prototypes for human lives.

There is relatively little Marian contextualization in *Crime and Punishment* (1866). True, Raskolnikov imagines Dunya praying about the decision to marry Luzhin before the icon of the Kazan Mother of God (and Luzhin contrives to schedule the wedding proximate to the Dormition, suggestive of the figurative death awaiting Dunya in that marriage), but the imagery is developed only in the sense that Dunya maintains her moral and physical virginity in the face of onslaughts by Luzhin and Svidrigailov. For her part, Sonya—who prostitutes herself out of compassion for others—is held up to Mary of the Lazarus story (to whom many came and, after witnessing Jesus' miracle, acquired faith), the same Mary who, as we saw earlier, became part of the conflated Magdalene persona.[69] These details, of course, come as props in a scheme of sexual politics that occupies a much vaster space within the novel.

The episode concerning the Swiss girl Marie, narrated to the Epanchin women by Prince Myshkin in *The Idiot* (1868), clearly draws on the religious myth of the fallen woman. Marie has been viewed as an incarnation of Mary Magdalene.[70] Marie, deflowered by a passing merchant, is ostracized by the village until the local children rally to her cause and raise her to the status of a sort of holy woman. Several scholars have noted the seeds in the Marie tale of the story in the larger novel of another "sinful woman," Nastasia Filippovna. Most recently, Michael Finke has argued that these parallels serve ultimately to announce a significant disaffinity between the two narrations. The Marie tale "becomes a generic model for Myshkin, and his unhappy place in the novel as a whole can be understood as that of an *author* attempting to shape a Petersburg story [revolving around Nastasia Filippovna] on the model of the Switzerland story."[71] Marie's story follows the trajectory from transgression to sainthood generic to the myths of the "sinful" Marys. Myshkin's failure to activate this tale in Petersburg can stand, in a sense, for the larger question of why Dostoevsky rarely imports the Marian figures into his novels with their wholesale religious connotations intact.

The Dostoevsky novel in which the Marian paradigm is called upon most fully is *The Devils* (1872). Two Marys—Maria Lebyadkina and Marie Shatova—act out versions of the "virgin" and the "whore." Lebyadkina, the saintly half-wit, vocalizes her reverence for the Mother of God, calling her "the hope of humankind." She is murdered after baring Stavrogin as an imposter, an act in which she imitates the Marian function as judge and conscience of the criminal. (Jackson suggests a symbolic relationship between the vandalized icon of the Mother of God at the Church of the Nativity of Our Lady and the murder of Maria Lebyadkina.)[72] Marie Shatova intially comports herself "loosely," abandoning her husband for an affair with Stavrogin abroad, but then moves to the other Marian pole, "coming to life" with the birth of

Stavrogin's son in the forgiving presence of Shatov—a short-lived resurrection that ends three days later with the death of all three. Susanne Fusso uncovers a link between the Sistine Madonna (much discussed in *The Devils*) and Marie Shatova, reading it as a "restorative parody" that honors the Marian image: "Thanks to the divine power of art, embodied in Mar'ia Shatova as a walking, breathing, birth-giving Sistine Madonna . . . the human being is once again, if only for a moment, not just a worm, not just a slave, but also a god."[73] This glimpse of redemptive value, central (of course) to Dostoevsky's thinking, remains necessarily compromised for its temporality. Nina Pelikan Straus sees the Madonna figure in *The Devils* quite thoroughly problematized, maintaining that Stavrogin's destructive involvement with women linked to the mother/Madonna by names that "begin with *Ma* (Matryosha, Maria, Mary)" represents "an unconscious mother complex addicted to paying back or destroying a primal female image."[74]

If the fixed religio-cultural orientation points of the Marian icon, locus of beauty and spiritual value, and the repentant harlot, model of salvation for all, appear frequently in Dostoevsky's novels, they appear more often than not riddled with disfigurement, disjunction, parodic curves, and tensions of other sorts. Explaining the ambiguities of this imperfect transfer, Nina Pelikan Straus writes: "In his letters and nonfictional writings, Dostoevsky clings to the model of Christ as the ideal man and to the icon of the Madonna as Christ's feminine counterpart." But while allusions to both images appear in Dostoevsky's novels, "his male and female characters are not construed in terms of them but in terms of what deconstructionists call *différance*"—in other words, final, authoritative meaning is always deferred in a "dialectic between modernism and traditionalism, skepticism and belief."[75] In his complex treatment of the two Marian prototypes, Dostoevsky would seem to provide some antecedent for Chekhov. The categorical distinction, however, should be fairly clear: the metaphysical striving of the former, his consuming desire to put stock in Christian certainties, remained forever alien to Chekhov.

Tolstoy, who studied Russian religious culture more thoroughly than any other Russian writer (save, perhaps, Leskov) knew well his culture's associations with the Marian framework. Tolstoy was preoccupied with the question of the relationship between the spirit and the flesh, precisely the dichotomy on which the Marian paradigm is founded. His works are peopled with a generous proportion of "Marys" whom he portrays with a marked fidelity to the premises of the religious paradigm. Thus, for instance, Konstantin Levin's irascible brother Nikolai in *Anna Karenina* (1877) lives with a woman he has delivered from the brothel named Maria Nikolaevna. Especially in his earlier prose, however, Tolstoy's "Marys" are fully developed characters whose resonances with the Marian figures, if they exist, are not direct. Such are Masha in "Family Happiness" and Mariana in "The Cossacks."

This indirection is true, too, of *War and Peace* (1869). Marie Sémon stops short of reading a Madonna-like character into Princess Mary, but does call her Tolstoy's "ideal heroine" and suggests of her epistolary style, "en reprenant ce lexique sentimentaliste, Marie le transpose de l'exaltation amoreuse à la religiosité."[76] Indeed, in volume 2 of the novel (part 2, chap. 13), Tolstoy gestures in the direction of the Virgin when Princess Mary, in her capacity of protectress to "God's people," hosts an elderly pilgrim at Bald Hills who regales the skeptical and jesting Pierre and Prince Andrei with her stories of miracles performed by the Mother of God. Undoubtedly Tolstoy chose the name Mary to adorn a heroine characterized by piety, humility, and faith in the loving nature of humanity.

Certainly questions related to woman's sexuality loom large in the nineteenth-century novel and are by no means always posed through Marian allusions. In late Tolstoy, however, the paradigm is woven into many works in a fashion that verges on a name fixation. In the most didactic of Tolstoy's novels, *Resurrection* (1899), Nekhliudov has an affair with a nobleman's wife, Maria Vasilevna; he almost marries the posturing social butterfly (or "inauthentic virgin") Maria Korchagina; he is urged to put Maslova into a house for "Magdalenes"; and he encounters at the novel's end the real Tolstoyan Madonna, Maria Pavlovna, who, born beautiful and rich, has left her life of privilege to live with the simple people, spreading comfort and love to all she meets. *Khadzhi Murat* (1912) presents two Marys: Maria Vasilevna Vorontsova freely pursues affairs with her husband's military subordinates, while the kind Maria Dmitrievna, the common-law wife of a low-ranking commander, intercedes on behalf of a Tartar, and rebuffs Butler's advances (an allusion Tolstoy spells out with the words "he was no longer the wonderful Joseph in relationship to Maria Dmitrievna"). The explicit conflict between spirit and flesh appears most clearly in "Father Sergius" (1911), a story that Chekhov obviously could not have known, but one that deserves attention for the way that it encapsulates the dichotomies of the Marian paradigm.

"Father Sergius" opens with an introduction to Stepan Kasatsky, an ambitious young man of the world who aims to enter the highest court society. Kasatsky woos Princess Korotkova, whose "angelic purity" enraptures him until, shortly before their wedding (and just at the moment when we learn her name is Mary) she informs him that she had been mistress to Nicholas I. Kasatsky abruptly abandons this "fallen woman," and enters a monastery on the feast day of the Intercession (of the Mother of God). He becomes Father Sergius and wrestles with temptations of pride and of the flesh for many years. The holiday of the Virgin's Intercession again steers his next move, from the monastery to a hermit's cell. Living as a hermit, Father Sergius vanquishes sexual temptation when visited by the alluring Makovkina by chopping off his finger, but some time later he succumbs to the seductions of the sensual young merchant's daughter, Maria. This fall leads him to suicidal thoughts, and then to Pashenka, the humble woman who "lives for God, imagining that she lives for people." The religious guidewires of the Virgin's protection and the whore's sirenlike call to ruin find a quasi-Chekhovian resolution in the third Mary, Pashenka's daughter Masha, who sits in a Madonna-like pose holding her small son, but whose burdensome demands on her mother belie the image. Unlike Chekhov's working of the motif, however, this dissociation serves an ideological function—that of introducing Sergius/Kasatsky to the imperfect world outside the church, where he ultimately finds God.

Any inventory of a figure as widespread as that of Mary in Tolstoy will necessarily be constrained. It should be clear, however, that Tolstoy rather steadily chose to engage the religious and cultural associations of the name Mary to characterize women in the general semantic fields of virgin and whore. Because of his ambivalence about sensuality, these depictions (especially in late Tolstoy) are charged with a greater degree of moral indignation than in the works of most of his predecessors. Tolstoy may be a "fox," as Isaiah Berlin claims, but the face of the "hedgehog" seems to peer through when he looks to the Marian paradigm.[77]

Along with his famous statement about the resemblance between Chekhov's literary form and impressionist art, Tolstoy is said to have stated, "As an artist, Chekhov can not be compared with earlier Russian writers—with Turgenev, Dostoevsky or myself."[78] While no value judgment concerning *literary* merit lies dormant in the observation, I make essentially the same point here. Despite colossal differences in genre, tone, and intention, in the works of the Russian canon before Chekhov we find that the Marian images and their offshoots occupy an overarching common territory. Each author transfers the value of the conventional religious images as they were understood in Russian culture either directly, satirically, or in some slightly altered form into the qualities of, and situations encountered by, his literary characters. This transference was often accomplished ingeniously and with tremendous sophistication. Nonetheless, in their use of Marian imagery all of these authors seem to stand by, in one way or another, the "diptych of Christian patriarchy's idea of woman."[79]

Chekhov was an enormous innovator, but not an overtly radical one. Without fanfare, his prose develops an original means of considering the significance of the polarized Christian Marys. He looks at the premises of the paradigmatic associations themselves—in essence, at the fact that they should hold such sway over the Russian imagination that even its most distinguished voices preserve them. Chekhov was able to approach the question phenomenologically in no small part because of his insider's view of the Orthodox religion. His Christian upbringing educated him in the many media of the faith: Scripture, liturgy, iconography, acathist, prayer, apocrypha, the saints' lives, spiritual verses, and *lubok* prints. Singing in the church choir (and, for that matter, clerking in his father's store as a boy) also brought him into close, everyday contact with the functions of religion in the lives of rank-and-file people. This is a vantage point from which Pushkin, Gogol, Turgenev, Dostoevsky, and Tolstoy never viewed Russian society.

If writers prior to Chekhov, by and large, meant to authorize an associative reading of characters placed beside Christian images, Chekhov uses this first tier (where, so to speak, the clue is supplied) as a springboard to a far more important second tier. Here he subverts the original associations through a variety of devices, including displacement, reversal, and inversion. Thus the proximity of a character to a Marian reference never sanctions a direct association, but rather a break with the stereotypical religious equation. By liberating this imagery from its conventional hooks, Chekhov creates room to explore psychological responses to the paradigm itself, or how the received cultural construct is "used" in life (at least, in life as represented by fiction). Pursuing this line of inquiry, the chapters that follow aim to open up some new vistas in the symbolic topography of Chekhov's prose.

Chapter Two

Early Prose:

Genesis of the Marian Context

> Under a kerchief that hides the locks
> Of light red braids,
> Masha asks a question of
> A man walking her way:
> "Excuse me, but might I ask
> By what name you go?"
> "It's early yet. I'm called a scoundrel,"
> Answers the rogue.
> —ditty from *Splinters,* 1882

CHEKHOV PENNED most of his early stories under the pseudonym Antosha Chekhonte (pronounced *Chekhonté*), a name that suited well the jesting tone of the popular press where his pieces appeared. In the early 1880s his feuilletons and short compositions were published in *Splinters* (*Oskolki*), *The Dragon-fly* (*Strekoza*), *The Alarm Clock* (*Budil'nik*), *The Spectator* (*Zritel'*), *Moscow* (*Moskva*), *The Companion* (*Sputnik*), and *Worldly Sense* (*Mirskoi tolk*). These stories entirely conform to the prescribed format and content of the lowbrow press: they are brief, they recount situations (often comic) of an anecdotal character, and the dénouement hinges on an unanticipated peripeteia.

One factor, however, that distinguishes Chekhov from his fellow "scribblers" (as he dubbed them) is his rich play with language. This playing is not only a matter of clever witticisms and adroitly orchestrated repartee: Chekhov also draws on the many idiomatic spheres of Russian speech, probing the intersections between different kinds of language and exploring the psychological ramifications of the speech-act. The province of speech that interests us here is a subtle plane of language grounded in the religious discourse of the culture, a plane that both corresponds to the obvious (and frequently humorous) meaning of a story, and goes beyond it. In this chapter we shall consider the nature of these Christian linguistic undercurrents in the early prose.

A substantial literature on the relationship between Chekhov's early and mature prose focuses on the many integral ties between the two.[1] Given this tendency toward continuity, one might expect the early stories to yield some material related to Marian imagery. Few of the stories Chekhov wrote between 1881 and 1886 explicitly evoke either of the Marian prototypes. Rather, intimations of the Christian paradigm are revealed through the use of language on the part of the characters or narrator, and/or by the narrative situation. Let it be said that the name "Maria" represents an essential ingredient in these configurations. Yet this is not a mere technical exercise. It is not true that the name—a patently common one, the use of which, moreover, may have kindled "in-jokes" with the author's sister—commands Marian associations in every case. Neither can one assert that elements of the complex (the veneration of a woman, for instance) are necessarily keyed to this cultural code.[2] The stories under consideration yield verbal clues keyed to the Marian vocabulary, treat perceptions of women as either lofty/superior/compassionate, or sexually tainted, and, through gender configurations, comment on the underlying culturally generated psychological impulses behind a character's behavior.

Already in the early prose the hallmark of these framing Marian background images is disjuncture. Articulated religious themes rarely surface, but the stories are replete with the residue of Christian discourse which permeates the Russian language. Highly cognizant of the multivalences of words, Chekhov observes how the ecclesiastical language, so prevalent in the mind of a population required to adhere to the Orthodox faith, bursts out of its semantic boundaries when imported into quotidian life. Meaning becomes transposed—or translated—in unexpected ways. In fact, the notion of translation will guide my initial discussion of the religious idiom in Chekhov's early prose. From there, five stories illustrate the genesis of the Marian context as manifest in the linguistic fabric of a story. Next we shall look at secular iconography and the Marian context in several stories; finally, two stories on the brink between Chekhov's "early" and "mature" periods will receive attention. It should become clear that Chekhov revels in the potentialities of language, in the plasticity of these interpretations of the Christian idiom.

Chekhov plays outright with the notion of translation in his early work. Several stories bear subtitles such as "Translation from the Portuguese," "Translation from French," "Translation from the Language of Children," and "The Works of Jules Verne, Translated by A. Chekhonte." In "Love Spurned (Translation from the Spanish)" (1883) Chekhov inserts a romantic serenade in Latin ("Imperfectum conjunctivi passivi!" sings the lovesick bard) that is then "translated" in a fictitious footnote from the (Russian) translator as, "If you don't appear, my blood will sully your window! I am dying!" (2:15). This tongue-in-cheek pseudo-mystification is a relative of the brilliant translations in *Eugene Onegin,* where Pushkin masquerades foreign words as Russian, proffers off-the-cuff translations, footnotes fictitious works, and so forth. S. G. Bocharov suggests that such "translation" in Pushkin's novel-in-verse illuminates the novel's multilingual planes by showing how meaning can be transposed (and nimbly manipulated) not only between natural languages, but between stylistic variations within the Russian language.[3] It is such translation effected within one's own language that especially marks Chekhov's play with words in the early prose.

Literal translation of Christian ideas constitutes the pith of some phrases. Thus an actor is defined as "a genuine Christian who observes fasts" in the farcical "3,000 Foreign Words That Have Entered Russian" (2:182). A brief snippet published in 1882 finds examiners grilling a clerk prior to promotion: "What is the meaning of the word 'Amen?'" they query; the clerk answers, "That'll do! Enough!" (18:37). The formulaic closure of the sacred text is translated into the language of the impatient churchgoer (and reflects as well on the clerk's desire to see the exam end). The wit in both instances resides in a linguistic common ground bred of a shared religious experience.

A frivolous tidbit from Chekhov's notebooks illustrates how the religious idiom can become psychologized through "translation" into personal terms: "When they sang 'Today is the beginning [*glavizna*] of our salvation' in church, at home he cooked up soup made from an animal's head [*glavizna*]; on the day of St. John the Baptist's beheading [*useknovenie*], he refused to eat anything round [which might resemble a head] and flogged [*sëk*] his children" (17:85). In this nearly untranslatable play on words, the subject interprets phrases from the liturgy as directives for his domestic comportment. Obsolete and obscure Church Slavic expressions are not left behind in church, but leak out into everyday life. The words are translated idiosyncratically into actions highly inappropriate to the religious context, but filled with a certain obtuse logic for the agent himself. As it happens, this phrase opens the troparion to the service of the Annunciation, and thus leads into the Marian theme.

The main linguistic current in "Tears the World Doesn't See" ("Nevidimye miru slezy," 1884) appears to derive from the principal Orthodox acathist to Mary. The story masterfully illustrates the importation of the Christian idiom into a household setting. As already noted, this acathist was repeated in church and at home countless times each year. The language and concepts of the Marian acathist were so deeply familiar to both Chekhov and his readers that he could assume his caper would be grasped by some.

In "Tears the World Doesn't See" the lieutenant colonel Rebrotesov and his pals, upon leaving a provincial club at two in the morning, begin to indulge in food fantasies, imagining how delightful it would be to have a bite to eat and a glass of vodka. Rebrotesov decides to invite his companions home. The story's core scene portrays Rebrotesov attempting to convince his slumbering wife to relinquish the larder key so that he might entertain his friends. One suspects that the title itself lampoons the liturgical phrase "All things Seen and Unseen" (*Mir vidimyi i nevidimyi*), since the spice of the story rests in the discrepancy between the public and private behavior of Rebrotesov and his wife.[4]

In the privacy of their bedroom, Rebrotesov faces his irascible spouse after waking her from a sound sleep and pleads his case: "The guests all respect you so much. . . . Dvoetochiev is a religious man, you know. . . . Pruzhina and the bursar are too. . . . They all say of you . . . 'Maria,' they say, 'Petrovna,' they say, 'is not a woman, but something,' they say, 'unintelligible [*neudoboponiatnoe*]. . . . The luminary of our district [*svetilo nashego uezda*]'" (3:48). Chekhov introduces the Christian theme in this otherwise patently prosaic context with Rebrotesov's incongruous identification of his drinking buddies as "religious" people. Laughably, both are bureaucrats—and Dvoetochiev holds the post of inspector of the theological institute. His humorous surname "Colon" (*dvoetochie*, literally, "two points") resonates with the story's bifurcated semantic play. Moreover, it seems not unplausible that Chekhov knowingly (and slyly) refers here to an omnipresent, and graphically pronounced, form of punctuation in the acathist: the colon (see Fig. 2).

Rebrotesov's description prepares the ground for the praises the "religious men" purportedly sing to his wife. Lines of the Marian acathist contain the words *neudobovoskhodimaia* and *neudobozrimaia:* "Rejoice, O heights *unobtainable* by human thoughts: Rejoice, O depths *unpenetrated* by Angels' eyes." Ieronim in "On Holy Night" cites this line, then covers his face and shakes his head in awe, repeating with amazement several of the acathist's compound words. Clearly Chekhov was intensely conscious—and appreciative—of the complex word morphology of the acathist. The dubious compliment attributed to Rebrotesev's friends (that his wife resembles "something unintelligible" [*neudoboponiatnoe*]) precisely echoes the verbal structure of the Church Slavic participles. Similarly, the acathist also honors the Virgin Mary as "the luminous sphere of the never-setting sun" (*svetilo nezakhodimogo sveta*). In Pushkin's poem "An Acathist to Ekaterina Nikolaevna Karamzina" he calls the addressee "a lofty luminous sphere" (*svetilo*). Chekhov cleverly maintains the acathist's grammatical structure in Rebrotesov's reworking of the epithet, "the luminous sphere of our district" (*svetilo nashego uezda*).

This nearly inconspicuous second plane of the story is rendered meaningful by the wife's name, Maria Petrovna. Chekhov underscores her name by the diminutives "Masha," "Mashenka," "Mashunia," and "Manechka" with which Rebrotesov showers her. But despite the acathist's promise that Mary is the *key* to paradise, Maria Petrovna in no way corresponds to a benevolent intercessor who might unlock the pantry and, satisfying the prophecy of the Magnificat, "fill the hungry with good things." Instead, she responds to her husband's plea with a string of curses. For his part, the pose that Rebrotesov assumes (he gets down on his knees and weeps as he presses his suit) turns the gestures of pious entreaty into buffoonery. His "translation" of the religious code clearly aims for nonspiritual ends; the food of which the men dream is distinctly not manna from heaven.

Failing to win the keys with his absurdly contrived rhetoric, Rebrotesov alternates between pleas for mercy ("I implore you . . . Manechka! . . . Forgive me! . . . Give me the keys! Manechka! Angel!") and expression of his derisive male scorn ("So it turns out that you're not life's companion, not your husband's consoler [*uteshitel'nitsa*], as the Scripture says, but . . . to put it crudely . . . a serpent you've been, and a serpent you are" (3:49). *Uteshitel'nitsa* resembles a huge series of epithets from acathists (including "alchushchikh kormitel'nitsa" [nurturer of the hungry]), while the serpent harkens back to the Garden of Eden, to Eve's so-called transgression, and to the evils of woman—in short, to the sinful sexuality associated with the Virgin's much-maligned counterpart. The acathist line directly preceding that which Chekhov parodies in Rebrotesov's speech reads, "Rejoice, O Contestation of Adam's fall: Rejoice, O Deliverance from Eve's tears." The hero's own name derives from *rebro* (rib), anatomy humorously evocative of the scriptural explanation of woman's origins. But Chekhov's story plainly debunks any myth that woman might be tearfully dependent on man by reversing the terms.

Rebrotesov vacillates between these two clichéd rhetorical positions. If Maria Petrovna resolutely refuses to assume the role of "consoler," however, her actions do resonate with the acathist's opening line, "O, Elected Commander Victorious!" (*Vzbrannoi Voevode pobeditel'naia*). She beats her husband soundly in retaliation for his insults, behavior that reflects ironically on Rebrotesov's status as a lieutenant colonel. Moreover, while the couple is arguing, a portrait of a general absorbs the attention of the guests: "The guests stood before a depiction of a general, regarded his astonished eyes, and debated who was older—this general or the writer Lazhechnikov" (3:49). Who, they wonder, would make the better commander in time of war? They are interrupted by the return of Rebrotesov with an injured cheek and black eye, back from his own private war.

The "trick" dénouement of the story finds Maria Petrovna issuing forth from the bedroom to prepare a meal for the company, "cheerful and radiant." She dons the guise of the welcoming hostess, thereby answering the praiseful words attributed by her husband to his unwitting companions with a luminous appearance that will immortalize her reputation. All of the guests envy Rebrotesov his conjugal happiness. Thus the Christian word, first unconsciously distorted by Rebrotesov in his zeal to obtain the keys, is appropriated again by his wife and translated into terms that will gratify her vanity. The Marian acathist that intends to portray a female ideal of goodness, compassion, forgiveness, and nurturance is turned on its head by Chekhov's characters.

Chekhov wrote "Tears the World Doesn't See" just after 11 August 1884, a period that corresponds to the holiday of the Dormition (15 August) when his sister Maria Pavlovna celebrated her nameday. This was a time at which the Marian figure came to the forefront both culturally and in Chekhov's personal life. The stories that follow exhibit fewer concrete links to Marian texts; they do, however, illustrate a versatile range of associations that Chekhov recognized (consciously or unconsciously) as property belonging to the Christian paradigm of the virgin and the harlot.

"The Sinner from Toledo" ("Greshnik iz Toledo," 1881) is subtitled "A Translation from the Spanish," a device that serves to distance its evaluation of uncompromising church dogma both historically and culturally. Set in Yaroslavl, this same story would doubtless have been rejected by the censor. The story takes place in the Spanish Middle Ages. A monk accuses the beautiful young wife of a Barcelonian sailor, Spalanzo, of being a witch. The story treats with lightness the absurd ends attained when Christian rhetoric is employed for selfish and obscurantist purposes.

The written word represents the font of authority in Chekhov's parody of Catholicism. Each of the male characters enjoys the reputation of an intellectually astute thinker. Spalanzo is renowned as a "most learned Spaniard"; the monk Augustine has authored a learned book; and the bishop is a "very learned man." Comic discrepancies mark these characterizations: Spalanzo is a lowly sailor, Augustine engages in a witch-hunt, and the bishop burns innocent victims at the stake. Belief in the righteousness of their actions clearly issues from the power wielded by a monologized Christian word.

Each act of the witch-hunt drama is accompanied by reference to a written document or inscription. An announcement posted throughout Barcelona offers exculpation of sins in return for the delivery of Spalanzo's wife, dead or alive. Prior to the accusations against her, lost in the city, the young wife inquires of Augustine the whereabouts of Saint Mark's street, a reference to the author of the Gospel. She recognizes Augustine, namesake of a foremost exegete of Catholicism, as the author of a book in which he damns women and expresses hatred toward men for being born of women, all in the name of Christ's love. In pursuit of the supposed witch, Augustine and three other figures dressed in black come out of gates marked with a long Latin inscription. It is the sight of the written announcement that drives Spalanzo to poison his wife, and the deed is committed in order to receive an indulgence, that is, a written document. Finally, the bishop, who creates two words from the Latin *femina*—*fe* and *minus*—on the grounds that women have less faith than men, rewards Spalanzo's action with a book he has written: "In this book the learned bishop wrote that devils most often possess women with black hair because black hair is the same color as devils" (1:115). This sounds especially foolish in Spain, where black is the most common hair color.

Ecclesiastical male *authority*, then, appropriates language and texts to the end of denigrating women because of her sexual appeal. In this sense, it is not surprising that Spalanzo's wife should be named Maria, a name connected with imputations of sexual immorality in Christian discourse (and, of course, wildly popular in Spain thanks to the Catholic Marian cult). This is the trap laid by the cleric's language. The sight of Maria's breast, her bared arm, and quickened breath in the moonlight incites Augustine's denunciation: "I swear by Saint January's blood that you're a witch!" (1:111). Repressed sexuality is thinly disguised by fanatical religious zeal. Maria, cliché of the gay beauty with her "thoroughly Spanish body," falls victim to the monk's rant. Later, the bishop draws on the same distorted "Christian" logic when he tells Spalanzo that Maria is not a Catholic's wife, but the Devil's: "She is Satan's wife! You poor man, hadn't you yet noticed that she has betrayed you many times for the evil spirit?" (1:112). Maria Spalanzo's fate is to die in the literally "lowly" state to which she is relegated, in the hold of a ship.

In this parodic sketch the faintest outlines of the Marian paradigm may be perceived, for Maria's "fall" has to do with images of chastity imposed upon her by men of the cloth. The source of these images is the language of Christianity manipulated by the priests as protection against the perceived threat of female sexuality. They hide behind an authoritarian religious code. The story remains on a purely comic plane because the characters are akin to cardboard mannequins depicted in an obviously fabricated world. Corrupted Christian rhetoric has far more serious consequences in Chekhov's later story "Peasant Women" (see Chapter 4).

Chekhov's "The Swedish Match" ("Shvedskaia spichka," 1883) also plays with texts, burlesquing the genre of the detective story. The story recounts a search for the murderer of Mark Ivanovich Kliauzov, whose disappearance from the bedroom of his provincial estate is attributed to shady dealings. In a manner that might be called "linguistic slapstick," the investigators begin to formulate their theories. Diukovsky, the investigator's assistant, builds a case against Kliauzov's sister based on her religious faith, excitedly recreating her motives for the murder:

> She murdered him out of Old Believer fanaticism! It's not just that she killed a useless weed, a profligate—she liberated the world from Antichrist—and this is just where she sees her service, her religious heroism! Oh, you don't know these old maids, these Old Believer women! Just read Dostoevsky! And see what Leskov and Pechersky write! . . . It must be she! She strangled him! Oh, you spiteful woman! Surely she was standing by the icons when we came in just in order to lead us astray? (2:212)

The pious sister, irrationally suspected of Kliauzov's murder, is Maria Ivanovna. Notably, she is intimately associated with icons: "They found Kliauzov's

sister, Maria Ivanovna, an old maid of forty, praying in front of the tall family icon-case" (2:210). Chekhov repeatedly (twice in the text, once more in an early draft) calls Maria Ivanovna "maiden" (*deva*), an epithet that contextually means "old maid," but distantly reverberates as well with the title "Virgin [*Deva*] Mary." This conjunction of words—Maria, icon, *deva*—conveys a devotional purity that doubles the humor of Diukovsky's accusations.

The comic device of tampering with cultural associations is furthered when Diukovsky misinterprets not only the religious context, but several literary "subtexts." He indiscriminately conflates Dostoevsky's pious Elizaveta Ivanovna (a victim of murder in *Crime and Punishment*), Leskov's murderess Katerina Lvovna in "Lady MacBeth of the Mtsensk District," and a whole array of Old Believers depicted sympathetically by both Leskov and Pechersky.

Finally, one more reversal in the story is worth noting. When Diukovsky comes to suspect another woman, Olga Petrovna, of Kliauzov's murder because she possesses a box of Swedish matches similar to the match found at the scene of the crime, the inspector heatedly defends her as a "a noble and honest woman" (2:216). We are led to believe that, just as Diukovsky misread Maria Ivanovna, he is again needlessly besmirching the reputation of a chaste woman. It turns out, however, that Kliauzov was not murdered at all, but that Olga Petrovna forcibly abducted and seduced him, hiding him from her husband in the sauna.

In this story of 1883, then, the two poles of behavior that interest us appear, the pious virgin and the "sinful woman." As yet they are not connected in a manner that creates a larger context of meaning; they are, however, already the subject of inverted meanings and reversed expectations—in a story, moreover, that is itself a parody of a genre that thrives on unexpected outcomes.

The language of Romanticism is solidly rooted in the language of Christianity. Countless amorous endearments in the languages of Christian culture derive from religious sources. The interchange in "The Grateful One" ("Blagodarnyi," 1883) refers to this interface. An old man grudgingly bestows a monetary gift on his secretary, Misha Bobov, at the behest of his wife, Misha's distant relative. Urged to express his gratitude where it is due, the young man visits his patroness in her sitting room. The hyperbolic terms of his gratitude lead to embraces and kisses, but this seduction scene is cut short by the entrance of the woman's irate husband. Clearly this sort of humor wholly satisfied the directives of the popular press, which encouraged the amplification of well-known circumstances into melodramatic extremes. The story also contains a modest play on the Marian theme.

Misha's direct speech dominates the story, the humor of which stems from the inappropriateness of his heightened romantic/religious rhetoric during what should be a brief courtesy call. He beseeches his sponsor, Maria

Semenovna, to thank the heavens for having sent her such an angel for a husband, then bestows upon her a "holy" kiss: " 'I'm kissing a saint who belongs to him. . . . This is a holy kiss. . . . Don't be afraid, I'm engaged. . . . It's nothing' " (2:46). Romantic discourse becomes ludicrously inflated with Christian diction as the overzealous protagonist drifts into the more familiar territory of religious vocabulary. The funny thing is that Misha's behavior is prompted by his own self-styled understanding of this language. As the ardency of his thankfulness increases, his physical attentions advance, foregrounding at once a latent connection between religious language and eroticism, and the utter absurdity of such an alliance.

Misha addresses Maria Semenovna twice as "You marvel!" (*chudnaia*). The point I make, here and further on, about words derived from the Russian root *chud-* has to do with its Christian origins. A root that initially referred to the miraculous in a religious vein spawned words (*chudo, chudesnyi, chudnyi*) that have come to convey "marvelous/wonderful" in a purely secular sense. Chekhov frequently uses these words unencumbered by religious coloration. But he also uses them liberally in texts where words and images drawn from sacred contexts appear, undoubtedly aware of the proximity of the root *chud-* to notions of the spiritually miraculous (compare the miracle-working/*chudotvornaia* icon). Could Chekhov have been oblivious to the resonance between Misha's address ("O, Chudnaia!") and phrases in Marian prayers such as, "O Miraculous [*Chudnaia*] Pure Virgin"?[5]

Indeed, the position of Misha's patroness accords roughly with certain features of the religious prototype. Maria Semenovna acts as an intercessor to procure for Misha the funds he needs to finance his betrothal (echoing the Marian role as patroness of weddings), although her financial benevolence occurs on the absolutely ordinary terms of allegiance to kin. Like the Virgin Mary, Maria Semenovna is married to an old man, and one to whom Misha ascribes characteristics of the righteous Joseph: " 'He's old and ugly, but what a soul he has. Just find me another such soul' " (2:46). The theme of a cuckolded Joseph, of course, was a joke for Pushkin in *Gavriiliada*.

This verbal seduction, a compulsive gush of the language of love threaded humorously with devotional intonations, overcomes Maria Semenovna quickly because of her romantic predisposition (she is reading a novel when he enters her parlor). The model of the sacred female ideal is at work here again, but Chekhov again flips the terms and pokes fun at another warped "translation" of its meaning. This is one way of understanding his subtitle for the piece: "A Psychological Study."

A simpler linguistic situation pertains in "The Stationmaster" ("Nachal'nik stantsii," 1883). A lovers' tryst between a stationmaster and the wife of the manager of a neighboring estate is interrupted by the arrival of her husband, Nazar Kuzmich. Believing that he is in for a whipping, the stationmaster tries to run, but an approaching train cuts him off. When the cuckolded husband catches up with the stationmaster, he has this to say:

> I've come to you on business, my benefactor! . . . It's important business . . .
> my Masha told me that you've become involved with her for pleasure. I've
> nothing against that, since all I get from Maria Ilinishna is a big fig, but if you
> reason the thing out right, you really ought to cut a deal with me, since I'm
> the husband, the head after all . . . as Scripture says. Prince Mikhail Dmitrich,
> when he got involved, used to pay out two twenty-five rouble notes each month.
> How much could you manage? (2:274)

Nazar Kuzmich (whose name, incidentally, means "devoted to God"), expresses no interest in his wife Maria's comportment as a "sinful woman." Rather, he altogether ignores the question of morality on which a conventional anecdote would hinge. He ignores linguistic conventions as well. The comic pastiche of phrases from different fields of diction (commerce, bureaucratic supplication, slang, Christianity) reflects the logic of his thoughts, devoid as they are of any hierarchy. Holy Scripture is summoned on a par with his wife's refusal of sexual favors to justify the financial deal. Language, in fact, becomes a sort of business tool: the ends of his rhetoric justify the means.

The semantic cluster related to the Marian complex is not large here. Nazar Kuzmich's reflexive evocation of Scripture is conjoined to the theme of sexuality via his attempt to "pimp" his wife. His usage of religious language is subverted hilariously. Furthermore, the text points to Maria Ilinichna as a sort of "loose woman," but it does not make the least impression on any of the characters. The customary consequences of the scriptural injunction ("the husband is authority"), which the stationmaster initially fears, turn out to be not moral indignation and physical punishment, but a financial penalty, and one that will rob future rendezvous of all romantic charm. Such dissociation between cultural/religious norms and human behavior becomes the subject of much more complex analyses in the later prose.

In the grouping of early stories to be considered next, Marian configurations relate in one way or another to iconography. Exposure to icons in the Chekhov home was a given. Pavel Egorovich, Chekhov's father, himself an amateur icon painter, actively acquired icons (the family collection included at least three icons of the Mother of God). In the course of researching his dissertation on the history of medicine in Russia, Chekhov collected copious notes on folk remedies in which we encounter a number of references to icons: "In certain cases . . . the people appeal to various saints: for instance, as a treatment for the plague or epidemics they turn to the Icon of the Bogolubsky Mother of God, . . . to cure the sick they appeal to the Icon of the Mother of God of all the Aggrieved" (*vsekh skorbiashchikh*) (16:305).[6] Given his exposure to iconography at home and in church, it is not surprising that Chekhov should have been interested in the psychology of the image in Russian culture.

Like the inert idioms of religious language, the fixed attributes of iconography provide a context for the depiction of characters and/or the situations in which characters find themselves. Savely Senderovich calls the icon an ideogram consistent in its configuration of meaning throughout Chekhov. The icon always appears in an environment of contrast, either as "part of a series of images that contain internal contradictions" or affiliated with "a double with an opposite and profane meaning."[7] He cites a number of examples in which such doubles appear, including the story "Failure" ("Neudacha," 1886), in which a young woman's parents plot to snare her a husband, but mistakenly snatch a writer's portrait from the wall with which to bless their daughter and her panicky beau. In his analysis of "On the Road" ("Na puti," 1886), Senderovich locates a key to the pervasive duality of meaning in a grouping of visual portrayals: "an icon lamp flickered in the corner above the table and fixed a red spot on the icon of St. George the Triumphant. From the icon stretched on each side of the corner a row of cheap woodcuts which maintained a strict and careful gradation in the transition from the divine to the secular" (5:462). In this "transition" lies an opposition between the sacred and the profane that underlies Chekhov's iconographic imagery.[8]

The sole story from the earlier works in which an iconographic image of the Mother of God explicitly appears is "During Passion Week" ("Na strastnoi nedele," 1887). Tension between the sacred and the profane indeed characterizes Chekhov's evocation of the icon here. The story's boy-narrator enters a church for confession and immediately sees an icon of the Crucifixion on which the Mother of God and John the Theologian flank the crucified Christ. At confession, the boy becomes preoccupied with observing an elegant lady who seems to have something shameful on her conscience. He follows her movements throughout confession and watches her emerge relieved and joyful. The next day the boy takes note of two female figures: the Mother of God, who now seems less sad, and the elegant woman in blue, the likes of whom he now dreams of marrying. The religious rite intended to facilitate spirtual purification in fact accelerates the boy's erotic awakenings, something suggested as well by the double entendre of the title, "During *Passion* Week."[9]

If the actual appearance of an icon of the Mother of God in Chekhov's early prose is rare, what might be called a shadow iconographic motif seems to operate more frequently. This can be felt in some textual configurations marking indisputably prosaic interactions. Thus in "The Correspondent" ("Korrespondent," 1882) the writer Ivan Nikitych returns home in the evening, *bows to the icons* in each room, then finds his daughter Manechka on her bed and pleads for a favor, to which she responds—directly eschewing the role of succor to those in need—"More punishment! Mother of God, when will this all finally end!" (1:191). In "Trouble" ("Beda," 1886) an errant husband returns from a five-day drunken spree expecting his wife Masha to rebuff him, for he had previously sworn off the bottle *in front of an icon*. "She is virtuous precisely because she won't forgive the sinful," he says, reversing terms associated with the Virgin's mercy (5:438). In the place of a wrathful reception, he finds himself welcomed and consoled. In these cases, it may be no more than a subconscious cultural bent that led Chekhov to associate the iconographic motif with a "Maria" and a plot situation keyed to woman's benevolence, but the coincidence is striking.

Three stories from Chekhov's early years look at the veneration of women in ways that indirectly call upon iconographic associations. These texts are nearly without firsthand pointers to a religious context, yet each involves the framing of a heroine who is the subject of inappropriate homage and adoration. If secular pictures stand alone here, their exalted status in the eyes of the viewer would seem to be conditioned by a cultural fidelity to the Marian image.

"In the Autumn" ("Osen'iu") was written in 1883. An example of Chekhov's "serious" early stories, "In the Autumn" tells the tale of a drunkard in a tavern whom a passing peasant recognizes as his former master when they meet one rainy night. Before the peasant arrives, the alcoholic pawns his last possession, a locket, for a drink. The meaning of the locket is subsequently explained when the peasant recounts his former master's biography, a tale listened to raptly by a group of pilgrims staying overnight in the tavern. Once a wealthy and sober landowner (the peasant tells us), Semen Sergeich fell madly in love with a city woman. She married him for money and during the very wedding festivities left him to return to her lover in the city. This tragic love has brought Semen Sergeich to ruin, the desperate ends of which the company has already witnessed as he exchanged the small, gold locket containing her picture for a glass of vodka provided by the innkeeper Tikhon.

The peasant calls Semen Sergeich an "unhappy martyr." Indeed, the inserted narrative does have some typological points in common with a saint's life: an eyewitness tells the tale of a man who, born wealthy, gives up his privilege to pursue faith in an ideal. But the situation is askew. A martyr suffers for his faith, while Semen Sergeich complains: "I've lost my faith, brothers! There's no one for me to believe in now!" (2:240). This absence of faith is related to the locket that Semen Sergeich relinquishes for drink.

Semen Sergeich's story is framed as a dialectic between the sacred and the profane by the setting in the tavern, where the prayers of the pilgrims create a counterpoint to Tikhon's mercantile activity. The picture in the locket that Semen Sergeich barters for vodka, and that Tikhon opens against his injuctions, is semantically aligned with the tavern: "Tikhon opened the locket and looked at the woman's head, which smiled out of a gold frame at the tavern, Tikhon, the bottles" (2:238). This is the head of Maria Egorovna.[10] The locket gently recalls small iconic medallions of the Virgin carried especially by wandering pilgrims. In Chekhov's dramatic version of this story, "On the Open Road" ("Na bol'shoi doroge," 1914), rejected by censorship and never published in his lifetime, a juncture between the pilgrims and the Virgin is directly voiced when the elderly pilgrim Savva insists that he will not die on the road: "The Mother of God won't allow me to die in foreign parts. . . . I'll die at home" (11:185). The play assigns Maria Egorovna an active role and paints her as a far more vicious character than does the story. In neither text, however, does the object of Semen Sergeich's devotion bear any resemblance to a Madonna. Hers is the head of an urban, worldly woman, and one who rejects his sincere love to mother children with another man.

In many saints' lives the Virgin's image is evoked periodically to reaffirm the subject's faith (this is true, for instance, in the famous life of Saint Sergius of Radonezh, although no connection with Semen Sergeich's patronymic is obvious.) In his drunken life, Semen Sergeich reenacts this sort of homage toward a "Marian" image: he carries the picture with him, regards it frequently, and twice implores Tikhon neither to look at, nor touch, the portrait of Maria Egorovna. This empty habit of devotion blinds him to the reality of Maria Egorovna: while he can say that "there's no one for me to believe in now," he remains completely beholden to the image.

When Semen Sergeich asks to borrow back the locket at the story's end, it turns out that Tikhon has scratched out the woman's face with his fingernail. Numbed by drink, Semen Sergeich does not percieve that the face is gone and continues to search for it. Tikhon's "iconoclastic" gesture, the physical defacement of the locket, actually reflects the status of the image as a source of value. The mechanics of veneration have possessed Semen Sergeich, luring him into an emotional dependence on Maria Egorovna's picture. Like alcohol, the locket represents a source of artificial intoxication. Reverence for the Marian image—so widely advertised in Russian culture as an emotional cure-all—is what does the protagonist in.

Suggestive contours of pictoral homage reside in another story of 1883 as well. "The Dowry" ("Pridanoe") is a curious story in which a narrator recounts his three visits to the Chikamasov home, each set some years apart. On the first visit, he notices an oil painting of a bishop on the wall that heads up a row of ancestral portraits. Returning seven years later, he observes that the bishop has been joined by a new portrait of the recently deceased general, the master of the house, and that the general's widow and his daughter are in mourning. Finally, on the last visit, he encounters the widow alone, and asks no questions after noticing her garb of deep mourning and "a portrait of the daughter standing in front of her on the table" (2:192).

The plot of the story, such as it is, concerns the ongoing efforts on the part of the Chikamosov women to sew and cache away a dowry for the daughter. But during the conversations in which Mme Chikamosov explains this activity to her guest, the daughter disingenuously insists that she has no desire to marry ("I'll never get married! Never!"; "I shall never, never marry!") (2:190,191). This young woman, referred to as "devitsa" (maiden/virgin) by the narrator, goes by the names Marie and Manechka.[11]

Nuptial rituals in Orthodox belief are presided over by the Mother of God, herself configured as the Bride of God.[12] By far the most prominent epithet describing the Virgin Mary in Orthodox hymnology, sung at the end of each ikos of the major Marian acathist, is "The Unwed Bride" (*Nevesta nenevestnaia*, known in Catholicism as the "Ever-Virgin"), a tribute to Mary's miraculous Immaculate Conception. The posthumous framing of Marie seems to perform a general parody of the notion of an eternal virgin and unwed bride.

Although Chekhov furnishes no icons in "The Dowry," he does provide a potentially apt reference. Each year the women buy material to sew Manechka's dowry at the market held on the holiday of the Ascension. Leonid Ouspensky writes of the "central position" occupied by the Mother of God in icons of the Ascension, calling her "the axis of the whole composition."[13] The Virgin's robe on this icon (in accord with convention) is dark blue; on his second visit to the Chikamosovs the narrator finds Marie's mother "crawling around the floor and cutting up dark blue fabric" (2:191). The Ascension symbolizes Christ's victory over earthly death, while the Mother of God represents the vitality of faith. Everything about this intimated link is displaced in Chekhov's story.

Instead of celebrating life, the Chikamosov house resembles a sepulcher. Family portraits depict the deceased, a display of drab and eerie faces: "from the bishop extended a row of forebears with lemony-yellow, gypsy-like physiognomies" (2:189). Manechka herself has died by the story's end. The very ordinariness of her death contributes to an irony: a woman mockingly evocative of the "Unwed Bride" so eulogized by the church puts an end to the Chikamosov patriarchal line by failing to marry and produce progeny, thus fully exposing the contradiction of the Christian command that women emulate the Virgin.

As does "In the Autumn," "The Dowry" interrogates the cultural habit of veneration provocatively. After her daughter's death, Mme Chikamosov continues to sew cloths for Manechka's dowry, keeping vigil by the portrait and remaining true to the dreams she has fabricated for the now-deceased unwed bride. The mother's morbid devotion reveals another potential for pathological distortion of an image intended as an eternal ideal. The question of women bizarrely idolized is taken up again, this time in a far more cheerful key, in a story of 1884 entitled "Maria Ivanovna."

Reader expectations are foregrounded as the subject of "Maria Ivanovna." The story opens with a scene that could be ascribed to either the sentimental, Romantic, or realist traditions: a young women of twenty-three sits on a couch of purple velvet in an elegantly furnished drawing room faced by a pale young man. Before the narration proceeds further, the voice of an indignant fictional reader breaks in and exhorts the story's author to answer for his predictable images and hackneyed style: "What a clichéd, stereotypical beginning!"; "They hand up to the public various rubbish, luxuriously furnished living rooms and some sort of Maria Ivanovnas with the chill of the grave!"; "Even so, they could have chosen more serious material. What's the sense in this Maria Ivanovna anyway?" (2:312–14). The fictional author takes up the battle cry, lecturing to the fictional reader at length on the importance of professional writers to the press, on the obstacles they face, and on how little readers appreciate their skills.

A brief dénouement to the fictional author's story turns the tables on the fictional reader. The young man undresses in front of the woman and goes to bed on the couch. In order to mollify the outraged fictional reader, the author explains: "The lady in the luxuriously furnished drawing room was painted in oil on canvas and hung over the sofa" (2:314).

The device of undermining readers' expectations was part of the daily arsenal of the popular press. What is interesting here is that the locus of this reversal is a devotional image. Before we find out it is a picture, the young man stands in front of his beloved and says: "I love you, you marvel (*chudnaia*), even now, when you give off the chill of the grave!" (2:312). (Recall the discussion of *chudnaia* above.) The commonplace name Maria to which the fictional reader so objects now finds justification precisely because she is the framed object of adoration. One wonders if Maria Ivanovna's surname, "One-cheek" (*Odnoschëkina*), might belong to the same referential field as Chekhov's subsequent image in "During Passion Week" of the Mother of God *depicted in profile* on an icon.

Maria Ivanovna, then, emerges as a literary device. This literal portrait reminds us that literary portraits resist the exclusively "realistic" interpretations that Chekhov's female characters have most often received. Even Chekhov's interpolated reader greets the anticipated love scene with boredom. One point of this study is to demonstrate the ways in which many of Chekhov's female characters are textual constructs, fictional portraits framed by cultural predispositions.

In these stories of the early 1880s, characters are clearly literary creations living in fictional worlds. Concern with language and literary topics, typical of Chekhov's early prose, finds expression both on the surface of the text (literature proper is parodied in "The Swedish Match" and "Maria Ivanovna") and on a more subtle plane. Beyond the obvious everyday situational humor or recognizable plot, a layer of connotation exists that is based on translations or redefinitions of the language of Russian religious culture. The characters use this discourse unwittingly, while the author points out the comic and tragic discrepancies between received texts and the uses to which they are put. In all of this, Chekhov defines himself as a remarkably astute cultural psychologist.

Two stories of 1886 published in *Petersburgskaia gazeta* cap this discussion of the early prose. The year 1886 is generally considered a watershed year in Chekhov's life. This was the year his works began to be published in Suvorin's *Novoe vremia,* the year of rapidly increasing fame emblematized by the admiring letter Chekhov received from Grigorovich, and the year that the pen name Chekhonte gradually gave way to the signature "An. Chekhov." It would, of course, be artificial to suggest that any one story directs the Marian theme toward Chekhov's "later" period (especially given that two stories to be discussed in Chapter 3 belong chronologically to this "early" group). Nonetheless, "The Uproar" and "A Dreadful Night" do move the theme into new territory.

"The Uproar" ("Perepolokh") appeared early in 1886, signed by Chekhonte. Similar to the stories discussed earlier in this chapter, no concrete indicators point to a Marian context. The intimations that do appear, however, concern both poles of the paradigm, a characteristic feature of the mature stories. "The Uproar" tells the tale of a young governess in a wealthy Saint Petersburg home who returns from a walk to find the house in a commotion and her room ransacked. She learns that the mistress has lost an expensive brooch and, horrified that she has been suspected of the theft, decides to leave the house. While she is packing, the master of the house comes to apologize and confesses that he stole the brooch. Astonished at this moral laxity, she remains doubly resolved to leave the household immediately, even though it means an uncertain future with her impoverished parents.

Having discovered that the mistress ordered her room searched, the governess becomes acutely aware of her legally defenseless status. The violation assumes very personal terms, for in the course of the search someone had pried into the governess' private life: a drawer was left ajar; the linen basket was rearranged; her bag, bookcase, table, and bed were left in disarray; and the lock on her money box had been forced. The young woman perceives the violation as a fall. She tells the maid that the act is "low," and, as if succumbing to this fate, she falls onto her bed. "Never had she been subject to such violence, never had she been so deeply offended as now. . . . She, a well-bred, sensitive young woman (*devitsa*), the daughter of a teacher, suspected of theft and searched just like a woman of the streets!" (4:333). This is a projection of the virgin-whore opposition. On the one hand, the young woman views herself as a *devitsa,* a respectable young woman (and virgin); on the other, she metaphorically assesses herself as a fallen woman (a streetwalker).

The governess is Maria Andreevna Pavletskaia, or Mashenka. Albeit at some remove from the text, the following associations belong to the cultural background against which the violation of Masha's physical space is described. An inviolate space surrounds and protects the Mother of God. This is true of icons, and is also expressed in the notion of the enclosed garden (*hortus conclusus*), symbolic of the Virgin's chastity.[14] A folk chant speaks of "the Mother of God's sealed lock"[15] (recall the forced lock on Mashenka's money box). The trespass assumes dimensions of sexual defilement in Mashenka's eyes.

Mashenka imagines a chain of injustices that might logically follow from the intrusion: "If they could suspect her of theft, that meant they could arrest her now, strip her down and search her, then conduct her under escort through the streets and lock her up in a dark, cold cell with mice and lice, just like the one Princess Tarakanova was put in" (4:333). Chekhov refers to the eighteenth-century adventuress, Princess Elizaveta Tarakanova, who was incarcerated and died in the Peter-Paul Fortress. She was immortalized in K. D. Flavitsky's painting (1864) and in G. P. Danilevsky's popular historical novel, *Princess Tarakanova,* published in 1882.[16] In the painting, Tarakanova is standing on her rumpled bed, hair and clothing in disarray, as mice scamper past and the waters of the 1777 Petersburg flood rise in her cell. Mashenka's master and mistress, both bewhiskered (he picks at his whiskers; she has barely perceptible whiskers), resemble the rodents of the painting. Tarakanova emblematizes the denigration of a woman of nobility to a fallen state, the worst fate that Mashenka can imagine.

Mashenka's capitulation takes place when she jumps up from the bed to take action. When Nikolai Sergeich comes to her room shortly thereafter, he pauses at her *closed* door. She meets Nikolai Sergeich's apologies for the "uproar" with compassionate understanding. In his ensuing attempt to dissuade her from leaving, our attention is drawn to Chekhov's choice of language: "Do you want me to get on my knees before you? . . . Or do you want me to tell you things I wouldn't even say at confession? Is that what you want? I'll bet you want me to admit things I wouldn't even admit to a priest on my deathbed" (4:337). Nikolai Sergeich presses a confession upon Mashenka; he exalts her by attempting to set her up as an absolving authority. At the same time, his total disregard for "maternal" authority surfaces with his admission that the stolen brooch had once belonged to his mother and that he now intends to sell it. He tramples roughshod over "sacred" values as he accedes to the legacy of his surname, Kushkin—from *kush*, a large sum of money.

In a final devotional gesture Nikolai Sergeich tells Mashenka that he admires her ability to feel disdainful: "I could sit forever and look at your indignant face" (4:337). Not only has he failed to comprehend her view of the committed offenses, a result not of contempt but rather of aversion to violence and fear of denigration; he persists in a perverse veneration of the image he has created of her. Neither Mashenka nor Nikolai Sergeich links thoughts or behavior to Marian sources, but related categories feed their reflections and actions.

The final line of the story reads, "An hour later she was already on the road" (4:337). Mashenka previously imagined herself a "streetwalker" who would be led along a "street" to prison. She has found her way past the abstraction of the fallen woman associated with the street, and sets out on the proverbial road of life. Mashenka, apparently a defenseless victim, is ultimately the only character to take responsibility for her own freedom. Her departure from the Kushkin household signals a modest liberation from the humiliating paradigm of the harlot and the virgin. It is Chekhov's insight that these projections can be self-imposed (streetwalker) as well as imposed from the outside (confessor). These suggestions of the Marian figures in relationship to the question of freedom presage questions that become particularly salient in "My Life" (Chapter 6).

"A Dreadful Night" ("Nedobraia noch'," 1886) might be considered something of an etude for the Marian theme in the later prose, given Chekhov's notation on a newspaper clipping of the story that it should not be included in his complete works (5:663). The author must have realized that the lack of a substantive plot would prove an inordinate challenge to the median reader who, as Virginia Woolf put it, feels that "stories ought to conclude in a way that we recognize." Woolf goes on to say that "in Tchekhov, we need a very daring and alert sense of literature to make us hear the tune."[17] The tune of this story is not easy to make out: one night the servants and mistress on a country estate watch a neighboring village burn down; the woman's husband comes home late from a party, learns of the fire, and leaves for the village; the mistress can't restrain her curiosity and soon goes off to see the fire herself. The final scene shows Maria Sergeevna watching the fire with two of the servants. A Marian motif helps elucidate the story.

The only obvious theme of "A Dreadful Night" has to do with the irrepressible, if inappropriate, excitement provoked by a major disaster: "Everyone realizes that they are witnessing a horrific calamity, they're all trembling, but if the fire were to end, they would feel let down. Such duality (*dvoistvennost'*) is natural and there is no point in reproaching egotistical humanity for it" (5:386). Dualities greatly interested Chekhov. The duality here consists of the discrepancy between an ideal of human behavior (namely, concern for the fate of neighbors) and the exhilarating thrill of spectacle. Chekhov incontestably meant to comment on this duality with a peculiar detail. Two characters, the coachman and the house servant, are both named Gavrila (Gabriel) and are paired together as "the two [*dvoe*] Gavrilas" (5:386). The double naming bridges the story's express theme to the Marian context: the name belongs most conspicuously to the Annunciation story.

As the story opens, the two Gavrilas and the estate watchman stand viewing the distant fire. One of them mutters: "Save us, have mercy upon us, Heavenly Queen! . . . Horrors, what horrors! The Lord's got angry. . . . Our Lady Mother . . ." (5:384). This entreaty mirrors a folk belief in the Virgin as deliverer from fire,[18] but resonates in other ways as well. The address to the Intercessor is followed by the information that Maria Sergeevna, the young mistress, is sleeping. Awakened by the din, Maria Sergeenva waves her hands in desperation, cries "My God, My God!" and declares that she has no idea what to do. The notion of an archetypal protectress clashes with the powerless lady of the manor. The story reflects at some length on the disjuncture between the ideals promoted by religious culture and a reality governed by prosaic, highly human thoughts and actions.

Topically the plot has nothing to do with the Annunciation story (it is set in the autumn and does not touch the subject of conception). But Chekhov knew well how closely associated was Gabriel with Mary, particularly through the Marian acathist wherein thirteen lines of each of twelve ikos verses replicate the Angel Gabriel's greeting, "Hail, [Mary]!" (*Raduisia*) (see Fig. 2). What's more, Chekhov, who complained that as a child he felt like a young convict when envied by outsiders for the beauty with which he and his brothers sang the Annunciation canticle "With the Voice of the Archangel" in church,[19] himself perceived how far at odds human experience can be from religious significations.

The coachman Gavrila in "A Dreadful Night" serves largely as a sign-post of duality, but the interaction between the servant Gavrila and Maria Sergeevna echoes lines from the acathist. The Archangel Gabriel is lauded as the "servant" of the great mystery, a possible Chekhovian pun on Gavrila's post in the household. Chekhov's servant Gavrila fancies that he knows best how to control the fire in Kreshchenskoe (an irony if held up to liturgical texts that image Mary metaphorically ablaze with her mission, the metaphor expressed by the icon of the Burning Bush).[20] When Maria Sergeevna wakes up, he says: "Hold it, brothers, I'm going to give her instructions" (*nastavlenie*) (5:385). Gavrila's plan is to take horses and men to the village, then to take charge of extinguishing the fire. This situation is quite the opposite of the sixth ikos of the Marian acathist that looks to the Virgin for instruction: "Hail, O Firey Pillar, instructing [*nastavliaia*] those in the darkness!" Similarly inverted, the dim light shed by the candle held by "Gavrila-the-servant" (Chekhov's words) when the group ascends to the attic to view the fire pales in comparison with the Virgin in the eleventh ikos, "a light-bearing candle that appears to those in the dark, for kindling the immaterial light, She instructs [*nastavliaet*] everyone in God's law." In Maria Sergeevna's room, too, only a "dim night-light" burns. There is a void in authoritative direction left by Maria Sergeevna's irresoluteness and Gavrila tries to take the lead. But neither offers anything by way of leadership. Although the characters live in a world deeply imprinted by Orthodox names, ideas, and language, "God's law" is simply not in the picture. In its place are profane echoes of religious images fueled by a human craving for excitement and gratification.

Maria Sergeevna herself initiates a thrill-seeking excursion: she leads the company up the staircase to watch the fire from the attic. Some symbolic overtones reverberate in this scene, especially in view of a motif shared with "The Teacher of Literature" (see Chapter 5): a staircase. In the acathist's second ikos, Gabriel greets Mary with the words, "Hail, O Heavenly Ladder" (*lestvitsa*); the Virgin holds a ladder in her hands on certain icons, foremost of which are those of the Burning Bush and the Uncut Mountain (see Fig. 5). The ladder of Jacob's dream (Gen. 28:12) is said to prefigure the Virgin, who would bridge earth and heaven with the birth of her son. Having made her way up the staircase (*lestnitsa* also means "ladder") to the attic, Maria Sergeevna notices the "earthy soil underfoot" and muses that it looks like a "set from a fairy tale" where "house spirits" (*domovye*) might live (5:387).[21] The ascent is associated with earthly and pagan phenomena. In other words, Maria Sergeevna has no point of contact with the "Heavenly Queen" evoked earlier by the men; she communes with them as an equal (the narrator explains that "the sight of misfortune brings people together" [5:386]). Oblivious to the stance of compassion and pity modeled by the holy Mary, Maria Sergeevna joins the servants, where "a thirst for powerful sensations gets the upper hand over fear and compassion for the woes of others" (5:386).

Once her husband has returned home, then left for the fire, Maria Sergeevna is overcome by impatience ("All the movement and chatter egg her on" [5:387]) and sets out for the fire, too. Significantly, she travels with the two Gavrilas. At the scene of the fire, Gavrila-the-servant cuts a figure mildly evocative (in the context) of an archangel: waving his arms, he stands tall and throws a long shadow. But Chekhov signals the patent rift between an "angelic" feat and Gavrila's pathetically ineffective shouts to rein in the fire by posing the latter "like a devil before matins" (5:388).

The "monstrous" scene that greets Maria Sergeevna indeed resembles hell, from the blinding flames and dark smoke to the chaotic sounds. The Mother of God, of course, participates in the domain of fire, hell, and sin as intercessor—her cardinal role in "The Virgin's Travels through the Torments." Maria Sergeevna remains a passive bystander. The final lines of the story read: "An unusual picture! Maria Sergeevna can not believe her eyes, and only the powerful heat reminds her that it is not a dream" (5:388). The popular folk text, "The Dream of the Mother of God," ends with sinners burning in "the fire."

This world of fire and sin reflects the unthinking conceptual framework of the servants who harshly judge the unfortunate victims of the fire: "And both the watchman and the coachman, as if wishing to foppishly strut their dignity in front of the mistress, begin to spout holy words: 'The Lord has punished them for their sins. . . . That's what's happening! A man sins and doesn't think about it. Such is man. But the Lord . . .' "(5:386). The breach between "holy" words and their "foppish" delivery, between compassion and thrill, pity and derision, between a Mother Intercessor ("Have mercy on us, Heavenly Queen!") and the impatiently curious Maria Sergeevna represents dualities especially palpable in the Orthodox faith (fortified as it is by daily religious observances), but characteristic in essence of "Sunday Christians" anywhere.

If there is an ironic tint to the narrator's pronouncement that "such duality is natural and there is no point in reproaching egotistical humanity for it," the words also convey a Chekhovian stance. Immanent dualities and contradictions in life are to be examined and acknowledged, not condemned. The divorce between articulated ideals and human actions, after all, goes far beyond religion. This story, then, serves as a good example of Chekhov's phenomenological approach to religious culture, an approach devoid of moral edicts that focuses, instead, on how religion *functions* in quotidian life. It also introduces us to some of the more complicated manifestations of Marian imagery characteristic of the later stories.

Commentators have previously observed components of the Marian complex in two stories written in 1886 and 1888. Savely Senderovich suggests that the address to Maria Ilovaiskaia, the heroine of "On the Road," where she is called "mother-miss" (*matushka-baryshnia,* an ethnographic detail on Chekhov's part), points to the paradox inherent in the Christmas configuration of a mother figure who is also a virgin.[22] Tolstoguzov remarks on the "holy harlots" Mary Magdalene and Mary of Egypt as a cultural symbol of contradictory unity in the story "Without a Title" ("Bez zaglaviia," 1888), arguing that the harlot in this story is transformed from a symbol of sin into a symbol of life-confirming salvation based on her prototype in the Apocalypse.[23] Notably, each identifies paradox as a key to understanding.

Chekhov's early prose includes a range of contexts that can be related to the Marian sphere of meaning, from the lighthearted and witty to the more reflective, even somber. There is, as well, a range of explicitness with which the associations appear. In some stories this amounts to a mere trace element of the paradigm. The mother in "Incident with a Classics Scholar" ("Sluchai s klassikom," 1883), for example, dubs herself a "sinful woman" whom God should punish when her son fails his Greek test, then calls on the Mother of God for strength to beat him. Elsewhere, as we have seen, the Marian code appears with greater articulation. The Marian context does not generally "stand on its own" in the early prose and has yet to assume the meaningfulness it does in the later prose. Nonetheless, through the distortions and reversals of the messages about womankind that Orthodoxy vigorously promulgated, it provides intimations of how the Marian theme will develop. Such is the difference between the work of Antosha Chekhonte and that of Anton Chekhov.

Chapter Three

The Two Marys in Four Stories

> How well I know that it is no honor or praise for
> you when someone so impure and depraved as I
> looks at your pure icon, for you kept your body
> and soul in purity, O Ever-Virgin.
> —Mary of Egypt's prayer

DURING HIS trip to Sakhalin island in 1890–91 Chekhov honed his skills as an ethnographer, commenting at length in his letters on the life of the common people. *Sakhalin Island,* Chekhov's published "travel notes" recording the journey, abounds in detailed descriptions of local life along his route.[1] This interest translates artistically into a sort of intuitive ethnographic orientation at the core of some of his stories. These are texts in which the author probes the workings of the Russian religious mind, presenting to the reader characters who, collectively, delineate the contours of popular belief (and popular beliefs). At the center of Chekhov's inquiry lie questions concerning the relationship between the texts of Orthodox culture and their reception on the part of the faithful. As noted earlier, Chekhov was duly critical of the claim on indisputable authority advanced by a biblical idiom when, in Bakhtinian terms, it functions as monologic discourse. The "absolute word," whether manifest in Scripture or iconography, fails to accommodate the diverse needs and experiences of Chekhov's characters.[2] Filtered through the individual consciousness (itself a product of ongoing exposure to liturgical text), the Christian word is subject to interpretations and translations that often lead it far afield of its original commands—and with consequences, in Chekhov's "serious" stories, more dire than in the early humorist pieces.

Clifford Geertz writes that one of the main methodological problems in writing about religion as an observer is "to put aside at once the tone of the village atheist and that of the village preacher, as well as their more sophisticated equivalents, so that the social and psychological implications of particular religious beliefs can emerge in a clear and neutral light."[3] The Russian intellectual tradition in the nineteenth century is marked by a remarkably consistent bifurcation between atheists and preachers, between defenders of utilitarian worldviews (Belinsky, Herzen, Chernyshevsky, Pisarev, Bakunin) and proponents of Christian thought (Gogol, Dostoevsky, Tolstoy, Leskov, Solovyov). In a subtle yet radical departure from his predecessors, Chekhov eschews both roles in favor of assessing the "social and psychological implications" of the religious beliefs held by the Russian people, a population reared in a mandated, state, "orthodox" church. Chekhov's nonpartisan stance is surely colored by his antipathy toward packaged ideologies, yet in many respects his self-proclaimed authorial motto holds true for this examination of a national religious mindset: "The writer's job is only to show who said what or thought what about God or pessimism, and under what circumstances. An artist should not judge his characters and what they say, but should be an impartial observer."[4]

Four stories spread throughout Chekhov's career investigate perceptions of the two Christian Marys in the Russian popular consciousness: "The Lady" ("Barynia," 1882), "Peasants" ("Muzhiki," 1897), "The Requiem" ("Panikhida," 1886), and "An Attack of Nerves" ("Pripadok," 1888). These texts consider the ways in which characters frame the world through cultural understandings of the female prototypes, and the ways in which characters contrive to adapt the religious figures to their own thoughts and needs. Chekhov details both the personal and cultural crises that ensue when the rigid Christian models for female behavior collide with incompatible ideas, or meet a hostile reception amid dismal conditions inhospitable to religious idealism.

It seems quite plausible that Chekhov's "The Lady" was conceived as a response to a tale written by a colleague from the ranks of the lowbrow journalists with whom Chekhov associated in the early 1880s. "The Lady" culminates with the death of a peasant woman at the hands of her husband. A typological resemblance connects Chekhov's plot to another story, published in the popular press nearly concurrently, in which a man kills his faithless lover. "The Lady" appeared in the August 1882 issues of the journal *Moskva* (nos. 29–31). It appeared one month after the publication in the same journal of M. Beloborodov's story "The Gremiachevo Meadows" (nos. 24–25).[5] Parallel subject matter and imagery urge us to consider Chekhov's story in relationship to the "The Gremiachevo Meadows," keeping in mind what Viktor Shklovsky wrote about Chekhov: "He found something new in that which is commonplace."[6]

The plots of the two stories bear comparison in three respects: (1) each introduces a peasant couple committed to one another in love; (2) in each story the couple is forcibly separated due to circumstances dictated by the man's father and brother, and the man is physically dislocated from the village; (3) in each case the male character returns to the village where, in a delirious state, he murders his beloved. Similar plotlines encourage the view that in writing "The Lady," Chekhov consciously undertook a reexamination of the theme of the Holy Virgin, which serves as the symbolic nucleus in Beloborodov's tale. The opportunity to see what Chekhov does compared to a run-of-the-mill writer is revealing.[7]

In "The Gremiachevo Meadows" Beloborodov harnesses conventional images of the Mother of God to the cart of a sentimental tale. His story opens with a lyric description of a chapel over a spring where, we are told, on the holidays of the icon of the Kazan Mother of God (8 July, 1 September, 22 October) village folk gather for prayer. Sergei and his Dunia, secretly in love, are to be pledged to one another by their fathers. The betrothal is scheduled for the feast of the Virgin's Intercession (*Pokrov*), a traditional time for weddings.[8] But Sergei's brother summons him to work in the city. Upon parting Dunia swears to Sergei: "May the Lord and the Most Pure Mother of God punish me if I take a different husband."

Sergei pines in the city for Dunia as the holidays of the Dormition (15 August) and the First of September (a regional holiday of the Kazan icon) pass by. He then learns that their fathers have quarreled and that Dunia has married another young man. Sergei returns to the village and burns down the peasant hut in which Dunia and her husband are sleeping. In a delirium, he climbs up to the chapel, where the Virgin appears to chastise him for his act: "The figure of the Mother of God, enveloped in a sort of heavenly radiance, disengaged from the large icon of the Kazan Virgin which stood directly across from the entrance illuminated by burning icon lamps, and, walking toward him with a raised arm, pointing her finger at him, uttered the words: 'Murderer, villain, incendiary!' " Sergei's dead body is found the next day in the ravine below the chapel.

Beloborodov deploys Marian imagery heavy-handedly. The progression of icons, holidays, and evocations of the Virgin could not escape even the most unpracticed reader. Securely anchored in the genre of the didactic tale, the merits of Beloborodov's story reside largely in the pleasure formulaic literature might offer an audience attuned to customary messages of religious morality. Beloborodov refrains from exploring the psychological ramifications of the blow dealt to those who believe in a traditional order when that order is disrupted, nor does he engage the question of belief in a benevolent protectress who punishes ruthlessly. It is highly instructive to see how Chekhov was challenged by the story to think about the psychology of the Orthodox peasant world.

It is almost certain that Chekhov, who made a point of keeping abreast of the periodicals in which his works were published, read "The Gremiachevo Meadows" before writing "The Lady." We know that Chekhov drew from all kinds of material at hand; he claimed that an ashtray could launch him into an interesting story. Because he was contributing to at least four other newspapers in the summer of 1882, his decision to place "The Lady" in

Moskva would seem to confirm a link with the earlier piece. In contrast to Beloborodov's preachy story, however, Chekhov's is an emotionally powerful tale that conveys the immense complexity of religious codes and moral questions in peasant life.

"The Lady" has most often been interpreted in sociohistorical terms as a portrayal of brutal class disparities.[9] Chekhov recounts the story of Stepan and Maria, a young peasant couple who enjoy the contentment of commitment to one another despite the constraints of a patriarchal household in which a despotic father and hard-drinking elder brother wield authority. When Stepan's physique attracts the eye of the divorced landlady on whose estate the family lives, however, the couple's peace is destroyed. The lady, Elena Egorovna Strelkova, drafts Stepan into service as a coachman. He tries to escape the sexual duties implicit in his assignment, but capitulates after a beating by his father. Stepan encounters Maria one evening after an unwilling tryst with Strelkova. He strikes his pregnant wife in the stomach "out of grief," then goes back to the stable, tormented by his act. Stepan's father orders him to return home after Strelkova refuses to supply the family with free lumber, but Stepan refuses. In revenge, his father drives Maria out of the hut. Learning of this act, Stepan goes to the village on a Sunday morning, gets drunk, and ruthlessly beats his brother. Deliriously dreaming of running away with his beloved Maria, Stepan runs home, where he finds her huddled on the ground. Maria's bitterness infuriates Stepan. He deals her a hefty blow that kills her. The story ends with the lady's Polish steward regaining his comfortable position as her lover, a position lost and reinstated "ten times a year." As devastating a portrayal as this is of destructive social and economic relations, the core of the tragedy must be located in a symbolic sphere.

In Beloborodov's story, faith represents a static entity with fixed meaning. Sergei and Dunia are judged by a preordained moral code, an a priori belief system shared by author, reader, and society. This complicity is facilitated by the Christian creed, the language of which aims to provide consensus and communication among the faithful. Chekhov recognizes that the situation is far more complex. Stepan and Maria live in a world which they both perceive on a very deep level in terms of a Christian worldview, but the language they share proves far more problematic than the discourse of Beloborodov's world. The limitations of language create the drama of the story.

The archetypal figure of the Mother of God wields ultimate authority in Beloborodov's aborted idyll. In Chekhov's story, we encounter the overpowering presence and categorical triumph of her counterpart, the sexually promiscuous woman. Elena Egorovna Strelkova, who divorces her husband after betraying him within days of the wedding, makes a hobby of seducing men. She is by no means, of course, a likeness of the repentant Christian harlot, although her name may hint sardonically at the archetype of female sensuality/sexuality that resonates in Chekhov, as Laurence Senelick demonstrates, by way of Offenbach's *La Belle Hélène*.[10]

Strelkova is a foreigner to Russian peasant tradition and Christian morality, a foreignness expressed linguistically by her French speech and her Polish companion. Moreover, the text hints that her life is governed by chance, a concept alien to Christian cosmology. She adorns Stepan's uniform with a string of charms and indulges in fortune-telling with cards to decide if the next day's weather will be suitable for her expedition of pleasure.[11] The opposition between Strelkova's world and the tenets of Christianity in which Stepan and Maria believe is developed with reference to perdition.

During Strelkova's visit to his parent's hut in search of her runaway coachman, Stepan lies under the icons, an implied source of protection from her far-ranging sexual appetite, a lust understood in cultural terms as demonic. Stepan's brother Semen aligns himself here with the landlady's cause (he calls her a "little devil" and tries to get Stepan to accept her offer).[12] Smoke figures prominently in the descriptions of both Strelkova and Semen. She smokes cigarettes and at one point pulls from her cigarette case a ruble to pay off Stepan's parents for convincing him to return to her. Semen smokes a small pipe, praises his good tobacco, tries to get Stepan to smoke, and muses that his brother will enjoy Strelkova's quality cigars. Were he to have the opportunity, he says, he would "suck the little devil dry." Semen says of Elena Egorovna: "The woman is fiery fire!" (1:258). Responding to these enticements, Stepan queries: "Isn't that a sin? . . . Even a poor man will go to Hell, to the devil, if he were to . . ." Semen, in a casual vein remote from his brother's earnestness, decries Stepan's stubborn refusal by telling him to "go to Hell."

Michael Finke demonstrates the recurrent pattern of the katabatic journey, the hero's descent to the underworld, in Chekhov's work, suggesting that classical/Christian paradigms of descent are always played out in Chekhov in a deeply ambivalent fashion.[13] The hero of "The Lady" imagines that he is "going to Hell" during his first evening "on duty" with Strelkova:

> Had there been stones under the wheels, they would have disintegrated into sparks. . . . Soon the bell-tower could no longer be seen. . . . Finally the village turned into a smoky strip and sunk into the distance. Stepan whipped the horses on and on. He wanted to fly further and further away from the sin which he so feared. But no, the sin was sitting over his shoulders, in the carriage. He couldn't escape. That evening the steppe and sky looked on as Stepan sold his soul. (1:264)

The church steeple gives way to a smoky haze, paralleling Stepan's perception of his act. Ambivalent, indeed, is this "descent," which in no way replicates a classical heroic descent in pursuit of knowledge or regeneration. It is a descent into alien territory where Stepan loses all bearings, and finds his rhetorical skills severely taxed.

Christian phraseology accompanies the actions of Maria, in contrast to Strelkova. She initially exacts the promise from Stepan that he won't go back to Strelkova's estate with abundant tears, with reference to sin and to her own impending motherhood. Her entreaties almost achieve the desired effect. Stepan says: "Leave me alone! Oh . . . Satan! I said it, and I won't go!" Despite his apparent affection, Stepan reacts to his nagging wife with a reflex that denigrates her, indicative of his powerlessness when faced with the mindless violence practiced by his father and brother.

A series of betrayals reveal Stepan's profound confusion. In accordance with the Christian duty of filial obedience (a habit with him), Stepan betrays his promise to Maria when his father, "resembling a deadman," comes out with a whip in hand and beats him. Returning to his "duties," however, Stepan immediately betrays this commitment as well, telling Strelkova that he'll "sell his soul to the devil" on the condition that she give nothing to his "accursed" father and brother. Caught in a three-way vise among the familiar rhetoric which he accepts (Stepan says to his father, "May God strike down my soul if I go . . ."), his subordinate position, and his own savage peasant proclivities, Stepan makes sense of the situation by considering it a fall into sin. This moral conceptualization vitiates the necessity of maintaining a humble stance toward his kin, at whom he lashes out with vengeance.

When Maria seeks out Stepan by the river, the conflict between his feelings and the external circumstances comes to a head. She approaches him just as he is recollecting "the bench on which he slept with his Maria and how he had been so content" (1:265). This sexually charged memory of Maria and the bed implicitly stands in opposition to Strelkova and the carriage, creating a painful contrast that confirms Stepan's self-assessment as a fallen soul. But he does not have the language to communicate these feelings. All of his speech falls squarely within the boundaries of peasant crudity or petrified Christian discourse. In complete ignorance of her husband's bitter thoughts, and restricted by a similarly limited vocabulary, Maria admonishes Stepan for his sins, threatening him with God's retribution. As he begins to walk away from these painful exhortations, Maria moves from the rhetoric of punishment to the rhetoric of forgiveness: "Darling! I'll wash your feet and drink the water! Let's go home" (1:265). This gesture of total devotion is a commonplace in Russian usage that derives from scriptural accounts of the sinful woman who washes Christ's feet to express her repentance (Luke 7:37–48). As noted earlier, popular belief imported from the West firmly identifies Mary Magdalene as that sinful woman. In the context of the story, the phrase is unobtrusively emblematic. Maria's very human emotions foreclose the possibility of either the Christian humility of a Magdalene or a Virgin-like pose of forgiveness, and she responds with malice to Stepan's blow.

The final tragic events take place on Sunday, but contrast darkly with the Christian meaning of the holiday: "The bells rang for mass. It was a Sunday morning [*utro bylo voskresnoe*], light, happy . . ." At the tavern where Stepan first goes, Semen baits him with comments about the sexual activity with Strelkova, leading to a fight. As Stepan stomps on his brother in a drunken frenzy, the church bells signal the Canon of the Eucharist (*Dostoino*), which features the hymn to Mary known as "Worthy is She" (*Dostoina est'*): "It is proper to bless thee, ever-esteemed Theotokos, most pure, and Mother of our God . . . thou, who incorruptibly gave birth to God the Word, verily Theotokos, we extoll thee."[14] This marks the moment when Stepan rouses himself and runs off to find Maria.

The "cue" of the Eucharist litany suggests that, just as Stepan regards Strelkova in the light of hell and damnation, a realm of meaning associated with the Holy Mother is relevant to Stepan's feelings toward his wife. Consequently, despite what has transpired between them, despite the communication gap, Stepan expects Maria to understand and forgive him. Discovering his wife huddled pitifully in the yard, Stepan suddenly fantasizes an escape to Kuban, the region of free Cossacks, "with this pale as death, downtrodden, passionately beloved woman" (1:271). But when he tries to convey this drunken plan, his *tongue loses the capacity to speak*. Thwarted by language, Stepan remains isolated in a world where physical gestures provide his only recourse to communication.

Having abandoned the rhetoric of humility altogether, Maria now expresses herself with her only linguistic alternative, the second pole of language available in popular Christian belief: she calls Stepan "accursed one" and claims that he has "sucked her dry," the expression Semen used earlier about Strelkova. Maria's expression of her sense of betrayal reaches its apotheosis with an evocation of the Mother of God: "You cruel ones! You've no pity for a Christian soul! You've worn me out, bandits. . . . You're a murderer, Stepka! The Mother of God will punish you!" (1:271). In "The Gremiachevo Meadows" it is the apparition of the Virgin that pronounces the word "murderer" and brings about Sergei's "just" death. Here, pronouncing the word "murderer," Maria calls upon the mythological Christian mother to exact justice—a mentality so satisfyingly rewarded in Beloborodov's tale. Her words, however, exercise no power. The incantational string of Christian clichés protesting her innocence makes of the Mother of God a piece of rhetorical artillery.

Maria's anger deafens her to Stepan's pained reception of her words ("Be quiet, for Christ's sake!"; "Be quiet, Mashka!"; "Don't tear at my heart!" (271–72). In response, Maria explicitly refers to Strelkova. For the first time the two women are adjacent in the text: "What do you need me for? You have a lady . . . Wealthy . . . Beautiful. . . . I'm a nobody, and she's a noblewoman . . ." (1:272). This is the moment that breaks Stepan. It becomes clear that Maria has no capacity to recognize his moral and emotional drama and to respond with the compassion and forgiveness for which he thirsts. Her language, although equally anchored in Christian conceptualizations, functions in a manner precisely the opposite to his own. Stepan, overcome by helplessness in a situation that does not correspond to expectations bred by Christian belief, tries to silence her, but underestimates the brutal force of his male peasant muscle.

In the final tableau, Stepan, sitting over his wife's dead body, "muttered incoherent [*bessviaznye*] words." The Russian "bez-sviaznye" (without connection) dramatizes the tragedy of "The Lady." Both hero and heroine embrace the language and images of conventional Christian belief, but the frozen, formulaic language they assimilate hardly suffices as a means of communication. The feelings of each remain beyond the other's purview. A language that promises common ground on which all can meet ends up emotionally stranding its speakers.

If human sinfulness is pitted against divine justice in "The Gremiachevo Meadows," moral absolutes have no place in "The Lady." The core of Chekhov's story concerns failure of communication between people who ostensibly share an identical symbolic discourse. The language of Christianity, seemingly infallible in its prescriptive (and proscriptive) formulas, proves deficient in the face of individual needs for self-expression. Moreover, those needs arise in a milieu that had typically been regarded by literate Russians—Turgenev's *Notes of a Hunter* notwithstanding—as a locus of simple, uncomplicated relationships. The exigencies of peasant life, in Chekhov's rendition, create an enormously complex drama.

Motherhood in "The Lady" is menaced by a literal miscarriage when Stepan strikes the pregnant Maria in the stomach. One must regard this action as the obvious victimization of a defenseless woman fostered by a violent, patriarchal culture. Yet I see its more essential function as the symbolic marker of an untenable, fracture-prone Christian discourse grounded in a maternal ideal tragically irrelevant to the emotional needs of the faithful—precisely the needs to which she theoretically ministers. In this sense, both women and men become casualties of belief in a cultural construct.

Julia Kristeva writes that "Christianity is doubtless the most refined symbolic construct in which femininity, to the extent that it transpires through it—and it does so incessantly—is focused on *Maternality*."[15] Russian cultural history speaks particularly eloquently of this preoccupation. The mythic proportions of Russian motherhood have been amply documented. One of the nearly unfailing reference points for representations and/or discussions of Russian motherhood is Marian iconography.

An icon of the Virgin becomes a narrational centerpiece for an inquiry into Russian motherhood in Chekhov's "Peasants." The Orthodox icon is a text of revelation written in a carefully determined pictorial language (and icons are "written," not painted). The lingual nature of the icon was preordained in patristics, where church fathers spell out the need to make holy pictures accessible to all as a guide to faith; that is, icons functioned as "books for a largely illiterate population."[16] The "writing" of icons represents a highly formalized art designed to orchestrate viewer reception.

In her discussion of a Western Madonna depiction, Rossetti's painting *The Girlhood of Mary Virgin,* Lynne Pearce insists that the laws of such a text's production and consumption mean to limit interpretation to one monolithic reading that promotes a vision of "female excellence." Pearce endorses a feminist intervention into such readings that would celebrate the "slipperiness of the sign" and defy the laws of apprehending sacred images in favor of claiming them for the viewer's own.[17] While Chekhov hardly champions a feminist gaze, his sensibilities are not altogether alien to this idea. In "Peasants," he "deconstructs" the Christian mythology of motherhood by showing how the unambiguous religious intentions projected by the icon are translated into disparate meanings by each female character. Each woman reads the icon in accordance with her own experience. In other words, Chekhov is highly cognizant of the icon's "slipperiness" as a sign.

Like "The Lady," "Peasants" has garnered substantial critical attention for its gloomy depiction of the social and economic woes plaguing the Russian peasantry. Christian imagery in the story has also attracted recent notice.[18] The story abounds in citations of Marian holidays, icons, and Scripture, and appeals to the Mother of God so organic to the peasant milieu that few critics have made special note of them. L. M. O'Toole does address the question, relating the presence of the Marian icon to "The Virgin's Travels Through the Torments." He asserts that Chekhov emphasizes "the special role of the Virgin in interceding on behalf of sinful man," and he reads the icon as "hope of an alternative way of life."[19] O'Toole certainly describes the unmediated value of the miracle-working icon in popular religious perception, yet an indication of an alternative way of life really doesn't present itself in "Peasants." Rather, Chekhov explores the phenomenon of an impoverished and downtrodden populace confronted with an idealized maternal image.

The Marian icon appears in "Peasants" as something of a cultural baseline from which to assess understandings of motherhood, the only natural function in this destitute world. When the Life-Bearing Mother of God visits the wretched, poverty-striken village of Zhukovo, filled with drunken men and oppressed women, its inhabitants "consume" the image in conformity with the designs of the Orthodox faith:

> By the way, in Zhukovo, this Slaveville, there once was a real religious celebra-
> tion. It was in August, when they carried the Life-Bearer [Icon of the Mother of

God] from village to village throughout the district. It was to come to Zhukovo on a quiet and overcast day. The girls left in the morning to greet the icon in their bright, festive dresses, and arrived with it toward evening in a religious procession accompanied by singing, while the bells across the river rang. A huge crowd of locals and visitors flooded the street, noisy, dusty and crushing. . . . The old man, granny and Kiriak all stretched their hands toward the icon, greedily gazed at it and said, crying: "Mother Intercessor! Intercessor!" All of a sudden everyone seemed to understand that it was not empty between earth and heaven, that the wealthy and strong had not managed to get everything, that there was still protection against insults, slavish bondage, against unbearable need and terrible vodka. "Mother Intercessor!" sobbed Maria, "Dear mother!" (*Matushka!*) (9:307)

The crowd embraces the Mother of God in her foremost role as benevolent intercessor, intermediary between earth and heaven. Yet a description of relentless drinking on the Marian holidays of the Dormition and the Intercession precedes the account of the procession of the Virgin, and the narrator tells us that everything returned to normal as soon as the icon left the village.[20] The wide gap between this pious interlude and daily life suggests that ecclesiastical meaning is transposed by the circumstances of individual women to reflect on the variety of possible meanings the iconographic figure can hold. While the significations read by the characters into the image of the Mother of God in this story tend to be more closely bound to the "rules of the text's production" than is the case elsewhere in Chekhov, they remain idiosyncratic translations of the original text's intent.

The "Life-Bearing" icon of the Virgin itself speaks of spiritual motherhood. That little girls first greet the icon and the peasants call it "dear mother" (*matushka*) underscores the icon as a cultural locus of motherhood and the feminine. The story's minimal plot (Nikolai Chikildeev falls ill in Moscow and returns with his wife Olga and daughter Sasha to his village, where he dies amid the squalor of the overcrowded family hut, leaving Olga and Sasha to make their way back to Moscow) urges the importance of relationships over action. Indeed, three generations of women in the Chikildeev family receive much of the narrative attention. The elderly grandmother (Babka) presides over the household of her three daughters-in-law—Maria, Fekla, and Olga—and a band of female grandchildren, including Sasha and Motka. Men are either passive (the old man), absent (Maria's Kiriak works in the forest, Fekla's husband serves in the army), or sick (Nikolai). The women do all of the work: when a hut catches fire, the village men stand idly by as the women haul water. The village has become a matriarchal society by default, wherein lies the centrality of the icon. Yet the iconographic ideal of female power and fortitude has gone awry. What follows (not an exhaustive reading of the story) is an attempt to illuminate the psychological ramifications of the icon in the lives of these female characters.

In "Peasants" there is no doubt that Chekhov intended to paint this Maria in relationship to the Mother of God. We recall that Maria mouths her plea to the Virgin separately from the others in front of the Life-Bearing icon ("'Mother Intercessor!' sobbed Maria, *'Matushka!'* "). The proximity of the two figures—the fictional character and the religious image—promises neither hope nor redemption. The moment is facilitated by a ritual familiar in its repetition, but alien to Maria as a daily source of comfort. Again, such a portrayal bears on the entire Marian motif in Chekhov; he uniformly dissociates Maria characters from the Virgin qualities, but at the same time insists on the model of the Virgin as the point of religious and cultural orientation from which to define their characters and plights.

Maria, whose husband Kiriak returns only occasionally to the village from his job in the forest, clearly leads the subservient and degraded life of an abused wife. Details of language illuminate the disturbing dimensions of her position by revealing the complete discrepancy between her debasement and the venerated Marian ideal, an important observation for a society that still today subscribes to essentialist understandings of gender based on woman's "sacred" biological ability to bear children. Early in the story, Kiriak arrives at the hut thunderously shouting "Ma-ari-ia!" and begins to beat her. When the newly arrived Nikolai and Olga are brought to his attention, he releases Maria, prays to an icon, and says: "'My brother and his family have come to the parental home . . . from Moscow. The first capital city of Moscow, the mother of cities . . . Apologies'" (9:285).[21] Moscow is lauded in Russian culture as the nation's matriarchal spiritual authority, its heart and mother. The frozen epithets about Moscow that issue from Kiriak's inebriated brain divert attention from his own bestial behavior toward Maria by rhetorically saluting a cultural icon of femininity. But the family greets his pronouncement with silence, evincing the irrelevance and hollowness of his words.[22]

The name Kiriak sheds light on his status as undisputed and feared master in his family's home. The Greek *kyriakos*, "the Lord's own," serves as one of the most common refrains in Christian prayer: "Lord have mercy" (Greek, *Kyrie eleison*). Chekhov's pairing of Kiriak and Maria, then, couples two of the most frequently invoked names from the Orthodox liturgy. It appears that Chekhov was not unaware of this connection; he treats the resonance of the name Maria in relationship to the liturgical setting. When Kiriak comes to beat his wife, he yells "Ma-ari-ia" thrice from afar, and she turns to the family, uttering, "In Christ's name, intervene, my own kin, . . . —intervene, my own kin." Her appeal reverses the Marian role of intercessor; moreover, it is made to kin (*rod*), a network of earthly relationships. Kiriak figures as the violent head of this clan; even in church Maria cannot escape him. There, she quivers from the sound of the deacon's bass voice, hearing in it only the shout "Ma-ari-ia!" The deacon's sacred utterances enter Maria's mind filtered through her domestic experience, defined as it is by terror of her husband, the "lord."

The namesake of the Mother of God in "Peasants" represents motherhood degraded to a state of abject physicality. Maria's body is plundered by the thirteen children she bears Kiriak, seven of whom die. The grueling physical exigencies of childbearing are completely divorced from spiritual belief or image. Maria, through no fault of her own, annuls the myth of hallowed motherhood. She wants to die, the narrator comments twice, and *was glad when her children died.* If we are startled by the poetic pronouncement of Innokenty Annensky, whose muse breaks the arms of young children and blinds them, or by Mayakovsky's famous line, "I love to watch children dying," this characterization in Chekhov shocks us for its plausibility as a description of real lives. He exposes rawly the futility of motherhood (and thus of future) in the eyes of the peasant mother so often idealized in Russian literature. We have only to think of the women Dolly encounters at the river near the Oblonsky estate in *Anna Karenina.*

It is not surprising that the prism through which Maria views motherhood should so thoroughly distort the cultural ideal, given the lack of any benevolent matrons among the elders. Babka, Maria's mother-in-law, provides a distressing example of a matriarch, something evident enough from her unkind behavior, and symbolically illuminated by her understanding of the Mother of God. Babka's telling "reading" of Marian icons exposes the limitations of her emotional/spiritual world. The evening prayer she concocts derives from a cultural tradition so centered on the icon that the object can come to replace the message. Standing before the family icons, Babka whispers: "To the Kazan Holy Mother, to the Smolensk Holy Mother, to the Three-handed Holy Mother" (9:306). Driven in everyday life by anxieties over physical survival, the primary vestige of piety left in Babka's consciousness is but the verbal shell of sacred meaning, a list of names that stands at a remove from epithets offering the solace sought in supplications to the Virgin.

A broader iconographic context in "Peasants" relates to the interface between the sacred and the profane. The walls of the Chikildeev hut sport bottle labels and newspaper clippings that have been hung by the icon in the corner, obscuring the boundary between secular and sacred depictions. In the house of the village elder, Antip Sedelnikov, the chief image on a wall of magazine illustrations is a portrait of the former Bulgarian prince Battenberg, which hangs "in the most prominent place beside the icons." Babka's husband takes it for an icon and "genuflects to Battenberg" upon entering the house (9:302). This jumble of images represents the leveling of secular and religious authority in the villagers' beleaguered lives. Babka's explanation for the heavy drinking in which her husband and Kiriak indulge faintly resonates with the portrait of the prince. She laments, "The Queen of Heaven got angry" (9:284).

78

The epithet "Queen" (*Tsaritsa*) conflates the holy figure with secular authority. Indeed, the family's destiny is controlled by local officials who confiscate the family samovar for debts and attempt to extract arrears. No hierarchy of value prevails in the Chikildeev home.

This disorientation concerning sources of authority and value inadvertently precipitates her own son's death at his mother's hands, a travesty of biblical events. The holiday of the Intercession (*Pokrov*) is the Zhukovo parish holiday. The day commemorates the spreading of the veil of maternal protection over all believers. On this holiday the old woman learns from the sacristan (sacred authority) about a former military medic (secular authority) with a good medical reputation (scientific authority). Intending to intercede, as it were, on behalf of her ailing son Nikolai, she travels to a nearby town and returns with the attendant. The medic never receives a name, but is repeatedly referred to as "vykrest" (a word usually indicating a Jewish convert to Orthodoxy), a sign in itself of inverted meaning. The "convert" lets Nikolai's blood and departs. Nikolai weakens and dies. Thus Babka's impulse to act out the role of the healing mother, signaled by the Intercession, misfires completely. Her life has been defined by onerous physical conditions, and she responds with a faith in the physical healing powers of the convert and of "all the doctors, medics and sorcerers within thirty versts" (9:308).

Reading of sacred text in a very literal sense characterizes another of Babka's daughters-in-law, Olga. She reads the Gospels zealously. Holy words she does not understand "touch her to tears," and words such as the Church Slavic *ashche* and *dondezhe* ("if" and "until") move her deeply (9:286). Olga's godliness appears proximate enough to qualities of the Virgin that the association has been accepted on face value.[23] But, as O'Toole recognizes, "the reader's positive view [of Olga] is gradually subverted by irony as the story progresses."[24] Her allegiance to sacred writings comes out of the popular mind-set typical of pilgrims (to whom the narrator compares her). A piece of folk verse captures this mentality:

> The Lord said to the sinners:
> "Sinful and accursed slaves!
> How is it you didn't know?
> Books were created for you,
> Everything is written in those books,
> About how to save your soul and gain entrance to heaven."[25]

Chekhov describes in Olga the pitfalls of a simple mind that latches onto text as a rigid truth.

Paradoxically, Olga's readings of Scripture are "deviant" because of her literal apprehension. She prescribes textual solutions to the harsh life encountered in Zhukovo, thus handily resolving hardships such as the beatings

Maria suffers from Kiriak: "In the Scripture they say: 'If someone hits you on the right cheek, turn your left cheek to him'" (9:285). Intended as solace, this central Christian commandment does little to alleviate Maria's suffering. It also resonates with Olga's daughter's paraphrase of Matthew 25:33, in which the righteous go to the right, to heaven, and the sinners to the left, to damnation. In both cases an unequivocal understanding of right and wrong masks the complexities of human lives. Olga's rejoinder to Maria's complaints about the arduous life in the Chikildeev home also offers little by way of aid: "They say: 'Come to me, all who labor and are heavy laden'" (9:286). Chekhov may have counted on his readers to recall that this citation from Matthew 11:28 continues, "Take my yoke upon you, and learn from me . . . for my yoke is easy, and my burden light." Later in the story Fekla complains about how little Olga works and hits her with the *yoke* that Fekla herself has just used to haul water up from the river. As attractive a character as Olga may be, her rote biblical citations, part and parcel of the folk religious experience, are problematized by their uselessness in ameliorating the women's arduous lot. The credulous naïveté of the pilgrim protects her from having to acknowledge onerous and difficult human relations, and allows her to bypass the stifling necessity, austerity, and afflictions borne by the village inhabitants.

Much is made in the village of the fact that Olga has taught her daughter Sasha to read. Increased literacy in Russia was a goal to which Chekhov devoted significant energy, building schools and donating books to the Taganrog library. Never, however, could this be construed as a push for literacy motivated by Tolstoyan didacticism. Rather, in Sasha, Chekhov shows how broad is the range of textual interpretation. He attends less to what texts hope to do for people than to what people do with texts.

The passage that Sasha reads from the Gospel when neighbors arrive for a visit is taken from the Book of Matthew 2:13, which relates the flight of Joseph, Mary, and the Christ child to Egypt.[26] Sasha reads aloud in Church Slavic, "Now when they had departed, behold, an angel of the Lord appeared to Joseph in a dream and said: 'Rise, take the child and his mother, and flee to Egypt, and remain there until I tell you'" (9:289). A rough analogy can be drawn between this passage and Sasha's family. The flight into exile of a father, mother, and child recalls the journey of Nikolai, Olga, and Sasha, who had arrived the day before to find that the family home seemed more like a place of exile from Moscow than the comfortable nest Nikolai recalled. Sasha's choice of text snugly fits her own life, in which Olga assumes the place of the spiritual Mother.

Just as Olga shares with Maria scriptural citations and religious lore, Sasha regales Motka, Maria's daughter, with her vision of the church. Sasha creates for God suggestive companions: "God lives in the church. People burn lamps and candles, but God has little red, green and blue icon lamps, like little eyes. At night God walks around the church, and the Most Holy Mother of God and Saint Nikolai go with him—pitter-patter, pitter-patter" (9:291). She pairs the Mother of God with the saint for whom her father was named, Nikolai. (Saint Nicholas enjoyed a very special status in Russian religious sentiment, often placed on a par with Christ or considered a deity.)[27] Sasha subconsciously fuses these central Christian figures with the principal players in her own life, her parents. Bent on imitating her mother, Sasha internalizes the Christian language with which Olga conceptualizes life. (Olga, we are told earlier, believes in the Mother of God; her speech is peppered with religious epithets such as "Saints alive!" and "Heavenly Queen!" [9:293].) Sasha thereby succeeds at creating images that are not there, just as she sees angels in the sky that Motka cannot make out. This "corrective lens" grants Sasha a childish temperament, absent in the sullen, bass-voiced Motka, whose parental legacy is so radically different.

If Sasha comfortably constructs a relationship between these benevolent holy texts and that which holds for her cardinal emotional value, she and her cousin Motka even more actively pursue an intervention that will assure negative consequences based on Scripture. This involves a "reading" of the Last Judgment. In his first notebook, Chekhov jots down a skeletal scene in which a grandmother whips a girl, who revenges herself by pouring milk in the old woman's soup in order to make her break the Lenten fast, a violation that guarantees the perpetrator eternal torments. The girl's name is Masha (17:33). The name is not accidental: in a Chekhovian reversal, Masha intercedes on her *own* behalf; she performs a malicious act much less characteristic of the merciful mother of "The Virgin's Travels" than of the vindictive Mother of God known to Russian popular spiritual verses. These verses "exclude all thought of mercy at the Last Judgment" and "turn the Mother of God into an implacable Judge."[28] This sketch resurfaces, embellished, in "Peasants."

On the evening of the day when Sasha explains to Motka her version of the Last Judgment (Olga and Maria will end up in heaven; Kiriak and their grandmother, in the "fire"), an opportunity arises to seek revenge on the old woman who, as in the notebook sketch, has just beaten the girls. Babka sits sucking on rye crusts that are soaking in a bowl when Maria comes in with a bucket of milk from the evening's milking. Milk, with its resonance of maternal nurturance, repeatedly accompanies the Marian theme in Chekhov's stories. In Maria's case, her milking cows conveys her own maternal function as a virtual beast of burden, the fate also of her counterpart in "The Lady" (Semen tells Stepan that his wife is a "foolish cow"). Later Maria feels anguish at the sound of the starving and bellowing cow near the time of the Annunciation.

The old woman transfers the milk to jugs for storage, pleased that the Dormition fast forces the family to abstain from milk. The Dormition setting (the observance of the death of the Mother of God), symbolically echoes her delight in the denial of maternal sustenance. Babka pours a bit of milk into a dish for Fekla's baby, then brings the jugs to the basement with Maria. Motka, inspired by Sasha's talk, splashes milk from the baby's dish into Babka's bowl. When the latter returns and starts in on her crusts, the girls "watched her and were pleased that she was breaking the fast and would now certainly go to hell" (9:294).

Ironically, Sasha and Motka have taken upon themselves the arbitration between heaven and hell that belongs in the religious mind to the Mother of God. Moreover, they rely on the authority of the Dormition fast, but with the inverted intention of sending the matriarch not "up" to heaven, but "down" to Hades. This personalized adaptation of the Christian text manifests itself on a subconscious level as well: falling asleep, Sasha imagines a Last Judgment in which a black devil with cow's horns chases her grandmother into the fire with a stick resembling that which the old woman used to chase geese. The detail of the cow's horns suggests that Sasha is desperately attempting to salvage some kind of power for the maternal locus of nurturance so thoroughly denigrated around her, although it appears in an ambivalent form. This entire Last Judgment episode emphasizes the adaptability of religious thought to personal exigency. Psychological motivation becomes inextricably bound up with the apprehension of text.

The texts through which the female characters of "Peasants" read motherhood into their lives neatly map the languages of the religious mind; the illiterate Maria and Babka appear adjacent to iconographic themes, while the literate Muscovites speak and act in reference to the scriptural word. In no case, however, are the laws of these texts' production obeyed, not because of willful misunderstandings, but because the cultural ideal that looms in the story's background in the form of the Life-Bearing icon is at such distinct odds with the social reality of motherhood. The icon that promises a better life mutates into the forms of life led by the women. No single "Mother of God" exists for Babka, Maria, Olga, and Sasha; only cultural translations of the image that move the sacred female ideal into the territory of human psychology uncharted by church dogma. That Chekhov breaks away from the icon and Scripture as sources of truth to investigate this unexplored domain speaks to his depth of understanding as an observer of culture.

One female figure in "Peasants" orbits outside the sphere of the Mother image. Not coincidentally, her actions trace the outlines of the paradigmatic counterpart, the sinful woman. The third Chikildeev daughter-in-law, Fekla, dallies with the estate bailiffs across the river. She returns from a tryst "with her hair let down" (9:287), one of the cultural and iconographic hallmarks of the harlot that Chekhov frequently evokes. Of course no direct correlation is in effect. When she returns naked to the hut one night and reports to Olga, "I came home with no clothes . . . just how my mother bore me" (9:300–301), we understand that sexuality and motherhood are integrated for Fekla as natural functions of the female body. By effacing the cultural dichotomy between female purity and physical degradation, Fekla in a sense counters all the claims of the Life-Bearing icon by relishing the rudimentary sensuality available in her harsh life. She provides a critical textual signal as well that constructs of holiness can only exist in relationship to constructs of sin. It is to the most explicit manifestations in Chekhov's prose of the "sinful woman" Saint Mary of Egypt that we now turn.

Two stories of the 1880s make clear Chekhov's conscious interest in the figure of the sinful-woman-turned-saint. The surprising number of Russian literary works treating Saint Mary of Egypt's life was detailed in Chapter 2. Most of these (the poems by I. S. Aksakov, B. Almazov, E. Shakhova) rework the hagiographic theme in order to edify and uplift the reader. Chekhov moves into deeper territory by exploring aspects of the very attraction in Russian culture to this particular saint. Once again, reception of text forms the centerpiece of these stories. In both "The Requiem" and "An Attack of Nerves" Mary of Egypt's *Vita* serves as a paradigm from which the heros are loath to disengage.

In "The Requiem," Andrei Andreich, a shopkeeper in a provincial village, words his request that a prayer be offered in honor of his deceased actress-daughter Mashutka (Maria Andreevna) in a manner that seriously offends the presiding clerics. He submits a diptych (on which requests for prayers are written) that reads: "For the peace of the servant of God, the fornicatress (*bludnitsa*) Maria" (4:352). The priests, who have read of Maria Andreevna's death in the newspaper—and are incongruently impressed by the worldly success that gains her such eminence in print—indignantly upbraid her father for what they perceive as abusive and sinful words.

Savely Senderovich shows that the meaning of names in "The Requiem" functions as the philosophical core of the story.[29] Father Grigorii, the priest, considers Andrei Andreich's requiem request to be blasphemous and a slur on the daughter's name; he associates the word "fornicatress" with its secular connotations ("a word that it would be indecent to say even out on the street" [4:352]). Andrei Andreich, on the other hand, regards the combination "the fornicatress Maria" as a sacred utterance evocative of Saint Mary of Egypt's repentance and consequent salvation: "But the Lord through his mercy did . . . that is, forgave the fornicatress . . . prepared a place for her, you can see from the saintly life of the venerable Mary of Egypt in what sense this same word, pardon me" (4:352). The model of the forgiven harlot affords the inarticulate Andrei Andreich hope for the salvation of Mashutka's soul.

Senderovich has demonstrated that the story hinges on a systematic set of dualities that, in toto, reveal the deep complexities and ambivalences of the Russian religious consciousness. These include the irreconcilable positions of the priest and Andrei Andreich, the contradiction between the priests' view of religious morality and their secular orientation, the immanent ambivalence of the religious belief that a sinful woman can also be a saint, and the opposition between Andrei Andreich's "genuinely religious consciousness" and the "repellent crudity of his nature" (when she was alive, he disdained his daughter, but he comes to appreciate her later through the redeeming paradigm of a saint).[30] I would add to this some comments on the duality between the Virgin and the harlot, and, in so doing, wish to weigh in Andrei Andreich as a character whose religious consciousness appears to be grounded in a stringent adherence to text with nothing of the emotional coloration that might connect it to the spiritual.

The restricted nature of the shopkeeper's spiritual understandings suggests itself from a number of clues. "The Requiem" opens with a reference to the Mother of God. The first sentence states that mass had just ended at the church of the Hodegitria Mother of God in the village of Verkhnie Zaprudy. The Greek Hodegitria (Russian, *Putevoditel'nitsa*) icon type shows the Virgin with Christ in one arm, pointing with the five fingers of her other hand to her son in order to indicate the path the faithful should follow, an illustration of the words, "He is the Path and the Salvation."

The emphasis on fingers in the story seems to relate to this image. Andrei Andreich finds the iconostasis and church routine to be "as familiar as his own five fingers," conveying his solid grounding in the images and "path" of the church. He invokes the name of the Mother of God in an analogous vein. Noticing the priest's beckoning finger, Andrei Andreich thinks to himself: "Who's he blinking at, God preserve him? . . . And who's he pointing his finger at? And he's stamped his foot, for goodness sake. . . . Holy Mother, what odd behavior! Who does he want?" (4:351). Andrei Andreich's language indicates that sacred words have become part of his everyday repertory, a verbal convention without spiritual substance. The informal "God preserve him" and "Holy Mother" represent a reflex action, a discourse as unthinkingly familiar as the icons in the church and his five fingers.

During the requiem that Father Grigorii performs in Mashutka's memory, Andrei Andreich recalls that the only contact that he had with his daughter in her childhood occurred when he "accidently ran into her somewhere near the gates or on the staircase landing" and would try to find time to teach her prayers and biblical history. I might point out that both gates and staircases represent epithets for the Mother of God ("Locked Gates," "Heavenly Gates," "Heavenly Ladder"), familiar figurations that might subconsciously feed Andrei Andreich's desire that his daughter strive toward a religious ideal, although nothing in her girlhood behavior justifies such an ambition. He thinks to himself, "O, and even then he was known as an authority on church regulations and the Holy Scripture" (4:354). The suggestion that regulations dwell in the same territory as Scripture points to Andrei Andreich's literalistic apprehension of matters of faith. He requests the requiem "For the peace of the servant of God, the fornicatress Maria" in observation of Orthodox regulations regarding prayers and services for the dead. In following this ecclesiastical directive he ironically stumbles across his own emotions.

Andrei Andreich recollects in detail the life of his daughter in the course of the requiem, including their complete lack of communication when she had visited him three years earlier. Appalled by her announcement that she had become an actress, the shopkeeper refrained from conversation with Mashutka until the last day of her visit, when, overcoming his shame at being seen before "honest people" with his actress-daughter, the two took a walk. He recalls her exultation over the natural surroundings, which contrasted with his own obstinate thoughts of how unprofitable was such empty land (earlier he describes her eyes as "kopecks," another hint at his mercantile mentality). Now he thinks that her tears and deep breaths then must have meant that she understood that she was not long for this world. At this moment, when his feelings become most acute, Andrei Andreich resorts to the "forbidden" word again "in order to stifle the burdensome memories": " 'Remember, O Lord,' he mutters, 'your deceased servant the fornicatress Maria and forgive her both willing and unwilling sins' " (4:355). He retreats into the familiar territory of ecclesiastical formula so as to repress this raw encounter, to curtail his own private mental requiem.

Thus another level of duality in "The Requiem" is presented through the polarity of the Marian images. Andrei Andreich's understanding of the models of both Virgin and harlot is grounded in a conventional religious consciousness based on custom and regulation. The Mother of God image can be associated with the "five fingers" of habit, while Mary of Egypt provides an equally familiar means to identify his dead daughter Mashutka. An "untouchable" in life because of the widespread social belief that actresses lead sinful lives, after death Andrei Andreich finds in the saintly prototype a secure domain that wards off the genuine grief he feels over the loss of his estranged daughter. This stringent textualism sustains a committed faith, but it is a faith at odds with the Christian commandments to love and forgive, acts Andrei Andreich found impossible to perform toward his living daughter. This form of traditional Russian religiosity, Chekhov recognizes, possesses an uncomfortable potential to divorce faith from life.

Chekhov treats another aspect of the Russian religious consciousness in his study of Vasilev in "An Attack of Nerves." The story opens with the law student Vasilev's ruminations on the women he expects to encounter on his first visit to a brothel. He has heard about "fallen" and "immoral" women who "sell their honor for money" only by hearsay and from books. But he decides that since they, too, were created in the likeness and image of God, they undoubtedly realize that they are leading sinful lives and hope to be saved. It's true, he thinks, that society rarely forgives one's past, "but God does not consider Mary of Egypt inferior to other saints" (7:199).

In the brothels Vasilev encounters gaudily dressed, boisterous, drunken women who express no discontentment with their lives and refuse to conform to his Magdalene-like image of long-haired pale women dressed in black, timidly and sadly awaiting salvation. This evocation reminds us of Chekhov's sensitivity to the cultural pose of the "sinful" woman. Maria Fedorovna in "The Duel" (Duèl, 1891), hypocritically assuming the role of mother/intercessor/confessor to Laevsky's lover Nadezhda Fedorovna, proclaims the latter a "horrible sinful woman" and suggests that any other woman would have "hidden herself from people, sat home under lock and key, and people would have seen her only in the holy cathedral, pale, dressed all in black, weeping, and, sincerely touched, everyone would say, 'O Lord, this angel who once sinned is again returning to you'" (7:402).[31] Anna Sergeevna in "Lady with a Dog" images her "fall" after the first night with Gurov with an analogous image: "Her long hair hung down dolefully around her drooping, pale face and she assumed a dejected pose, like a sinful woman in an old painting" (10:132). In both "Lady with a Dog" and "An Attack of Nerves" the perception of sinfulness issues from textual sources: in the case of Anna Sergeevna, a painting; in Vasilev's case, books.

Class difference has no bearing on the level of sophistication with which Chekhov's characters read religious texts; however, it does matter, "An Attack of Nerves" seems to suggest, in ultimate outcomes. Like Andrei Andreich (a shopkeeper), Vasilev does not belong to the peasantry, the traditional locus of Russian religiosity. But unlike Andrei Andreich, who remains unconscious of the paradoxes inherent in his apprehension, Vasilev's status as a member of the intelligentsia and training as an analytical thinker (he is a student of law) lead him to a state of crisis once his empirical inquiry disproves the premises of the books in which he has sought knowledge.[32] Marena Senderovich pinpoints the problems of the textualism with which Vasilev frames women, and the Christian concept of women on which he expounds, as the determining factor in his "attack of nerves":

> At the moment of a clash with life, there occurs a collapse of both the scientific and religious world-view of Vasilev. All his *a priori* concepts and ideas become displaced: the prostitutes whom he encounters in the brothels do not have anything in common with those fallen women about whom he has read in the Gospels. Scientific methods of problem solving . . . turn out to be powerless to improve the world. Finally he—who considers himself a Christian, a loving person, who views the world from the heights of evangelical morality—he

comes to feel hatred and becomes incapable of putting his Christian ideals into practice. His Christianity has proved to be no more than pedantic erudition.[33]

This analysis reiterates the chasm between Christian convictions and individual consciousness that distinguishes Chekhov's foray into the religious mind. Chekhov's dexterous intellect never seems to exhaust the large range of psychological and philosophical angles from which to view this phenomenon.

Like the reworking of Beloborodov's theme in "The Lady," "An Attack of Nerves" attests to the ways in which Chekhov's methods differ from those of the literati surrounding him. He wrote the story for a literary collection in memory of the writer V. M. Garshin, and intentionally selected "Garshinesque" subject matter. Chekhov refers to his future hero Vasilev in a letter to Pleshcheev as "a man of Garshin's ilk."[34] Chekhov expands on the subject of the prostitute that Garshin treats in "The Event" (1878) and "Nadezhda Nikolaevna" (1885). Garshin defends the prostitute as a victim of unjustly moralistic censure and castigation on the part of society, claiming for her a "human face." Garshin's position, of course, echoes a literary history in which Russia's intelligentsia attempts to "save" fallen women.[35]

In his "response" to Garshin, Chekhov rejects the idea of moral judgment one way or the other in favor of an examination of the forces that create a moral viewpoint in the first place. Garshin's position, after all, equals Vasilev's view of women, although the polar opposite, in its self-righteous claim to "understand" the situation. It is characteristic of Chekhov that he should turn to the prototypical harlot image in Russian religious culture as a means to examine these questions.

"An artist should not judge his characters." Chekhov's withholding of judgment (insofar as it succeeds) permits an understanding of female characters that goes beyond a facile sociology to examine the underpinnings of culture. What Chekhov judges bleakly is the culture itself that would encourage the hegemony of a monolithic Christian discourse inscribed in texts that claim to administer to all human cares. Chekhov dissents from the literature of Christian ideals in favor of examining the acute tensions, contradictions, and difficulties of belief.

All four stories—"The Lady," "Peasants," "The Requiem," and "An Attack of Nerves"—foreground the question of reconciling a faith that offers a fixed blueprint for life with the infinite and unpredictable range of human shame, complacency, desire, anger, envy, regret, and sorrow. Chekhov breaks down the at once expansive and vague notion of "belief" into its constituent components. We view at close range translations from the "absolute word" of Orthodoxy into cultural vernaculars and recognize that monologic integrity of Christian discourse is rendered dangerously vulnerable by the unwittingly "deviant" readings it receives. As a result, we see that the religious mind can scarcely be considered "religious" in the conventional sense. All of the corre-sponding synonyms—"pious," "godly," "devout," "spiritual," "sacred," and so forth—must be qualified by circumstances and perceptions that psychologize rather than totalize. Although he carried out his fieldwork at the desk, then, just as in an ethnography, Chekhov uncovers the inner stuff from which a culture is shaped.

Fig. 1: Icon of the Crucifixion. XIX century. Mary Magdalene and the Mother of God depicted at the foot of the cross. Insets pair the two at the removal from the cross and placement in the grave. [Arkhangelsk Museum of Fine Arts.] *The Russian Icon of late XVIII–XIX cc.* Saint Petersburg, 1994.

XIII. АКАѲИСТЪ ПРЕБЛАГОСЛОВЕННѢЙ ВЛАДЫЧИЦѢ НАШЕЙ БОГОРОДИЦѢ И ПРИСНОДѢВѢ МАРІИ.

Кондакъ 1.

Взбранной Воеводѣ побѣдительная, яко избавльшеся отъ злыхъ, благодарственная восписуемъ Ти раби Твои, Богородице: но яко имущая державу непобѣдимую, отъ всякихъ насъ бѣдъ свободи, да зовемъ Ти: радуйся, Невѣсто Неневѣстная.

Икосъ 1.

Ангелъ предстатель съ небесе посланъ бысть рещи Богородицѣ: радуйся! и со безплотнымъ гласомъ воплощаема Тя зря, Господи, ужасашеся и стояше, зовый къ Ней таковая: Радуйся, Еюже радость возсіяетъ: радуйся, Еюже клятва исчезнетъ.

Радуйся, падшаго Адама воззваніе: радуйся, слезъ Евиныхъ избавленіе. Радуйся, высото, неудобовосходимая человѣческими помыслы: радуйся, глубино, неудобозримая и Ангельскима очима. Радуйся, яко еси Царево сѣдалище: радуйся, яко носиши Носящаго вся. Радуйся, звѣздо, являющая Солнце: радуйся, утробо Божественнаго воплощенія. Радуйся, Еюже обновляется тварь: радуйся, Еюже покланяемся Творцу. Радуйся, Невѣсто Неневѣстная.

Кондакъ 2.

Видящи Святая Себе въ чистотѣ, глаголетъ Гавріилу дерзостно: преславное твоего гласа неудобопріятельно души Моей является: безсѣменнаго бо зачатія рождество како глаголеши, зовый: аллилуіа.

Икосъ 2.

Разумъ недоразумѣваемый разумѣти Дѣва ищущи, возопи къ служащему: изъ боку чисту, Сыну како есть родитися мощно, рцы Ми? Къ Нейже онъ рече со страхомъ, обаче зовый сице: Радуйся, совѣта неизреченнаго таиннице: радуйся, молчанія просящихъ вѣро. Радуйся, чудесъ Христовыхъ начало: радуйся, велѣній Его главизно. Радуйся, лѣствице небесная, еюже сниде

Fig. 2: Acathist to the Most Holy Mother of God. First two kontakion and ikos verses. From an Orthodox Prayer Book. Petrograd, 1915.

Fig. 3: Icon of Saint Mary of Egypt with Scenes from Her Life. 1629. The saint prays to the Mother of God in the desert (center) and at the entrance to the Jerusalem cathedral (top right). Tretiakov Gallery, Moscow.

Fig. 4: *Lubok* print of Saint Mary of Egypt with Scenes from Her Life. 1894. I. D. Sytin Collection, Russian National Library, Saint Petersburg.

Fig. 5: Icon of the Mother of God, Uncut Mountain. XVI century. The icon is based on prophecies from Daniel 2 and Genesis 28, where Jacob's dream of the ladder prefigures the Virgin's role as mediator between earth and heaven. Tretiakov Gallery, Moscow.

Fig. 6: Icon of the Annunciation. XV century. Orthodox Church calendar for 1991.

Chapter Four

Distortion of Text in "Peasant Women"

> One word upon parting. . . . Advise all preachers,
> including your own self, that the word of a preacher
> should correspond to the preacher's deeds.
> —Triletskii to Platonov in *Fatherless* (11:113)

STORYTELLING HOLDS a revered place in Russian folk
custom. Chekhov, who listened attentively to the many tales he heard in
the course of his travels, fully appreciated both the tradition that produced
(and reproduced) oral narration, and the sway held over listeners by the
storyteller's art. During the trip to Sakhalin, in particular, Chekhov "tuned in"
to folk narration. One of the stories he wrote shortly after returning from the
journey to Sakhalin in 1890 is "Peasant Women" ("Baby," 1891).

"Peasant Women" is about telling stories, interpreting stories, and about
the persuasive power of language. The most prominent story-within-the-story
is the tale of Mashenka, related by the merchant Matvei Savvich to his hosts
at a roadhouse. Of his account he says to the roadhouse owner Diudia, "This,
granddad, is an extraordinarily detailed story" (7:342). One can discern in
the fabric of both the frame story and the framed narration, both of equal
and substantive length, numerous details drawn from other stories as well,
religious stories well known to the peasant world from the plots presented on
icons and in Scripture, acathists, and oral verse. The most obvious allusion in
this vein is Matvei (Matthew) Savvich's narration of the events in the life of
Maria and her son, a self-styled gospel that violently falsifies the precepts of
the evangelist's text. In "Peasant Women," perhaps more than in any other
story, Chekhov takes on explicitly the question of a well-meaning Christian
discourse gone irredeemably awry.

The story's title warns us that a tale of gender relations will follow. It
is an overwhelmingly tragic tale. As we shall see, only at the end of "Peasant
Women" does a yardstick appear to suggest that the normative features of
Judeo-Christian culture might offer legitimate grounds for a woman's self-
determination. The stories themselves (the frame and framed narrations)
introduce unabashed patriarchs who glory in their authority over women.
The "evangelist" Matvei Savvich has earned unanimous critical condemnation as a "sanctimonious bully and hypocrite."[1] Diudia bolsters his position

of supreme power in his roadhouse tsardom with scraps of Scripture and punctual observation of daily prayers. The meaning of names again figures centrally. The peasant women bear three of the most prominent—arguably even *the* three most prominent—female names of Russian Orthodoxy: Maria, Sofia (Divine Wisdom), and Varvara (the Great Martyr). By incorporating the texts associated with these three religious figures into his story, and reworking them, Chekhov would seem to suggest in "Peasant Women" not that Russian Orthodox Christianity's view of women is immanently corrupt, but that Christian ideals are easily corrupted through the manipulation of language and distortion of text. How individuals position themselves in relationship to sacred texts, and what this comes to mean in their apprehension of the world, are the questions posed in this reading.

Because of the story's double structure, a brief paraphrase of "Peasant Women" is not a simple task. Matvei Savvich arrives for the night at Diudia's roadhouse with the young boy Kuzka. Diudia runs the roadhouse and trading post with his wife Afanasevna, son Alyosha, and two daughters-in-law, Sofia and Varvara. As darkness sets in, Diudia and Matvei Savvich fall into conversation. The latter launches into the tale of Mashenka, the boy Kuzka's mother and his own former lover. Mashenka, Matvei Savvich recounts, gets married to his neighbor, Vasia, who soon leaves for Poland as an army recruit. After Kuzka's birth, Mashenka and Matvei Savvich consummate their mutual attraction and come to "live as man and wife." Two years later Vasia falls ill and returns home. He forgives the errant couple, but when Mashenka refuses to disengage her affections from Matvei Savvich, he beats her brutally. Matvei Savvich, happy to be free of the entanglement, inveighs against Mashenka's sinful ways. Vasia dies, prompting rumors that he was poisoned by his wife. The arsenic found in his disinterred body incriminates Mashenka, who is sent to jail. A jury remains split on the question of Mashenka's guilt, but Matvei Savvich's testimony helps convince them to convict her to hard labor. She dies en route to Siberia and Matvei Savvich adopts Kuzka.

Back in the frame story, the household settles down for the night after Matvei Savvich and Diudia have performed their evening prayers. Varvara returns from a tryst with the priest's son and regales Sofia with tales of her sexual exploits. She then suggests to Sofia that they follow Mashenka's example and poison Diudia and her own husband Alyosha, but soon dismisses her own suggestion and they fall asleep. The story ends with the morning household clatter and the departure of Matvei Savvich's cart from the yard.

V. V. Rozanov, the most famous Russian critic of Christianity from within Christianity, holds a broadly misapplied Christian creed accountable for the tragedy of Mashenka and her son. He sardonically writes:

> Everything is as peaceful as in an epic. The boy born [to Mashenka] sticks around on the cart, not wanted by anyone. "Everything's as it should be";

"everything in the Christian manner." "The Christian manner": 1) you've sinned—a person can't live without that, Christ came to earth in order to expiate such sins; and therefore 2) "you need to repent after the sin" and "return to the path of good." . . . "Everything truthfully, in the Christian manner," and the woman and her boy are left to think: "We should forgive him,"—because the ancient *eye for an eye* is replaced by the higher law of gospel love.[2]

Rozanov's use of quotation marks intentionally imitates the Russian cultural penchant for citation of "indisputable" authority.

Those who use this authoritarian discourse most overtly are Diudia Kashin and Matvei Savvich. "A dog's death to a dog," says Diudia of Mashenka before retiring to his room, where he "lit a candle, put on his glasses and stood in the corner with a book" and "read and genuflected for a long while" (7:348). Diudia follows his facile aphorism with religious study; Matvei Savvich authors his own parable of the fallen woman. These acts epitomize their proclivity for contorting biblical teachings to suit personal needs. Bakhtin writes of the Middle Ages that "the primary instance of appropriating another's discourse and language was the use made of the authoritative and sanctified word of the Bible, the Gospel, the Apostles, the fathers and doctors of the church," language enclosed in a variety of "intonational quotation marks."[3] At issue is the psychology behind the appropriation of others' speech, a practice observed unswervingly in Matvei Savvich's tale.

THE GOSPEL ACCORDING TO MATTHEW

The narrator of the frame story issues a warning that the traveler "turned out to be loquacious and eloquent" (7:342). Apparently a casual account, Matvei Savvich's tale in fact represents a carefully crafted text. He calls his narration an "istoriia." "Istoriia" means "story" or "history" in Russian, the latter a genre identification that makes implicit claims at recording the past truthfully. Matvei Savvich's patronymic derives from the Greek word for "elder" and he casts his speech as that of an authoritative patriarch. Yet he cuts a figure so patently hypocritical that Karlinsky calls him "the closest we come to an out-and-out villain in Chekhov's writings."[4] He has usually been judged within a purely moral context; however, his most villainous acts concern the manipulation of language.

With hubris, Matvei Savvich uses language that suggests his own kinship with the Christian saints. Harnessing the biblical language of sin, he claims that in the affair with his neighbor's wife the devil is to blame ("the unclean spirit led me astray, that enemy of the human race"), and that in this he is no worse than the holy fathers ("Not only we sinners, but the saints themselves went astray") (7:344). The manner in which he colors his subsequent actions— from the sermons he preaches to the ruble he thrusts upon Mashenka as she departs for Siberia "for the salvation of her soul"—bespeaks a man faithfully fulfilling the duties set before him by his image of the righteous man. This role rests on a mentality entirely beholden to *Script*ure; that is, a conception of scripted human behavior grounded in the written word. But Matvei Savvich reinterprets the language of Christianity to his own ends.

When Matvei Savvich goes next door to view Mashenka and Vasia's ill-fated reunion, he reports to his audience: "I preached exhortations to her as if inspired by a heavenly angel" (7:346). This comment, apart from conveying his self-righteousness, strikes at the heart of Matvei Savvich's relationship to language. Language issues not from the individual consciousness, but from sources external to the speaker. He crafts his speech as though it were impersonal, relying on proverbs, scriptural quotations, and Church Slavonicisms to bolster his authority.

The aphoristic language used by Matvei Savvich relays his static apprehension of the world. Stock phraseology in Matvei Savvich's speech masks the individuality of personal actions. A house without a wife is "just like a man without an eye"; work around the yard is "not a woman's affair"; when Vasia is drafted, he says, "Trouble's come, leave the gates open" (7:343). The most emblematic adage uttered by Matvei Savvich concerns Mashenka's guilt in the death of Vasia. He uses an idiom meaning, "It was as clear as twice two is four"; literally, "the affair was as clear as offering a drink" (7:347). The certainty conveyed by this hackneyed turn of phrase is offset by Chekhov's ambiguity and wit: not only does the story withhold a guilty verdict, but the murder in question could only have been committed by "offering a drink." Matvei Savvich's pithy maxim contains within it "proof" of the crime, rendering language itself the prosecutor.

Early in the story, the narrator tells us that Diudia's elder son works as a mechanic at a factory and that "he's gone far up the mountain and you can't touch him now" (7:340). Chekhov links the aphoristic mindset explicitly to the peasants with the words preceding this adage, "the peasants say of him." Matvei Savvich is implicated in this mode of thinking. But this is far from the valorization of folk sayings and peasant speech that marked the burgeoning ethnographic studies in Russia at the end of the nineteenth century; neither does it correspond to the enthusiasm for such language in Slavophile and populist literature. For Chekhov, Matvei Savvich's inflections reveal a mentality frozen in the grip of inflexible linguistic rubric. The adage does not add local color to his speech, but glosses over complexity and warps perception.

Something similar holds true for Matvei Savvich's use of scriptural citations; only here the situation is more weighty because of the revered status of the Christian word in Russian culture. Like the aphorisms, references to Scripture blend into Matvei Savvich's speech seamlessly. Directly after listing the material bounty of Mashenka's dowry, he reports of her new mother-in-law: "And the old woman, in accordance with her foreboding, on the third day after the wedding went off to Heavenly Jerusalem, where there are neither illnesses nor sighs" (7:343). The Church Slavic phrasing of the original is stripped of its lofty metaphysical value by its matter-of-fact delivery. Notably, the root for "heavenly" (*gornii*, "mountainous") echoes the peasant aphorism, "he's gone far up the mountain," a leveling of vastly discrepant fields of diction.

Much more insidiously, Matvei Savvich maneuvers Mashenka into the position of victim, using Scripture as his weapon. Upon receipt of the letter in which Vasia announces his return from military service, Mashenka admits that she had been forced to marry him, had never loved him, and wants to remain with Matvei Savvich. He responds, "You, I say, are devout, and have read what's written in the Scriptures?" (7:345). Diudia interrupts with his answer: if you've been married to a husband, you should live with him. Matvei Savvich immediately "translates" Diudia's words into a scriptural formula, paraphrasing (significantly) the Gospel according to Matthew (19:5–6): "Man and wife are one flesh." This moment underscores the nature of Matvei Savvich's rhetorical strategy. That which Diudia announces in "plain Russian" finds expression in an elevated biblical style, the *author*ization for his version of past events.

Matvei Savvich ends his diatribe by threatening Mashenka with the Last Judgment. "Anyway it's better, I say, to suffer at the hands of your lawful husband in this world than to gnash your teeth at the Last Judgment" (7:345). The logic of this statement allows Matvei Savvich to ignore his own role in the love triangle. Indeed, Chekhov displays a keen mastery of the psychology behind allusion to Scripture. The number of readers who have believed Matvei Savvich's version of events testifies to the persuasiveness of his rhetoric. (Vasia calls for his own death after beating Mashenka; thus his death may have been a suicide.) Despite the story's inconclusiveness on the matter, the assumption has reigned in criticism that Mashenka did, indeed, commit the murder of her husband.[5] This viewpoint has even been interpreted as a reflection of Chekhov's own understandings: "one of the men in 'Peasant Women' [Matvei Savvich] utters what one might expect to be Chekhov's own verdict on the affair: 'the female sex causes a deal of evil and harm of all kinds in this world.' "[6] If anything, Chekhov expresses compassion for those victimized by Matvei Savvich's "loquacity and eloquence."

The affair between Matvei Savvich and Mashenka begins in a manner that disregards Christian principles, and not only the injunction against coveting one's neighbor's wife. Their first meeting as lovers takes place on Holy Thursday as Matvei Savvich makes his way to the market. Indulging in trade and adultery on the day commemorating the Last Supper bespeaks blasphemy (especially in light of Judas's betrayal on that day, motivated by thirty pieces of silver). The day observed as the prelude to Christ's execution, however, feels to Matvei Savvich like a holiday: "I started complimenting her, as if I weren't standing at the gate but was at a nameday celebration" (7:344). Could Chekhov have been attracting attention to the significance of *names* in the story? The incident resonates with one other religious text as well: in a *Vita* otherwise devoid of temporal designations, Mary of Egypt appoints the Thursday of Holy Week for a meeting at the Jordan with Father Zosima. If Chekhov had this in mind, then an allusion embedded in the lovers' initial encounter correlates with the Christian texts that Matvei Savvich subsequently imposes on Mashenka once their affair has ended, texts of the harlot.

The archetypal image of the whore prevails in Matvei Savvich's speech. In what he perceives as a flourish of oratorical genius, he admonishes Mashenka, in Vasia's presence, to perform the ritual act of repentance recommended by the popularized Christian story of the sinful woman:

> I bowed low to Vasia and I say: "We're guilty before you, Vasily Maksimych, forgive us for Christ's sake!" Then I got up and I say these words to Mashenka: "You, Maria Semenovna, should wash Vasily Maksimych's feet and drink the water. And be his obedient wife, and pray to God for me that he, being merciful, might forgive me my sins." (7:346)

The words, "I'll wash your feet and drink the water" close the tale "Akulka's Husband" in Dostoevsky's *Notes from the Dead House*, a tale of male violence and female victimization that Chekhov may well have had in mind when writing "Peasant Women." In "The Lady" the same linguistic formula was advanced by the desperate Maria in an attempt to win back her husband Stepan. The derivation of the idiom, as I mention there, is the scriptural account of the sinful woman of Luke 7:37–48, a figure conflated in the popular mind with Mary Magdalene. Matvei Savvich imposes the entire weight of repentance, for herself and for him, on Mashenka's shoulders. The sinful woman, as the most prominent cultural icon of repentance, is appropriated by the false patriarch to absolve himself of his own disregard for Christian law.

After the beating that Mashenka receives, begun by Matvei Savvich and finished by a savage Vasia, the victim lies wrapped in bandages on the bed, locus of the sexual relations that led to her denigration. Vasia weeps in the next room, for he now regards the beating he gave his wife in a fit of rage to have ruined his life, while the unrepentant "real" villain continues to ply his verbal art: "I say, 'Hello, Maria Semenovna!' Silence. . . . I sat by Mashenka for about a half an hour and read her the law. Put the fear of God in her. 'The righteous in this world,' I say, 'will go to Heaven, but you will go to fiery Gehenna along with all the harlots'" (7:347). The culture offers a ready-made formula, rhetoric of the fornicatress, that permits Matvei Savvich to deny all responsibility in the love affair. The abnegation of personal accountability facilitated by such timeworn utterances is made clear earlier in Matvei Savvich's response to Vasia's conscription: "It's God's will, there's nothing you can do" (7:343). This recalls Levin's vow in Tolstoy's *Anna Karenina* to combat passive resignation among the peasantry, to fight against "this seemingly elemental power, which he could find no better name for than 'God's will be done.'" Both authors recognize the devastating effect of this mentality on Russian life. The notion that *volia* (in Russian, both "will" and "freedom") operates outside of the human sphere of influence has frightening implications. Matvei Savvich's command of Scripture constitutes a natural extension of "God's will," creating a narrow world of limitation.

Chekhov's reading public reacted with a vehemence to "Peasant Women" that confirms the depth of the cultural belief in the Christian censure of female sexuality—a belief so strong that no one noticed the travesty it was subjected to in Matvei Savvich's hands. Reportedly, peasant readers soundly endorsed Mashenka's guilt: " 'All of us accuse Mashenka. . . . We all say she is guilty. She seduced him to sin.' "[7] Clearly, Matvei Savvich's discourse seemed natural to these readers. The publishing industry itself was well aware of these issues. Shortly after the publication of "Peasant Women" in Suvorin's *Novoe vremia*, Chertkov's publishing house Posrednik became interested in the story. An editor approached Chertkov with his marketing plan: "As a brighter conclusion to Chekhov's 'Peasant Women' . . . I'm thinking of including a little story called 'Ali the Righteous' about a repentant woman and the absolution of her sins through the birth of a child."[8] The whole society was complicitous in encouraging the association between Mashenka and the loose woman. Her steadfast refusal to comply with her former lover's prefabricated interpretation of her life made of Mashenka a menacing heroine.

The reception of the story suggests the need to look more closely for other Christian texts referentially encoded in "Peasant Women." While Mashenka receives top billing in the story, the plural title prods reflection on the story's other peasant women as well. A detour through their lives will precede a rereading of Mashenka's life, for the nature of the Christian texts lingering near all of them bears on an understanding of the story. Varvara and Sofia, although silent at its reading, become active interlocutors of Mashenka's tale when alone.

THE FRAME STORY

Readings of "Peasant Women" often see the fates of the women in the two stories (the frame story and the inserted text) as parallel tales of female entrapment. Yet in the symbolic space of the story, this kinship is, I believe, largely an appearance. It is true that structures of enclosure can be found in both frame and framed narrations—and the combined inventory of images they present is sobering. Women are confined to houses and yards by windows, window frames, fences, and gates. Women are implicitly compared to animals contained by birdcages, birdhouses, fish traps, bridles, and reins. Ultimately, prison walls enclose Mashenka. The manner in which the women in the frame story react to that enclosure, however, distinguishes them from their sister in misfortune.

The Great Martyr Varvara and Divine Sophia number among the most celebrated female figures of Eastern Orthodoxy. Saint Varvara, the martyr who as a young woman defied the paganism of her father Dioskor in order to embrace Christianity, met a gruesome death at the hands of her persecutors. Sophia was said to embody Divine Wisdom. In the Chekhovian world, one accurately anticipates that the associations between these holy women and their namesakes will not be straightforward.

Let us begin with Varvara. The story presents her as a self-confident young beauty who has been married to the cripple Alyosha, Diudia's son, and has thus gained a perch in a wealthy home. She eschews any onerous work, does not sleep with her husband, and earns money by selling her favors to travelers and carrying on with the local priest's son. Cathy Popkin reads Varvara as a peasant woman who refuses to be exploited, who takes charge of her own female pleasure, and who "revels in her own authorship, her own authority, in contrast to the unfortunate Mashenka whose story has been wholly appropriated by Matvei Savvich, man of business."[9] This modern and optimistic appraisal of Varvara unfortunately corresponds poorly to the Russian world that Chekhov knew. Her authorship of a life script notably erodes in the face of the texts from which it derives. Seemingly a peasant *émancipée*, Varvara's apparent freedom and self-determination are to a large extent illusory.

An unusual gesture Varvara makes during a break in Matvei Savvich's narration provides a clue to the nature of her perceptions. Following the moment in the late evening when the entire company listens quietly to the sonorous high note reached by a tenor voice wafting over from the church, Varvara shields her eyes with her hand "as if from the sun" (7:345) and looks at the church. This gesture, gratuitous in the darkness of the night, suggests a grave misunderstanding of figurative illumination. She identifies the singers and it becomes clear that the two voices that shortly before broke off into raucous laughter belong to the priest's sons, with one of whom Varvara dallies each evening. Varvara mistakes the excitement of this illicit liaison for freedom.

Lurking in the background of Varvara's actions is the Orthodox hagiographic account of the Great Martyr Varvara (Velikomuchenitsa Varvara). The figure of Saint Varvara appears more than once in Chekhov's work. Her nameday is cited in "O, Women, Women!"; the young communicant in "During Passion Week" first notices the side-chapel dedicated to Saint

Varvara and later dreams of suffering torments imposed by Dioskor; and the old peasant who speaks to Egorushka in "The Steppe" tells him that all who wish to repent must turn to the Great Martyr Varvara. Chekhov could not but have been familiar with the details of her saintly life (something demonstrated, if nowhere else, by this story). The language used by both the (unidentified) frame-story narrator and by Varvara herself alludes to the saint's tale, not necessarily consciously, but as an index of the images latent in the Russian religious mind. That Varvara is distinguished by her lack of correspondence to her holy forerunner means nothing directly in terms of the sacred and profane (that is to say, Chekhov casts no moral judgment on her behavior), but it does provide a measure of her character.

Saint Varvara is a beautiful young woman who is locked in a tower by her wealthy, pagan father Dioskor to protect her beauty. Chekhov's Varvara is a beautiful young woman who works in the upper story of her wealthy father-in-law's house. The latter, no hostage in this home, is free to come and go as she pleases. A Christian priest visits Saint Varvara in the guise of a merchant and baptizes her. The saint's father discovers her faith when she insists that three windows be built in a *banya* (baptistery) in honor of the Holy Trinity. (These three windows become the focal point of the acathist sung in praise of Saint Varvara.) The *merchants* who visit Chekhov's Varvara in the *upper room,* where she often sits at the *window,* enjoy her services as a prostitute.

Determined to serve the Lord, Saint Varvara "would better be deprived of life than give up her virginity."[10] Varvara diverges from the saint's motto of chastity in every way as she promotes the virtues of sexual infidelity and glibly refers to suicide as a means to escape a life of toil: "It'd be better to pine away in maidenhood, to accept kopecks from the priests' sons, to beg for alms, it'd be better to jump head first into a well" (7:350). Of course no puritanical messages accompany this perspective on Varvara. Saint Varvara does not embody an ideal for Chekhov, but she does represent a life of articulated worth in which the heroine fights for her beliefs rather than endlessly griping about the prevailing order (and refusing to engage in the activity that constantly emerges as paramount in Chekhov's life: work).

Saint Varvara undergoes the martyr's customary slate of ghastly tortures (she is whipped, singed with hot wax, smashed with a hammer, and exhibited naked) before her father chops off her head. Varvara, on the other hand, receives neither punishment nor reprimand for her loose, easy, and "un-Orthodox" behavior. Responding to Sofia's excited remark that sexual promiscuity is a sin, Varvara disdainfully remarks, "So what . . . Who cares? Let it be a sin. Better to be killed by thunder than to lead such a life" (7:350). In the saint's *Vita,* her father Dioskor is killed by a thunderclap for his wicked deeds. Varvara's comment links her to the pagan potentates, whose great failings were the worship of false idols and their fondness for gold.

Varvara's displacements of the hagiographic motifs can be read as a guide to the world in which she lives and the choices she makes within it. Unwilling to settle for the traditional order (Diudia mumbles, "They're all trying to live by their own wits, they don't obey, and it turns out their way" [7:348]), she embarks on what appears to be a new path of sexual choice and self-determination. The inverted parallels with the *Vita* suggest, however, that she remains within an old paradigm of female saintliness and sin.

Varvara behaves as a genuine harlot, collecting money from any willing customer for her favors. Her indiscrimination is indicated by the declaration, "it's easier to sleep with a viper than with that lousy Alyosha" (7:350). It is not entirely unlikely that Chekhov points here to the trope in the acathist to Saint Varvara that compares Dioskor to a viper, compounding the association between Varvara and the pagan world. Her husband, in fact, is the only man with whom she refuses to sleep. Varvara seems to be swimming against the current, but she actually negotiates a course similar to that of the harlot, a role familiar, and ironically acceptable, to the surrounding society and the story's pseudopatriarchs. As Popkin notes, "Varvara's charms are harnessed explicitly to keep Diudia's customers satisfied."[11] Varvara, then, shares the fundamental understandings of Diudia's household, carrying on her trade out of view at night, while her vocal opposition to her parents-in-law is tolerated because she poses no threat to the status quo.

Varvara's dallying occurs with the priest's son literally in the shadow of the church, a detail highlighted by repetition: "the church cast a broad shadow, dark and terrifying, which encompassed Diudia's gates and half the house"; "in the shadow near the church fence someone [Varvara's lover] was walking" (7:349). This shadow serves at once as a sign that the church holds no moral sway in the circumstances, that this activity is tacitly sanctioned, and that the affair occurs in metaphoric darkness. The church, like the saint's life, represents an orientation point in Russian life that, although it does not speak of any objectively moral good, at its best had been a font of meaning for believers. The shadow it casts recalls the absent sun, from which Varvara shields her eyes in the dark night as she looks thence.

If Varvara, despite her demonstrations of independence, fails to violate patriarchy's limits, then Afanasevna, Diudia's wife, and Sofia, his other daughter-in-law, are so thoroughly its servitors that they discharge their duties without a grumble. Afanasevna's investment in the values of the Kashin household is revealed by her name: her patronymic alone (or the "male" part of her name) suffices as identity. Afanasevna, and her complement in the inner story, Vasia's mother Kapluntseva, epitomize that which Mashenka, Varvara, and Sofia could opt to be: the traditional, subservient peasant wife who grows into the role of the family matriarch.

Sofia, who accompanies Afanasevna in the chores of evening and morning milkings, does not accept this system of values entirely. She unthinkingly subordinates herself to Afanasevna, but nurses her grief privately. Her lack of emotional well-being is paralleled by her poor health. On Sundays, the perennially ill Sofia does not go to church for spiritual healing, but to the hospital for medical treatment. Sofia's name, of course, figures as one of the central symbols of the Orthodox religion. In elite culture, the concept of *das Ewig-weibliche* was promoted by Chekhov's contemporary, the philosopher V. S. Solovyov, nearly to the status of a cult. Sonya Marmeladova in Dostoevsky's *Crime and Punishment* ranks among the most famous of heroes in Russian letters as an incarnation of Christian wisdom.

Chekhov's dull-witted Sofia has nothing to do with divinity. Her behavior decidedly clashes with the qualities of her Christian name. Far from Divine Wisdom stands Sofia's blunt mind, manifest in her passive acceptance of a subservient position and in the readiness with which she entertains Varvara's entirely contradictory ideas. In addition, abandoned by her husband and deprived of her child, Sofia has been forced to part with any suggestion of the feminine nature (*zhenstvennost'*) that Divine Sophia represents (in Solovyov's view). Rather, Sofia, as Varvara states it, is nothing more than a workhorse. Time and again horses show up as agents of economic activity in the male world of the story.

Well versed in a view of the world that corresponds to that of her surroundings, Sofia responds to Varvara's sexual activity and to her suggestion that they poison the Kashin men with the expected litanies: "What prattle"; "It's a sin!"; "A sin!"; "What prattle, God be with you"; "That's awful, God will strike you down" (7:350–51). At the same time, Varvara easily persuades Sofia with her alluring picture of sexual freedom that true life is located outside the gates in the arms of the priest's sons. Sofia regrets having missed out on such good times in her own youth, and begins to laugh as she hears a "free life stretching out from the sad song" that emanates from beyond the church (7:350–51). Sofia does not detect the falsity of the promise held by Varvara's blueprint for freedom.

Living within the world of their oppressors, Varvara does not menace the patriarchy despite her audacious behavior, while Sofia falls its unredeemed victim. Only in the framed narration does a woman take her bid for self-determination seriously. The measure of independence and self-fulfillment characteristic of the saint's life that so poorly matches Varvara finds its fit in Mashenka.

THE LIFE OF MARIA

Within the parameters of Christian thinking, two of Chekhov's peasant women behave as sinful women: Varvara and Mashenka. As we have seen, Varvara's brazen nocturnal philandering excites no reaction. It conforms to a stock model. Mashenka's comportment, on the other hand, and the seriousness with which she regards her love for Matvei Savvich, evokes a hail of rebuke and castigation. The threat she poses has to do with her unwillingness to live with the role proffered her, to be "played out in parables and in the teachings."[12]

When Matvei Savvich parades his picture of the sinful woman before Mashenka ("you'll go to fiery Gehenna, along with all the harlots"), she lies before him on the bed bound in bandages, only her nose and unmoving eyes visible. This image of Mashenka loosely evokes a mutilated icon (the prominent nose and eyes). There is no immediate reference to the Virgin in "Peasant Women" (as is present, in one form or another, in the other Marian stories). Associations that do occur are so indirect as to remain pure conjecture.[13] In contrast to the prototypical barrenness of the "sinful woman," however, Mashenka is a devoted mother: in prison, holding and pressing Kuzka to herself, she assumes a Madonna-like pose. The image of motherhood and innocence functions as a counterweight to her behavior as an unfaithful wife. Both Marian figures operate at least distantly in Chekhov's depiction of Mashenka.

Mashenka diverges from the Christian formulas in a manner completely different from Varvara and Sofia. She moves outside of the paradigm altogether. A roughly hewn sense of self-determination serves as Mashenka's hallmark, expressed in her willingness to laugh. Upon her initial amorous encounter with Matvei Savvich on Holy Thursday, Mashenka laughs in response to his compliments. She later uses laughter to advocate her right to self-fulfillment when countering Matvei Savvich's efforts to convince her that Vasia's return means the end of their involvement: "I love you and I'll live with you until death. Let people laugh. . . . I won't pay attention" (8:345). Mashenka invites ridicule in the name of pursuing her yearnings, unwilling to give up the integrity of her freedom before a society that nearly unanimously endorses submission to a counterfeit collective moral code.

Stalwart resistance to prevailing norms typifies the life of a saint. If Varvara renders profane all allusions to her saintly namesake, Mashenka's life story is informed by certain contours reminiscent of the martyr's existence. Her cause, however, completely diverges from, and even opposes, the crusade in the name of faith undertaken by Christian martyrs. The latter refuse to accept their tormentors' pagan belief, while Mashenka's resistance is the outcome of her refusal to accept the widespread values concerning female submission and self-sacrifice promoted by the "Christian" culture.

Hagiographic convention requires evidence of the saint's tenacious commitment to the tenets of the faith, something Matvei Savvich portrays in Mashenka's stubborn defense of her right to be herself: "The woman wouldn't listen, she dug in her heels and there was nothing you could do! 'I love you'—and nothing else" (8:345). Mashenka's aspirations in fact (literally and ironically) echo the paramount command of Christ: "Love thy neighbor." She adheres, however, not to the religious tenets, but to the religious patterns of behavior. Mashenka accepts the torments inflicted upon her by Matvei Savvich and Vasia in silence, a mark at once of the futility of response and of an obdurate refusal to acquiesce. As he preaches to her of her wrongdoing, he tells us first that she "is silent," and then that "not a word did she say, she didn't even blink an eye, as if I were speaking to a pillar" (7:347). The martyr invariably responds to torments in Christian literature with stoicism and silence.

Mashenka's subsequent imprisonment is also associated with stock motifs of hagiography. It recalls a widespread feature of the saint's life: incarceration in prison and suffering at the hands of pagan tormentors. Matvei Savvich, in essence, belongs to the category of those who belie Christian principles. In prison his verbal attacks do not abate as he continues to plague Mashenka: "Oh, Masha, Masha, a fallen soul! You didn't listen to me when I taught you good sense, so weep away" (7:348).

Chekhov's depiction has something in common with the modern saints portrayed by Leskov, Dostoevsky, and Tolstoy, insofar as human failings and strivings participate in those portraits. Nothing extraordinary distinguishes Mashenka. She is neither humble, nor pious, nor compassionate. Her actions are of the most ordinary human sort. In refusing to remain in a marriage she entered against her will and in committing adultery, she presents her convictions in very simple, straightforward language. She attempts to uphold her desire for a meaningful existence and maintains the integrity of her feelings in the face of an onslaught of stifling rhetoric.

All of this appears foreign to both the characters in Matvei Savvich's narration and to his audience. Mashenka is the outsider in a world that accepts decayed Christian values as a primary point of orientation without noticing that the foundation has rotted. So the situation is inverted. Mashenka deflects the light of Christian martyrdom because she is pursuing a direction (individuality) that nobody understands; the people around her, self-acknowledged bearers of Russia's Christian culture who avail themselves of the language and symbols of that culture, pay no heed to the fact that their religion triumphed only after centuries of struggle, movement, and martyrdom.

This understanding of Mashenka is reflected in her son Kuzka. Matvei Savvich calls him "Kuzma-bessrebrenik" (7:347). *Bessrebrenniki* comprise one of four rankings or categories of saints in the Orthodox Church, those who tend to the ills of humankind and wholly shun material wealth or gain. One of the best known of these saints is Kosma (always paired with Damian in iconography and hagiography), from whose name "Kuzka" derives. The charitable attitude toward money characteristic of these saints (*bessrebrennik* literally means "without silver") plays out ironically in Kuzka, who himself is without means and who is beholden to a merchant bent on the accumulation of wealth and on cultivating him as a shop-assistant or merchant. Kuzka's name also shows up in a number of rhymed folk sayings dealing with childhood misfortune: "Kuzma has a bitter lot"; "Kuzenka the little orphan."[14]

In spite of the conversation in which Sofia avers that the boy could not possibly remember his mother, Kuzka clearly bears the burden of that memory with him, his only possession not subject to appropriation. He rides into Diudia's yard wearing "a long black frock coat with large bone buttons" (7:340), garb reminiscent of mourning, as if he carried on him his mother's memory and his lost childhood. Later Afanasevna describes him as "all bones" (7:349). Silent like his mother, during Matvei Savvich's story, Kuzka sits by the gate, staring at the sky, "and in the twilight resembled a stump" (7:348). This recalls Matvei Savvich's complaint that his advice to Mashenka fell on deaf ears, "as if I were speaking to a pillar (*stolb*)." The stunted stump, a remnant, as it were, of the felled pillar, makes it clear that the mother's tragedy has not left the son unscathed. Whether or not authorial intent, the "pillar" recalls the common praise of the Virgin as a "Pillar of Clouds," a "Fiery Pillar," a "Pillar of Faith," and a "Pillar of Virginity." Mashenka's pillarlike pose and motionless eyes belie less an iconographic Madonna than an emotionally pained and estranged woman, for whom virginity, sin, and Gehenna have no meaning. The pillar, too, is a frequent metaphor for the church and the stump describes the humiliated state of the House of David prior to the Virgin birth.[15] These later associations participate only generally in the story's ironically inverted Christian context.

Mashenka, then, is a uniquely unreligious martyr, unwilling to compromise her feelings. Her simple exertion of free will involves a readiness to accept responsibility for her actions and to suffer for her integrity; she accomplishes this by disputing the rhetoric of a language saturated with Christian phrases, slogans, and innuendos, a language manipulated by the speaker into a trap. In Mashenka the prototypes of the two Christian Marys are conflated into the paradox of an innocently simple mother and "sinful" woman. Her death reflects a sad vision of the possibility for realizing value beyond the fixed roles doled out by fraudulent patriarchs. Yet her gropings toward a life of personal fulfillment represent a promising direction in Chekhov's ever-modest estimates of what life can yield.

"Peasant Women" ends with a curious scene on the morning following the telling of Mashenka's story. It stands out as essentially unrelated to the narrated story, but in it the motifs from a number of Christian texts converge as a final appraisal of the state of affairs in the Kashin household:

> The morning tumult began. A young Jewess in a brown dress with flounces brought a horse into the yard to water it. The well shaft creaked mournfully, a bucket clattered. . . . Sleepy, sluggish Kuzka, covered with dew, sat on the cart,

102

and as he lazily donned his coat, he listened to the water splashing out of the bucket in the well and huddled up from the cold. "Hey lady," yelled Matvei Savvich to Sofia, "Whack my boy, get him to harness up!" At that moment Diudia yelled from the window, "Sofia, take a kopeck from the Jewess for the water! Those lousy people take it for granted!" (7:352)

In the Old Testament, the well—source of a precious commodity in arid land—frequently symbolizes the abundance of the Lord's blessings. The well was a communal source of sustenance, and the sharing of water with strangers a sign of elevated spirit (as in Genesis 24, when Rebekah is betrothed to Isaac after offering Abraham's servant water from the city well). The presence of the Jewess by the well in Chekhov's story suggests a link with the Old Testament.

Diudia's demand for money from the Jewess signals the well's corruption. The "lousy" Jews whom Diudia berates were the biblical owners of wells, the Old Testament forebears of his own faith, and exemplars of an orderly patriarchal existence in which all were nourished from the well—a way of life, it can be argued, in which women occupied a respected position. Diudia claims of the water in the well that the lousy Jews "take it for granted." The Jewess, too, comes from outside the yard and wears a feminine dress "with flounces," setting her apart from the Russian peasant women. Her independent appearance contrasts with the subservience of the browbeaten Sofia. Of course Diudia does not fail to exact a price from her as well. Chekhov's well is clearly a tragic parody of its biblical counterparts.

Mindful of this context—and, perhaps, as well of the New Testament encounter at Jacob's well between the Samaritan woman and Christ, who offers her the "living water" of eternal life (John 4:12–24)—the final scene reverberates variously throughout Chekhov's story. First, we recall Matvei Savvich's sham truisms, "You, Maria Semenovna, should wash Vasily Maksimych's feet and drink the water" and "the affair was as clear as giving a drink." Second, we recall Varvara's prescription for escaping the peasant woman's predicament: "better to end it all head first down a well." Third, as if in response to the figuratively chilling water of Diudia's well, Kuzka huddles up from the cold at the sound of the water in the well. (He apes a gesture made earlier by his mother in prison, who huddles up to the wall and quivers.) A far cry from "living water," Chekhov's water is polluted by a perverse association with death.

One last puzzling detail at the end of "Peasant Women" can be illuminated, I believe, through the acathist honoring Saint Varvara. Sheep run up and down the street outside the yard during the morning bustle, untended by a shiftless shepherd, and three enter the yard. The acathist sustains a comparison between the saint and a sacrificed lamb, who ultimately escapes her tormentor Dioskor and "runs to the kind shepherd Christ." Compare:

ACATHIST: "Rejoice, You who have entered the yard of the righteous sheep who stand on His right."
CHEKHOV: "Three sheep ran into the yard and knocked around by the fence, unable to find the gate out." (7:352)

Like the biblical well, the yard (*dvor*) of the acathist is reflected in warped forms in both the frame and narrated stories. The entire action of both stories takes place within the yards of Diudia, Matvei Savvich, and Vasia, the first two of whom attempt to "lord it over" the peasant women with their "Christian" exhortations.[16] Ironically, the saint's namesake Varvara is ordered to chase the three sheep out of the yard. She replies: "Sure! As if I'm going to work for you, you tyrants [literally, *irody*, or Herods]!" Varvara's flippant remark once again locates the pseudo-Christian patriarchs in the symbolic field of the persecutors of Christians (Herod, Dioskor).

The passage also draws attention to a triplet motif (three sheep) that is strung throughout the story (and might be related to the Trinity and resurrection themes that saturate Saint Varvara's acathist). In "Peasant Women" Chekhov sabotages the resurrection theme, so prevalently signaled by the number three (and so earnestly engaged) in many works of Russian literature. Within the framed narration, Vasia's arrival home on the eve of Trinity Sunday is marked by Mashenka's neglect to decorate the fence and gates with greenery (decor of renewal and resurrection). The Trinity setting ironically reflects on the Vasia–Mashenka–Matvei Savvich love triangle that explodes upon Vasia's return. Kuzka is three years old when Vasia suddenly reappears among them on Trinity Sunday. Matvei Savvich reports that Kapluntseva, Vasia's mother, ascended to "Heavenly Jerusalem" on the third day after the wedding. After his death, Vasia's body is disinterred after three days to test for poison. Finally, the three months that Mashenka spends in prison end not in a return to the living, but in death.

The backdrop for this labyrinth of Christian associations, which Chekhov may not have consciously mapped out in its entirety, but from which he seems to have drawn quite deliberately, are the opposing images of two pre-Christian worlds: the "faithless" world of pagan rulers and the harmoniously devout world of the Judaic tradition. Theoretically the legatee of the latter, Chekhov depicts the Orthodox religion in this rural Russian manifestation as more in line with the lawless, authoritarian norms of the pagan world. This reversal of terms underlies the story's whole symbolic structure, to which names provide the passkey. Matvei Savvich, Diudia (whose Christian name is Filipp), Sofia, Varvara, Kuzka, and Maria each appear as a contorted version of their respective saintly prototypes (evangelist, apostle, divine wisdom, martyr, *bessrebrennik*, harlot). Hebrew names—or else names precious to the heart of Eastern Orthodoxy—have reached them, but the concepts from which those names derive are distorted beyond recognition.

These, then, are Chekhov's peasant women. The oppression of women in a patriarchal peasant society comes as no news to anyone. However, Chekhov does not suggest in this story that such oppression occurs because of Christian dogma, as is usually assumed; rather, it comes from a decayed Christianity, the language of which has been thoroughly adulterated and falsified. In the final analysis, the tragedy of the story has to do not only with hypocrisy, but with the paralysis of thought and feeling generated by language and images heedlessly and spiritlessly accepted and projected on the world. At the heart of the discussion lies the question of the responsibility of the individual for the consequences of his or her own words. Only Mashenka, in her primitive manner, takes on this challenge.

Mashenka demonstrates the only will to wrestle with the power of this darkness. And Tolstoy's play *The Power of Darkness* (about a peasant household in which a woman poisons her husband) does figure in the story's background. But Tolstoy's play, published five years before "Peasant Women," champions a flat, moralistic finale when it points to an exit from the darkness in the form of Nikita's repentance. In Dostoevsky's dark "Akulka's Husband," too, Akulka's bow of forgiveness to Filka Morozov provides the Christian answer. In Chekhov's peasant world the Christian "alternative" has been appropriated and deformed so thoroughly that it is no longer viable. V. V. Rozanov felt that this rang true for all of Russian society, which, hiding behind " 'Our ancient truth, our Christian truth,' " was incapable of assessing the importance of "Peasant Women": "The sluggishness of the Russian soul . . . is exclusively responsible for the fact that no one wailed over the story, no one ran into the street and began to scream, and in general no one created the kind of scandal after which you can no longer hide an awl in your pocket."[17] Rozanov's outrage may not be Chekhov's; but each eschews unthinking solutions couched in Christian ideology. Instead Chekhov's sophisticated realism delves into the psychology that underlies the manipulation of text.

Chapter Five

The Nature of Illusion in
"The Teacher of Literature"

> I played this morning with titles [for a book on
> Chekhov]. . . . A vrai dire, j'aimerais mieux "Le
> Message Implicite": mais qui comprendrait?
> —Charles Du Bos, *Journal*

IN 1894, three years after the appearance of "Peasant Women," Chekhov published "The Teacher of Literature." Interrogation of the functions of language and textual citation moves to a different plane in this story, both because it is set in a bourgeois social milieu and because Chekhov addresses the question of the role of literature proper in formulating understandings of life. Perhaps because of his early activity as a "lowbrow" writer, or perhaps because his loyalties were divided between literature and medicine, scholarship has not always fully appreciated the extent to which Chekhov's writerly compass was set on matters of literariness and on the Russian and European literary canons. Chekhov's works teem with references to Dante, Shakespeare, Goethe, Pushkin, Lermontov, Gogol, Turgenev, Dostoevsky, Tolstoy, Leskov, and countless other writers. The recognition of this intertextual horizon in Chekhov is now rapidly widening.[1]

Oddly enough, the radical futurist Vladimir Mayakovsky was one of the few writers to recognize in Chekhov a fellow literary epicure, pronouncing him a "master of the word," a "strong and spirited artist of the word," a "King of the Word."[2] Mayakovsky accurately foregrounds the "word," for in Chekhov it can be no more than a word that points the way to literary subtexts of substantial significance. The persuasive authority of borrowed words—and the unforeseeable uses to which they are put—are of central concern in "The Teacher of Literature."

"The Teacher of Literature" follows a year in the life of the gymnasium (high school) literature teacher Nikitin, who falls in love with Maria Shelestova (Manya), the daughter of a wealthy local family in a provincial town. Nikitin's courtship takes place during outings on horseback and social gatherings at the Shelestov home in the company not only of Manya, but of her older sister Varya, too. Nikitin proposes to Manya and is accepted. After the wedding, he settles happily into provincial life, absorbed by teaching duties and adoration of his new wife. After a year of bliss, however, cracks begin to appear in the existence Nikitin had considered so ideal. He begins to recognize that his wife and her family value nothing beyond the satisfaction of physical comfort. Gradually he understands that "happiness is no longer possible for him in the two-storied house" and that "the illusion had dried up" (8:331). He conceives a hatred for Manya, writing in his diary: "My God, where am I?! I am surrounded by banality! . . . I must escape, escape from here this very day or I'll go out of my mind!" (8:332).

Chekhov initially published the story in abbreviated form in 1889 as "The Philistines" ("Obyvateli"), a title that conveys the text's manifest theme of provincial life as a vacuous morass from which escape is a dubious prospect. Indeed, the baseness of *poshlost'* (banal and vulgar commonality, philistinism), a major theme in Russian social thought, especially preoccupied Chekhov, who identifies the 1889 story as "a frivolous trifle from the life of provincial guinea-pigs."[3] Assumptions that the author's central aim is the condemnation of *poshlost'*, however, eclipse an equally important question: Why does the banality of life in the provincial town elude, and delude, Nikitin for so long? What is the immanent nature of the illusion that "dries up"?

We can initially tackle these questions by attending to the change in the story's title: "The Teacher of *Literature*" highlights the role in the narration of Nikitin's profession. "Literature" (*slovesnost'*) was, to be sure, standard nomenclature in nineteenth-century public education. Related as it is to the root for "word" (*slovo*), the title also sparks interest in the functions of language and quoted texts in the story. As might be anticipated, the provincial town is peopled with individuals whose atrophied linguistic talents represent the very essence of philistinism. That Nikitin, however, *teacher* of the verbal arts, comes up short on the counts of oratorical skills and an articulated understanding of literature is a much more serious matter for Chekhov. It is this symbolic linguistic plane of the story that offers insights into the nature of Nikitin's illusions.

Through references to literature proper and to literary genres, Chekhov develops the idea that his protagonist is beholden to stock understandings of the written word upon which he patterns his life. In particular, Pushkin's *Count Nulin* serves as a subtext for Nikitin's behavior. Predictably, the Marian theme has a place in this analysis as well. Indeed, Chekhov emphasizes his choice of "Maria" as the heroine's name with a series of derivative nicknames (Maniusia, Manya, Masha, and Marie Godefroy) that can be related both to Chekhov's citation of Orthodox texts, and to another literary reference: a poem by A. K. Tolstoy. Unlike Matvei Savvich in "Peasant Women," however, Nikitin comes to realize that construction of the world around him based on these cultural prescriptions is false. I shall suggest that there is an "implicit message" in "The Teacher of Literature" and that it has to do with forging an identity independent of the models offered by literary and religio-cultural scripts.

LITERARY TEXTS

Chekhov's early work frequently pokes fun at the common person's garbled understandings of the Russian classics (remember "The Swedish Match"). A more consequential plane of misreading occurs in Chekhov's works as his career progresses. Characters who lay claim to an extensive knowledge of literature are more often than not exposed as poseurs. In their company stands Nikitin. Nikitin receives a teaching post at the gymnasium in a provincial Russian town after completing his education in Moscow, credentials that would imply training of the top caliber. Nikitin's erudition is repeatedly called into question, however, when literature is at issue.

At its most obvious, this theme is presented in the feelings of intellectual inadequacy Nikitin experiences when confronted by the shocked reaction of Shebaldin, a local pseudointellectual, upon learning that he has not read Lessing's *Hamburg Dramaturgy*. Nikitin ruminates to himself: "It's really quite awkward. I'm a teacher of literature and have not yet read Lessing. I'll have to read him" (8:316). In all probability Chekhov should have known of Tolstoy's pronouncement from a speech of 1883: "In nine out of ten cases, when the name of Socrates, the book of Job, Aristotle, Erasmus, Montaigne, Dante, Pascal or Lessing is mentioned in conversation . . . neither interlocutor will be familiar with their ideas."[4] In any case, Chekhov enjoyed a running joke with Suvorin about being brought to task by Svobodin for not having read Lessing.[5] That Shebaldin's passion for Lessing is an obsolete and unproductive view of literature is suggested by his nickname, "The Mummy." That Nikitin's subconscious repeatedly feeds him apparitions of Shebaldin popping up to reproach him for this shortcoming suggests that he fails to discern the dry pedantry of Shebaldin's view.

In an argument about literature with Varya, Chekhov ironically comments upon Nikitin's qualifications as a specialist in the field of literature. His rejoinder to Varya's claim that Shchedrin and Dostoevsky outstrip Pushkin as psychologists is the lame remark, "Shchedrin is one thing, and Pushkin is another" (8:314). Attempting to establish Pushkin's grasp of psychology, Nikitin recites passages from *Eugene Onegin* and *Boris Godunov,* the showy tactic of a schoolboy who has nothing substantial to explain. Later, when it is Varya's turn to "confess" during the parlor game of "Fate," Nikitin avers that he "knows her sins" and teases her about Polyansky, a man attentive to Varya, by misquoting a Lermontov epigram. While his students read Gogol and Pushkin aloud, Nikitin engages in daydreams of Manya.

This surface theme of literature reduced to humdrum judgments, or altogether misconstrued, bears on the inner structure of the story through several subtexts. The most important is Pushkin's poem *Count Nulin,* a clue to which is supplied in a deceptively offhand manner. In the first line of Chekhov's story, three horses are led out: Manya mounts the white Velikan, Varya mounts Maika, and Nikitin mounts the black horse, Count Nulin.[6] *Count Nulin,* an elegantly funny narrative poem composed by Pushkin in 1827, portrays the dandified Nulin, who stops at a squire's estate for the night on his return from Europe to "Petropol'" and attempts to seduce the squire's lovely wife. Given this plot, Chekhov's cursory mention of Nulin's name would seem but a slightly comic detail. Yet the similar shape of the names *Nikitin* and *Nulin* animates further inquiry. In fact, it does turn out to be a false lead—that is to say, Nikitin corresponds poorly to the Pushkin prototype—but the mismatch appears to be intentional.

Count Nulin reverberates in "The Teacher of Literature," first, on the level of plot. The opening of Pushkin's poem finds the country squire, Natalia Pavlovna's husband, mounting a horse and riding out for the hunt; at the outset of Chekhov's story the Shelestov party mounts horses and leaves for a ride. The two households have a common passion for horses, dogs, and hunting (Nikitin proposes to Manya next to a cupboard containing hunting gear). Each embodies a certain type of typically Russian provincial existence into which Nulin and Nikitin step as outsiders.

Count Nulin is also a spoof on the effect that literature has on ways of imagining life. In Pushkin's work, Nulin and Natalia Petrovna behave according to the dictates of their reading lists: she reads sentimental novels; he reads the Romantic works of Walter Scott, d'Alincourt, and Lamartine. Pushkin originally planned to call his narrative poem *A New Tarquin,* a reference to Tarquinius's ravaging of Collantinus's wife in Shakespeare's *The Rape of Lucrece.* Pushkin parodies Shakespeare's plot by turning a tragedy into a comedy: he refashions Tarquin's sexual conquest of the chaste and faithful Lucrece as Nulin's blundering effort to seduce Natalia Petrovna, who rebuffs him with a slap in the face. Chekhov, apparently conscious of the literary legacy, takes a further step in this textual series by sketching Nikitin in the shadow of Nulin, but subverting the meaning once again.

Count Nulin, after an evening spent with Natalia Petrovna, is annoyed with himself when he returns to his quarters for failing to make a sexual advance on his hostess.[7] In an analagous situation, back in his quarters after an evening at the Shelestov home, Nikitin, no aristocratic rogue, chides himself for having missed the opportunity to make a marriage proposal. In the wake of this initial failure to propose, Nikitin lies on his sofa and indulges in a fantasy of a letter he will write to his future wife, Manya, when called away on business to Petersburg: "That's how I'll start my letter: My dear little rat. . . . That's it!

My dear little rat, —he said, and began to laugh" (8:319). This strange and seemingly uncalled-for epithet acquires meaning by reference to Pushkin's poem, for this imagined epistle is a reverse echo of Nulin's seduction plan. Lines from *Count Nulin* read:

> Thus at times a cunning cat,
> The maid's mannered favorite,
> Steals after a mouse from his perch:
>
> . . . .
>
> Sharpens the claws of his crafty paws
> And—bam!—snatches up the poor thing.
> (lines 252–55, 258–59)

> (Tak inogda lukavyi kot,
> Zhemannyi baloven' sluzhanki,
> Za mysh'iu kradetsia s lezhanki:
>
> . . . .
>
> Razinet kogti khitrykh lap
> I vdrug bedniazhku tsap-tsarap.)

This image of mouse as sexual victim parodically echoes lines from *The Rape of Lucrece:*

> Yet, foul, night-waking cat, he doth but dally,
> While in his hold-fast foot the weak mouse panteth.
> (lines 54–55)

Nikitin's fantasy is fashioned in this Nulin/Tarquin mode. Nikitin's imagination conjures up a trip to Petersburg (Nulin, we recall, was also headed thence), although Moscow is the city familiar to him. And he pictures a nocturnal "assault" on the bedroom when he returns home to Manya unexpectedly. Even Chekhov's description of this fantasy mimics Pushkin: "or, even better, he'd be cunning: He'd return noiselessly at night, the cook would let him in, then he'd sneak to the bedroom on tiptoe, quietly undress and-plunk!-into bed" (*ili, eshche luchshe, on skhitrit: priedet noch'iu potikhon'ku, kukharka otvorit emu, potom na tsypochkakh proidet on v spal'niu, besshumno razdenetsia i—bultykh v postel'!*) (8:319). The many lexical rhymes with *Count Nulin* leave little doubt about the intentionality of the evocation: "cunning paws" (*khitrie lapy*) / "he'd be cunning" (*on skhitrit*); "maid" (*sluzhanka*) / "cook" (*kukharka*); "steal up" (*kradetsia*) / "sneak . . . on tiptoe" (*na tsypochkakh proidet*); "bam" (*tsap-tsarap*) / "plunk" (*bultykh*). The point here is that Chekhov transforms Nulin's mischievous erotic metaphor into a fantasy of consummated love in Nikitin's conscious mind. But in Nikitin's imagination, Manya unexpectedly assumes the features of a rat rather than a mouse. His fantasized escapade involves returning to the bed of a pernicious rodent, not a victimized female.

Chekhov's reversal of Pushkin's text foregrounds the question of sexuality. Nikitin is dissociated from the aggressive sexual role allotted the "cat" by both Shakespeare and Pushkin. Chekhov's protagonist repeatedly expresses his hostility toward the Shelestov cats, considering them at one point the sole obstacle to his happiness. That cats usually sit on the staircase adjacent to the site of Nikitin's proposal of marriage may thus be considered an ominous sign. Instead, Manya becomes associated with the white cat. A small-scale Chekhovian event reinforces this reversal: Manya orders that a scrap of cheese be sent to the servants' quarters despite remonstrations on Nikitin's part that it is only fit for a mousetrap. The theme from the letter fantasy ("my little rat") is realized as Manya proves herself the dominant partner. Nikitin turns out to be analogous to the mouse, caught in the trap of his misapprehension of Manya.

The motif of sexual maturity also resonates in Nikitin's preoccupation with his age. On several occasions he is mistaken for a very young man, barely old enough for marriage. Early in the story Nikitin fumes at being taken for a student: " 'How swinish!' thought Nikitin. —This fellow also takes me for a suckling!' " (*molokosos*) (8:312). *Molokosos* (literally, "milk-sucker") conveys a psychologically puerile state that aptly describes Nikitin's romantic interest in Manya. Not coincidentally, Chekhov borrows the word from Pushkin. At the end of *Count Nulin* Natalia Petrovna's husband has his say:

> He said that the count was a fool,
> A *suckling* (*molokosos*); that being such,
> He'd make the count yelp,
> He'd hunt him down *with dogs.*
> (my emphasis)

The husband's comic and empty threat is reversed in Chekhov's story. Nikitin is almost literally "hounded by the dogs" of the Shelestov household. The Shelestov dog Mushka takes an instantaneous dislike to Nikitin, growling at him aggressively at every opportunity.[8] The dog Som drools on his pants, staining his lap in a suggestive manner. The cats and dogs that come with Manya's dowry turn his new home into a rank menagerie. Nikitin, in response, feels intense hostility from the outset toward the family's "abundance of dogs and cats, and the Egyptian doves, who cooed in a big cage on the terrace" (8:313).[9] Although he hopes to exude Count Nulin's bold sexual confidence, this unflattering comparison severely compromises Nikitin's manliness.

Finally, Nikitin's inclination to shape his life according to elementary understandings of literature appears in the metaphors with which he describes his married life. These consist of a series of trite comparisons with literary genres. He writes in his diary about his wedding: "And I thought—recently my life has taken shape with such poetic beauty!" (8:324). Later he adds that he has now achieved the happiness that once seemed possible only in novels and stories. Nikitin subsequently thinks of his past and future as a "fairy tale" (8:326). Domestic life with Manya reminds Nikitin of "pastoral idylls" (8:327). This string of clichés reflects the level of Nikitin's literary sophistication. The vehicle of his ruminations is, appropriately, his diary—a supreme example of life focused in text.

Chekhov, then, suggests a relationship between Nikitin's complacency as a provincial teacher of literature and his impending identity crisis both through an affiliation with the Pushkin subtext and by calling into question his qualifications as a literary specialist. Indeed, as Nikitin starts to openly admit his deep dissatisfaction with life, he comes to the startling recognition that he has no talent for, nor interest in, the vocation of pedagogy. Moreover, he recognizes that "he knew nothing about the meaning of that which he taught" (8:331). Nikitin, it turns out, is uninterested in the subject matter and dislikes children—both qualities fatal to a pedagogical career. Part of the "illusion that dries up," then, is the illusion of his professional identity, exposed by his deficient ideas—in Chekhovian terms—about the value and meaning of literature.

An upset of literary convention on the level of textual imagery marks the psychological instability of Nikitin's position. We noted that Manya mounts a white horse and dotes on a white cat, whereas Nikitin rides the black Count Nulin. Contrasting white and black imagery is a traditional cultural and literary convention, indicative of the opposition between good and evil, innocence and vice. A classic example of this opposition appears in *The Rape of Lucrece*. Shakespeare contrasts the innocent Lucrece's "snow-white dimpled chin," "breasts, like ivory globes," "white sheet," and "modest snow-white weed" to Tarquin's aggressive sexual conquest, imaged as "so black a deed," "the blackest sin," "a black-fac'd cloud," "black payment," and "black lust." Chekhov problematizes these habitual straightforward sexual characterizations by outfitting the men in white coats and the women in black riding habits (*amazonki*) when the horse party leaves the Shelestov yard at the outset of the story. Black *amazonki* (traditional women's riding attire) insinuate robust females with nothing pure or innocent about them. The conventional values attached to black and white images become redistributed in Chekhov's text in a way that, I will eventually attempt to demonstrate, correlates with the inverted functions of textual pointers to the virgin and the harlot.

Riding next to Nikitin on her "proud white animal," Nikitin views Manya with "joy, tenderness, and rapture" (8:310) as the embodiment of all feminine virtues. But, as Karl Kramer has noted, Nikitin's "emotional response bears no direct relationship to the stimulus."[10] Intrusive signs keep infringing on this vision. First, he thinks that her (black) riding hat is not becoming. As they ride along, looming in the distance are black garden plots and apple trees in the cemetery on which the white blossoms have faded away (perhaps a pointer to the moribund status of a polarized black-white dichotomy). Still further, in what may be a Chekhovian pun on Nikitin's idealized vision of marriage (*brak*), Manya calls Polyansky's horse "defective" (*brak*ovannyi) because of the white spot on its left leg. (Nikitin later throws his *left leg* onto the back of the sofa as he begins to engage in fantasies of marriage to Manya.) Nikitin, who "understands nothing about horses," tries to dissociate Manya from her equestrian passion, but it clings to her like the nickname Marie Godefroy, the coarse circus trick rider Manya so admires (Chekhov refers to Godefroy in a letter as "ordinary and vulgar").[11]

Chekhov develops this disjuncture in Nikitin's mind in a manner redolent of the symbology of dreams. As the Shelestov horse party returns home, he feels the full measure of his happiness riding next to Manya: "He was so happy that the earth, the sky, the city lights and black silhouette of the brewery all merged in his eyes into something very fine and gentle" (8:313). The anomaly of a brewery's black silhouette in this lyric vision deflates the fantasy by pointing to an artificial source of figurative intoxication. The brewery again appears in an imagined episode that follows the "my little rat" fantasy. Chekhov charts the transition to this dream with the words: "The air became completely light/white (*vozdukh sovsem pobelel*)" (8:319). Manya is sitting on the porch of the brewery (an unlikely environs for a romantic tryst). She takes Nikitin's arm and they walk to the public garden, where he sees oaks and nests that looked like hats (recall Manya's unbecoming black hat). The raven nests (*voron'i gnezda*) phonetically mimic "the raven-black (*voronoi*) Count Nulin." Shebaldin peeks out of a nest and shouts, "You haven't read Lessing!"

Nikitin's subconscious mocks his preoccupation with a lofty Manya by delivering a series of contrapuntal blows. This dream cluster of black images (the brewery, ravens, and hats) not only undermines his conscious romantic perceptions, but links intellectual inadequacy to the construct he has created of his beloved. In her study of "An Attack of Nerves," Marena Senderovich suggests that the reversal of the meaning of black and white in the story reflects the reversal of positions initially assumed by the hero, that the black-white relationships in the consciousness of Vasilev resemble *"the black-and-white of a book page."*[12] While Nikitin's textual orientation on life is only a distant cousin to Vasilev's bookishness, it also comes in a context in which understandings of the written word are at stake. (Nikitin's dilemma, like that of Vasilev, "is characterized by an insoluble contradiction between high ideals, accepted fully and without compromise, and reality.")[13] In both cases a crisis ensues when the polarized thinking of the protagonists breaks down.

At the end of part 1, after the marriage proposal but before the wedding, the events of the story's first paragraph are repeated verbatim in Nikitin's final dream. Once again the black Count Nulin and white Velikan exit from the stables with Maika. The repetition itself suggests that the rut of the hero's perceptions has changed little (in fact, Nikitin is "quoting" the narrator of his own story). But Chekhov has exposed Nikitin's inner world, his inability to conceptualize his life outside of a rigid set of polarized understandings, by establishing the discrepancy between Nikitin's conscious formulations and unconscious visions. His subconscious and the world around him invert, subvert, and resist dichotomization, as we shall see in a consideration of the veiled religious context latent in the story.

THE MARIAN CONTEXT

In a gesture of a sort germane to Chekhov's poetics, Nikitin ends his intellectual face-off with Varya about Pushkin's status as a psychologist by shouting out a scriptural citation from the Annunciation scene. The phrase is delivered in an entirely colloquial tonality, so much so that its source easily escapes notice. This semiconcealed sign alerts us to the presence of a Marian motif in "The Teacher of Literature." It also suggests that not only Manya, but that Varya, too, might be considered in relationship to the Marian paradigm. This expansion of the paradigm's reach merits a slight digression as a prelude to a discussion of the Marian context in the story.

Thus far Marian significations have revolved around essentially one character (except in the case of "Peasants," where the icon reflects aspects of all the female characters). The situation becomes more complex in these later stories of the 1890s. Savely Senderovich has demonstrated the means by which Chekhov distributes features of the Saint George legend among different characters within a story.[14] In a similar vein, Chekhov expands the dual poles of the Marian paradigm to full potential by touching both a "Maria" and additional characters with its tones. A story published six months before "The Teacher of Literature" illustrates this point *graphically*, in a literal sense.

The heroine of "A Woman's Kingdom" ("Bab'e tsarstvo," 1894) is the wealthy heiress Anna Akimovna who lives alone in a grand house. Among her servants are *two* Marys: "downstairs Masha," confined to the servants' quarters or "woman's kingdom," and "red-haired Masha," her attendant in the upstairs, or stately, realm of the manor.[15] The "two Mashas" themselves barely participate in the plot, but their presence provides a bifurcated outline of the dilemma of sexuality in Anna Akimovna's personal life. The story is set on Christmas Day, holiday of the Virgin birth. The heroine craves "a husband, children" (8:282). In conversations about marriage, however, her simple plea is ignored. The lawyer Lysevich (upstairs) recommends that she enjoy "debauchery" by taking on a string of paramours. Spiridonovna (downstairs) pronounces prayers to the Mother of God upon her arrival, then extols the virtues of female sexual pleasure.[16] Tempted by the alluring call of sensuality (her "hair cascaded loose" at the talk of marriage [8:290]), Anna Akimovna agrees to marry the workman Pimenov; but running up the *stairs* (possibly another wry play on Jacob's prophecy) to the "upper kingdom," she reneges on the agreement, capitulating to the disgust of the servant Mishenka over the thought that a lady might marry a commoner. (Mishenka comes in at midnight carrying candles and laughs at Anna Akimovna's plan to marry Pimenov, a scene that parodies the parable of the ten virgins awaiting the midnight bridegroom [Matt. 25:1–13]). Thus the dialectic between virginity and sexuality signaled by the "two Mashas" plays itself out in the life of Anna Akimovna: she ends up, on Christmas Day, a misunderstood virgin without husband or child. The irony is compounded by her name and patronymic: the Virgin Mary's parents were Anna and Joachim (Akim, in Russian), and the couple was troubled into old age by barrenness.

In "The Teacher of Literature," too, then, more than one female character is refracted through the paradigm of the two Marys. Both Manya and Varya seem to be viewed unconsciously by Nikitin through this prism, that is, in terms echoing the virgin/harlot dichotomy. His perceptions relate to the question of textualism insofar as they involve the imposition of religio-cultural texts on individuals who themselves are clearly divorced from the associations. It represents, as well, an extension of the question of polarized thinking. This part of the "illusion" in Nikitin's life is, perhaps, the most important one to overcome before he can identify the *poshlost'* of his surroundings for what it is.

Playing at fidelity to literary convention, Chekhov opens "The Teacher of Literature" as a traditional tale of love, engaging the reader in Nikitin's romantic obsession with Manya. Some earlier stories (as previously noted) observe the intersection between romantic love and the cultural habit of Marian adulation. So, here, Nikitin's passion is tinted with hints that Manya appears to him as a sort of "Madonna." Such, for instance, is his attention to her eyes: "Large, motionless eyes" peer at Nikitin from under the "confession shawl" during the parlor game of "Fate" played at a Shelestov soirée. Later, at dinner, he notices how she "gazed at him motionlessly, without blinking" (8:317). That Chekhov considered motionless eyes to be a striking feature of the icon is clear from the story "Grief" ("Gore," 1885), where the dying Matryona "gazed sternly and motionlessly, just as saints on icons gaze" (4:232).

Nikitin's marriage proposal to Manya is interlaced with details that recall a Marian liturgical epithet, and then apocryphal accounts of the Annunciation. The presence of a staircase (*lestnitsa* also means "ladder") in the small entryway where the proposal takes place is noted thrice, a flag of significance in Chekhov's economical prose. The prophecy of Jacob's ladder (Church Slavic, *lestvitsa*) prefigures the Mother of God, who would bridge heaven and earth with the birth of her son (see the discussion of "A Dreadful Night" in Chapter 2 and Fig. 5). In Nikitin's mind, his plea for Manya's hand is to be just such a moment of attaining "heaven." The episode develops in a symbolic manner. Nikitin never actually ascends the staircase. On his way "up" he is interrupted from mounting the "narrow wooden staircase" by the sudden entrance of Manya. She slams the door to the nursery so hard that the staircase shakes.

Chekhov notes of the entryway, "there were doors here" (8:321). The slammed door, in this symbolic reading, reverberates ironically with an Annunciation metaphor. Mary is the "Impassable Door" (icon type), "Door of Salvation" and "Doors of the Venerable Mystery" (both acathist lines). The Annunciation is depicted on the doors of all church altars, or "Heavenly Gates" (*tsarskie vrata*).[17] Need it be said that Manya, who passes like a tornado through the door, does not deserve to be credited with the mystery Nikitin sees in her.

The proposal itself reiterates a detail that, like the staircase, is mentioned a momentous three times. This is a piece of blue fabric that first appears in Manya's hands, is then grasped by Nikitin, and, finally, falls to the floor when he moves to embrace Manya. This piece of dark-blue fabric has been discussed at some length by critics, but it is hard to agree that the scrap of material functions as a mark of triviality or represents an altogether extraneous detail.[18] Recall that in "The Dowry" Marie's mother cut dark-blue fabric in order to sew an outfit for her daughter, the "unwed bride."

Apocryphal versions of the Annunciation find the Virgin Mary spinning a thread for the temple veil when Gabriel appears to her. In iconographic depictions of the Annunciation the thread and spindle are shown *falling away* from Mary's hand when she turns from her work to accept her "spiritual assignment"[19] (see Fig. 6). Dark-blue—the color of the fabric that falls from Manya's hands—is a sacred color in Eastern iconography and the color of the Mother of God's robe on icons. (Decades later Akhmatova refers twice to the Mother of God's dark-blue cloak in the poem "By the Sea" [1914] and S. Klychkov writes of the Mother of God wearing a dark-blue dress in his novel *The Storyteller of Chertukhinsk* [1926].) Textile and thread are metonymically associated. Nikitin hears the sound of a seamstress's scissors coming from the nursery when he enters the hall to make the marriage proposal. Manya, like Mary, emerges from her girlhood occupation (the temple, the nursery) to participate in a "coming of age" event.

The parallels here, of course, are in no way analagous to the amorous "Annunciation" of Batiushkov's lover in "To Masha," although this is the romantic tradition against which to read the scene.[20] Nikitin's proposal of marriage can best be read, however, against the background of the biblical event. The proposal takes place in a profane mode and inverts the sacred value of the Annunciation at every step, revealing the deep discrepancy between Nikitin's striving for an ideal that conforms to his cultural milieu and the reality of the Shelestov home, utterly devoid as it is of true intellectual, emotional, or spiritual values. The miracle of the moment at which the Virgin Mary drops the thread concerns the Immaculate Conception; the moment at which Manya drops the blue fabric heralds erotic contact between Nikitin and his fiancée. The proposal has to do with the physical initiation of Nikitin into a world of sensuality at odds with Christian views of the ideal.

If the scene of the marriage proposal maps a distinct breach between Manya and the prototype in whose shadow she is being cast, Varya's position relative to this glorified vision of womanhood, too, is shown as if in a distorting mirror. She is held up to the light of motherhood and virginity, but frustrates the associations on both scores. Varya has taken the place of her deceased mother in the Shelestov family, and is also a "virgin": "She called herself an old maid (*deva*), which meant that she was sure that she would get married" (8:314). Again the word *deva* surfaces contiguous to the Marian context. Varya's is a portrait of dubious womanhood in conventional terms, for the emphasis is on substitution for the real mother and on barrenness.

That Varya fails to conform to Nikitin's vision of exalted womanhood is clear from their literary debate. (Note that interpretation of text on the level of plot parallels the question of the meaning of text developed on other planes.) Nikitin's common view of Pushkin is matched by Varya's insistence that Pushkin is "a great poet and nothing more." To escape the deadlock that the argument reaches, Nikitin yells: "I won't argue anymore! . . . Of his kingdom there shall be no end! Basta!" (8:315). His exclamation of frustration is an exact citation from the Annunciation scene in Luke 1:33. These are the biblical words of the Angel Gabriel, who proclaims to the Virgin Mary that the reign of the Son of God shall be eternal. The impetuous—and foreign— exclamation "Basta!" intrudes on this citation as an index of its inversion. The Christian prophecy issues from Nikitin's mouth as a profanity, a curse, as it were, on his own inability to articulate a convincing argument in his supposed field of expertise: literature.

In disgust at his intellectual impotence, Nikitin harnesses a quotidian expression bearing reflexes of Christian rhetoric to reject Varya's claim to a voice in the domain of the intellect. The reversal of the sacred text, couched as it is in casual language with offensive overtones, is meaningful: it is precisely Varya's lack of femininity in terms of the Christian model (a yielding, submissive nature) that diminishes her "eligibility" for marriage and motherhood. The image Nikitin projects on Varya, in accordance with his (mis)understandings, is the complementary opposite of the Virgin.

Varya's thwarted desire for marriage leads to this association with a "fallen" woman, although, again, nothing in her behavior justifies the allusion. Chekhov's design is evidenced by the presence of a citation from Aleksei Konstantinovich Tolstoy's poem of 1857, "The Sinful Woman" ("Greshnitsa").

Chekhov first refers to this poem in "A Liberal Fellow" ("Liberal'nyi dushka," 1884), where a browbeaten performer is called "immoral" for suggesting that A. K. Tolstoy's poem be recited on a Christmas program, a clever play on the contrast between the virginal mother and the harlot. (Later, in *The Cherry Orchard,* the poem is recited at the fête in act 3 and reflects on Liubov Andreevna Ranevskaya in an ironic manner.)[21] The reference to the poem appears to be an incidental detail in "The Teacher of Literature": it is used to characterize Shebaldin's hackneyed acting ("he himself took part in performances, always playing, for some reason, comic servants or reciting 'The Sinful Woman' in a singsong voice" [8:316]). The actual significance of this minor detail underscores the necessity of regarding every word in a Chekhov story as a critical component of its semantic structure.

The poem is about a beautiful, young prostitute who boasts to a crowd that she will seduce Christ, but who, upon seeing him, immediately repents. In short, this is a reworked version of popular tales about Mary Magdalene. At the moment of spiritual awakening and repentance, A. K. Tolstoy's sinful woman drops her wine glass on the floor and collapses at Christ's feet:

> The ring of a goblet falling from hands
> sounded out in the silence . . .
> A moan is heard from her constricted
> breast, the young harlot pales,
> Her open lips tremble,
> She fell down, sobbing,
> Before the sacred figure of Christ.
> (lines 203–9)

Chekhov's seemingly random mention of this poem turns out to be important because he invokes this scene at the moment of Varya's hysterical collapse: "Varya, Manya's sister, ran into the study with a *wine glass in her hand* . . . she apparently wanted to run further, but suddenly she burst out laughing, then *sobbing,* and her wine glass began to *roll across the floor with a ring*" (8:325; my emphasis). In both texts, the same action occurs at a moment of crisis: each woman drops a glass of wine that rings out as it hits the floor, and each breaks into sobs. The scene occurs just as Nikitin's Marian adulation of Manya has reached its apotheosis in the wedding scene.

A wedding in Chekhov needn't necessarily draw on cultural associations with the Virgin, patroness of weddings, although it is worth noting that in his play *Tatiana Repina* (1889), a parody of the Orthodox wedding service, Chekhov cites many parts of the marriage liturgy that invoke the Mother of God (12:83–93). Some of the priest's lines from that play are repeated in "The Teacher of Literature." It is at the wedding that Varya suddenly feels her own unwed status acutely. Varya is no more a "sexually compromised" woman, of course, than is Manya the embodiment of Marian virtues. Rather, Nikitin, conditioned by the texts of his culture, projects upon Varya the role (and text) of the fallen woman, and the dualistic paradigm that serves as a foundation upon which he constructs his own bliss is thereby solidified.

This citation from A. K. Tolstoy's poem, which appears in Nikitin's diary at the opening of part 2, signals a change in contextual orientation for the story overall. Recall that fabric falling from Manya's hand seems to situate the marriage proposal in relationship to a sacred text about the Virgin. Here a glass falling from Varya's hand alludes to a secular text about a sinful woman. Indeed, at the wedding itself Nikitin is disconcerted by the old general's description of Manya as "a rose" (*rozan*) for what it implies about her sensuality. (The rose as a symbol of the Virgin—a Roman Catholic convention—was replaced by the white lily in Orthodox theology; the rose's thorns, it was felt, suggested the taint of sin.)[22] Moreover, Nikitin finds himself preoccupied with the Varya incident as he writes about the wedding, and this hinders him from reading his account of the event to Manya. In other words, the text in which he has cast himself as hero is somehow marred by signs of female "sinfulness," just as, earlier, the black brewery trespassed on his bright prenuptial fantasies. These images come back to haunt him.

The trajectory of the evolution in Nikitin's thinking is embedded in two interesting details encountered well before his actual change of heart. The first is the pair of Egyptian doves that dwell on the porch of the Shelestov home. Within the context of the Marian network in Chekhov (and here it is necessary to rely on past stories), "Egyptian" resonates with the "sinful" Mary; on the other hand, the dove appears on icons of the Annunciation to represent the Holy Spirit descending to the Virgin. At first Nikitin is repelled by the Egyptian doves. Later, in a paroxysm of delight over Manya, he blindly projects his own emotions on the birds ("only the Egyptian doves moan in this house, and that because they have no other way of expressing their joy!" [8:318]). The Egyptian doves, then, represent the immanent duality in Nikitin's perceptions, something underscored by the presence of two birds.

The second detail is a Marian holiday. Immediately following the account of the wedding, Chekhov embarks on a description of Nikitin's felicitous married life, but only subsequent to noting that Nikitin resumes his teaching duties just after the Dormition. This signpost both reaffirms the salience of the paradigm to the story, and positions within the text a warning of the eventual disintegration of Nikitin's illusions about Manya (the holiday signifies the death of the Mother of God).

Nikitin comes to view Manya in the light of the sinful woman as his eyes open to the visceral quality of her life, confined as it is to the satisfaction of physical urges and desires. Early on, Manya's behavior uncouples her personality from his inviolate vision of her. During the parlor game of "Fate,"

Nikitin is instructed to play the role of a priest at confession. Entranced by the sight of Manya's large, motionless eyes as she comes to "confess," he poses the question, "How have you sinned?" (8:317). Her response is to screw up her eyes and show him the tip of her tongue—actions that defiantly undermine the iconographic association.[23]

In "The Lady," "Peasants," and "Peasant Women" Chekhov draws cows, milk, and domesticity into the Marian theme.[24] Another indication of Manya's dissociation from qualities of the Virgin, and association with the animal world, comes in a motif of milk. The Virgin Mary's status as a nurturing spiritual mother was sometimes portrayed in terms of the suckling breast. Popular prints depict the Mother of God moistening the lips of the faithful with milk from her breast. Chekhov must have been aware of the Russian *Maria Lactans* icon, which made a highly publicized journey through Russia from 1893 to 1896, coincident with the writing of this story.[25] A troparion to the canon of the Annunciation reads "The nature of the milk that you dispense, Pure Virgin, the human tongue cannot explain."[26] The curious scene in the early pages of "The Teacher of Literature"—where the equestrian party requests fresh milk at the Shelestov farm, but then refuses it ("no one drank the milk; everyone exchanged glances, laughed, and galloped away" [8:312])—prefigures, perhaps, the disaffinity between the frivolous Shelestov clan and Nikitin's sober-minded passion.

The meaning of the dairy enterprise that Manya founds must be located on the symbolic plane:

> With three cows, Manya set up a genuine dairy business. She kept a lot of pitchers of milk and pots of sour cream in the cellar and the pantry, which she saved to make butter. Now and then, as a joke, Nikitin asked her for a glass of milk. This gave her a scare, since it violated her sense of order, but he would embrace her with a laugh and say: —Never mind, I was just joking, my golden one, just joking! (8:327)

Remote from maternal benevolence, Manya's milk is hoarded and turned into solids, a petrified parody of the milk that flows from the Virgin's breast (an acathist line reads "Rejoice, for honey and milk flow from Her!"). Manya's refusal to give Nikitin milk becomes a symbolic gesture, a sign of her unequivocal dissociation from Nikitin's ideal.

Emblematic of the onset of change in Nikitin's understandings of Manya is the scene in which he pontificates to her on the nature of his good fortune. With unbridled egotism, Nikitin insists that he has created his own happiness, a statement that is ironically true in the sense that he has constructed his happiness from a profusion of borrowed texts. As he tells her this, Nikitin plays with Manya's hair, unbraiding and then braiding it again. Nikitin's actions have sensual overtones, but they coincide as well with the symbolism of the Virgin (one braid is the Orthodox prescription for the modest female) and the harlot (whose depiction with loose hair has been encountered throughout Chekhov as a cultural leitmotif).

In Joyce's "The Dead" the hero's epiphany occurs in early January on the feast day of the Epiphany. For the Orthodox, the feast of the Epiphany (or Theophany) is called *Kreshchen'e,* or Baptism. Nikitin's critical realizations about his misconceived life, too, are ushered in by this day. On Epiphany Nikitin's intense dislike of the Shelestov animals comes to light. But the actual holiday is marked by a failed celebration: "The police wouldn't allow anyone out on the river for the Blessing of the Water since, they said, the ice had swollen and darkened" (8:328). The swelling ice and dripping roofs anticipate an incipient thaw in Nikitin's frozen perceptions, but the aborted religious rite also directs us away from the notion that he is about to experience a genuine spiritual ephiphany in the Christian sense (something that might occur in Dostoevsky or Tolstoy).

His awakening of understanding comes as Nikitin stands in the rain after an evening of card-playing at the club. Card-playing, Nikitin's new pastime, points back to the parlor game of "Fate," played with two decks of cards. R. L. Jackson has suggested that cards in other Chekhov texts serve as a metaphor for the abnegation of will and capitulation to fate.[27] It is the comment by Nikitin's card partner about his unearned wealth that jolts him into the realization that he has *not,* as he earlier claimed, consciously created his own happiness, but that forces over which he wields no control orchestrate his life. His "baptism" in the rain, then, is both an ironical antibaptism—insofar as it portends his impending move away from the projections of artificial, even fraudulent, Christian images on the life around him—and a figurative baptism/initiation into a new sphere of values.

When Nikitin arrives home from the club, his view of Manya and their domestic life is completely altered. After a spat with his wife, he lies awake imagining a different and meaningful life that, importantly, he conceives as a world *beyond the icon lamp:*

> "He mused that besides the soft light of the icon lamp, which smiled at this quiet domestic happiness, besides this little world, in which he and that cat lived so peacefully and sweetly, a wholly different world existed. . . . And suddenly, in anguish, he passionately wanted to get to that different world, to work, himself, somewhere at a factory or in a large workshop, to speak from a podium, to compose, print, stir things up, to tire himself out, to suffer." (8:330)

The collective beliefs and values from which his sensations of happiness derived now seem to him monotonous (*odnoobrazny;* literally, "of one shape"). It is worth noting that *obraz* can also mean "icon."

Nikitin now regards Manya, lying on the bed beside the white cat, with her neck, full shoulders, and breast exposed, and for the first time understands the appellation "rose" that the brigadier general had used about Manya in church. (Incidentally, pictures of the "sinful" Mary of Egypt and Mary Magdalene often show them in scant garb with shoulder and breast exposed.) Nikitin repeats the word "rose" to himself as if to verify the identification. Nikitin comprehends that she whom he imagined in the light of Virgin really belongs to the world of spiritless sensuality associated in Christian doctrine with the whore. Nikitin has moved irrevocably beyond his mindless idealization of Manya, and has arrived at the opposite pole.

The story's final paragraph is saturated with signs related to Marian devotion that no longer exercise authority in Nikitin's life. The date of 20 March and the rays of the sun may be Chekhov's pointers to the Annunciation (celebrated 25 March and represented as a ray of light descending on the Virgin from heaven). The epithets that describe his surroundings—garden, miraculous, joys—can be coded not only to romantic delights, but also to Marian praise. But Nikitin sees no value in the scene that evoked euphoria in him a year before. He now dreams of returning to Moscow, not to the Petersburg of his "Count Nulin" fantasy. In the last lines, he recognizes Manya's obsession with milk—"boring, worthless people, pots full of sourcream, jugs of milk, cockroaches, stupid women" (8:333)—as a perversion of real value. Nikitin's misogynistic comments may be abrasive, but they come as a reaction to the lofty religious paradigms that have manipulated him.

If, when Tolstoy's Ivan Ilych discovers that life has been "not right" (*ne to*), a revelation of the need for spiritual value ensues, Nikitin's "not right" finds no decreed solution. When the protagonist detects that "the illusion had dried up," in the foreground is his awareness of the need to embrace a *conscious* life (*soznatel'naia zhizn'*). The series of texts that define, and confine, Nikitin's life prior to the "baptism" operate as subliminal cultural prompts to his behavior. Nikitin's act of self-liberation at the end of the story has to do with moving beyond the "scripts" offered by the Russian literary and religio-cultural traditions. In crafting this fate for his hero, Chekhov acts as a teacher of literature in his own right.

If we consider that, from the earliest Marian story, most characters "buy into" the paradigm in one way or another, Nikitin's ability to challenge the a priori cultural attitudes that determine his thoughts assumes added significance. Finding one's way beyond perceptions grounded in culture and literature is, in Chekhovian terms, a juncture of self-discovery, an important moment of advancement for the individual. The illusion that dries up in "The Teacher of Literature," then, is the illusion that the intelligent individual can base a satisfying existence on predetermined ideas, images, and or texts of any kind. In its place comes the much more difficult bidding to discover and structure meaning of one's own.

Ironically, the Russian reading public thirsted for just the kind of messages that Chekhov eschews. A young woman named Aurelia Groman wrote to Chekhov in 1899: "You say that each must bear his cross. But who will show us how to bear that cross? In your works we see ourselves as in a mirror. They show us our faults with the precision of a photograph, but we don't know how to improve ourselves."[28] In response to "The Teacher of Literature" an acquaintance from Yalta wrote to Chekhov: "Give us at least a few major chords—encourage us, give us some hope!"[29] The thoughts Chekhov tenders, however, do not encourage readers with "major chords," with prescriptive paths to happiness. Instead, Chekhov advocates accepting the uncertainty and responsibility for self that come with a mature apprehension of life. In so doing, he turns the quest for answers back on the individual.

Chapter Six

The Nature of Conviction in "My Life"

> "My Life"—that's what touched me and created
> a deep impression. Such simplicity, power,
> unexpectedness . . . And how new it is! How
> original! And what language!—just like the Bible.
> —I. E. Repin, letter to A. P. Chekhov

WHATEVER THE painter Repin may have had in mind when he compared the language of Chekhov's "My Life" ("Moia zhizn'," 1896) to the Bible, his comment was on mark insofar as a Christian frame of reference animates the text. Past scholarship has tuned into the story's Christian thematics largely in relationship to the Tolstoyan principles of simplicity and physical labor embraced by the protagonist, Misail Poloznev. While the question of Tolstoyism is undeniably relevant to "My Life," the language of the story urges another approach to the Christian context as well. This reading will not be overconcerned with assessing the philosophical positions occupied by the characters per se, territory that in any case has been covered in the critical discussion. Rather, my interest is in how texts of religion feed (secular) behaviors and help to carve out an individual's philosophical position. To put it another way, the focus here is on what Elaine Pagels calls the "mental architecture" of Christianity that has proven so influential in determining the contours of conceptualization in European cultures.[1]

Northrop Frye quotes Blake's definition of the Old and New Testaments as the "Great Code of Art," understanding this to mean that the Bible in Western cultures has generated a mythological universe of assumptions and beliefs unconsciously embraced. "Practically all we can see of this body of concerns is socially conditioned and culturally inherited," writes Frye.[2] Chekhov moves along these tracks in "My Life," where the comportment and views of his protagonists are coded to Old and New Testament texts, but in camouflaged "socially conditioned" and "culturally inherited" ways. Of course, if an authorial bias in favor of Judeo-Christian beliefs or traditions is implied by Blake's statement, Chekhov takes a different route, approaching the question as a phenomenologist. He is interested here in how the Orthodox Christian cultural inheritance makes an imprint on the modern consciousness.

"My Life," one of Chekhov's longest stories, is the first-person account of a social rebel, Misail Poloznev, who renounces the life of the provincial petit nobility to follow a creed of toil and self-abnegation that he believes will equalize class disparities and expose the hypocrisy of his father's entrenched, self-righteous faith. He becomes a day laborer and housepainter while his sister Kleopatra remains at home to cater to their widowed father's stringent demands. In his garb of a simple workman, Misail engages the interest of Maria Viktorovna Dolzhikova, his wealthy and flamboyant young neighbor who is enchanted by his ideals of physical labor and an unpretentious existence. After a rocky courtship, the two get married in a village church, imitating a peasant wedding at her insistence. They settle in a dilapidated country estate, Dubechnia, a gift from Masha's nouveau riche, businessman father Victor Dolzhikov. There Misail tills the land and Masha orchestrates the construction of a village school. Visits paid by the doctor Vladimir Blagovo, a married man living in Petersburg, end in an illicit love affair between Blagovo and Kleopatra. Meanwhile, the country idyll disintegrates: Masha becomes disillusioned and leaves for town, then for Petersburg, then for America. Misail moves back to the town and settles in the humble quarters of their childhood nurse with the now-pregnant Kleopatra, who gives birth to a girl before she dies. Misail continues to ply his trade as an honest painting contractor while raising his niece. Into this plot are woven numerous conversations about, and meditations on, the big "Russian" questions—faith, conscience, progress, truth, and freedom—built around arguments about how to best be "useful" (*polezno* appears as an anagram in the surname Poloznev).

At its most overt, the "Christian" positioning assumed in relationship to these questions is expressed by Misail's father. Poloznev Sr. works as an architect and offers his children moral blueprints in the form of lectures concerning the need for young people to return to religion. Poloznev Sr. complains: "God saw fit to punish me with you children, but I endure this trial with humility and, like Job, find consolation in suffering and constant work" (9:278). Job, on the contrary, was punished with the *death* of his children. Poloznev's godliness is sabotaged by many such details. Misail describes his father's face as that of "an old Catholic organist" (9:192), a sign in Orthodox culture of falsity. Like the priest in "The Requiem," Misail's father evinces a far greater concern for the world of social opinion than for that of the spirit. This conspicuous sanctimony, a reminder that the adulterated Christian patriarchy of "Peasant Women" was not confined to village life, serves as a measure for the positions of other characters in the sense that it demonstrates how the mental filtering of Christian text can create a worldview divorced from Christian principles.

The relationships to Christian text on the part of Poloznev's son, Misail, his daughter Kleopatra, Maria Viktorovna, and Doctor Blagovo are far less obvious, and far more interesting. If critics have already attended to the philosophical reverberations of Tolstoyism and the Book of Ecclesiastes in the lives of these characters,[3] our attention turns instead to the Marian theme and to related Old Testament "subtexts" from the Book of Daniel. As in "The Teacher of Literature," two female characters and the male protagonists adjacent to them are illuminated by Marian motifs: the behavior of both Maria Viktorovna and Kleopatra is delicately keyed to the Marian figures, while features of the paradigm are refracted in both the personal formulations and intellectual positions of Blagovo and Misail. Nikitin's diary, too, finds an analogue in the memoir format of "My Life." In contrast to the earlier work, however, the Marian context here is not always projected by the protagonist. Misail's autobiography has the effect of exposing the roots of Christian conceptualization in the speech and actions of others through the use of ample dialogue.

What Chekhov seems to suggest through these indicators is that the lives and beliefs of the four central characters of "My Life" are guided to one extent or another by Christian formulations—or, more precisely, are cast according to the molds of cognition and models for demeanor presented in Orthodox texts. Faith and spirituality of course, are not the focus. At issue are the means by which the "mental architecture" of Christianity shapes the behavior and beliefs of those who espouse utterly contemporary, late nineteenth-century social or political views, and act in accordance with their times.[4] At issue, ultimately, is an understanding of the appeal held by all-encompassing ideologies for the Russian mind.

MISAIL AND THE BOOK OF DANIEL

The character positioned closest to Christian texts is the narrator, Misail Poloznev. Chekhov's decision to configure "My Life" as a first-person narrative ("Notes of a Provincial" as the subtitle reads) links the tale to a Russian tradition of self-revelatory texts penned in a religious vein. The genre—a self-documented life of rebellious piety that promotes certain philosophical propositions—recalls Tolstoy's penchant for self-examination and possibly mimics Tolstoy's own brief piece entitled "My Life" and published in 1892. The Russian prototext of this sort is the seventeenth-century autobiographical/hagiographical "Life of the Archpriest Avvakum by Himself." Avvakum was a Zealot of Piety, and there is something of the zealot in Misail as well. Different, of course, are his strivings. Misail stands not on religious principles, but on socioeconomic theory, throwing the gauntlet to capitalism and class divisions by insisting that every individual should earn bread by his own labor. Patterns of perception bred by Orthodoxy, however, seem to fuel these modern, secular views. Chekhov signals an important related text with the hero's name, an appointment that solidly announces the elevated status of names in this story.

The protagonist's patently uncommon name comes from the Old Testament. The story of Nebuchadnezzar and the three pious youths—Hananiah, Azariah, and Mishael (Misail)—is recounted in the Book of Daniel (3:1–27). According to Scripture, the pagan king ordered the Babylonian aristocracy, including the captive Jewish youths, to gather and pay homage to an enormous gold idol. Learning of the unwillingness of the three youths to comply, Nebuchadnezzar had them thrown into a fiery furnace, from which they issued unharmed because of their faith. The tale figures prominently in the Russian religious tradition, in which the popular *Furnace Drama* (*Peshchnoe deistvo*) was acted out annually in folk renditions on the feast of the youth-saints (17 December). The seventeenth-century writer Simeon Polotsky enshrined the play in the early Russian theater repertoire.

At least two lines of inquiry emerge from this biblical passage. The first concerns Misail's rebellious stance toward the illegitimate authority of material wealth, a direct echo of the convictions of his religious forebear. The second relates to the drama theme so prevalent throughout "My Life," and to the notion that the relationship between Misail and Maria Viktorovna plays itself out according to a "script." Each will be considered in turn.

Chekhov touches the Scripture from Daniel in many ways through the name. Misail rails repeatedly against the unearned and ill-begotten wealth and power of the nobility in his town, echoing the central theme of the Book of Daniel, in which the opulent life of luxury led by the Babylonian satraps is repeatedly disparaged as a precarious, corrupt, and godless existence. By his choice to live in a humble manner and to subject himself to financial hardship, Misail can be associated with the Jewish youth of the *Furnace Drama* who expose the emptiness of meaningless affluence. Both the Jewish youth and Misail pit themselves against an intransigent "establishment." A seemingly random detail in one of Misail's longest diatribes against the vacuous town residents ties into this question. Bemoaning the lack of local cultural life, he notes that only "Jewish youth" (*evrei-podrostki*) visit the municipal library (9:205). In other words, "Jewish youth" are set apart as those who, in his view, savor higher values.

Chekhov's most marked pointer to his protagonist's scriptural mentor is Misail's remark that during his first days as a laborer his feet became hot while painting the roofs of houses "just as if I were walking on a scorching stove" (*po raskalennoi plite*) (9:216). The phrase "a scorching oven" (*raskalennaia peshch'*) describes Nebuchadnezzar's furnace in Orthodox literature. The pleasure Misail takes in painting roofs above all else ("I liked nothing better than painting the roof," he says of the sojourn in Dubechnia [9:245]) underscores his abiding fidelity to the feat modeled by the three Jewish youths. This "trial-by-fire" locates his convictions, a Christian ethics cast in terms of a modern theory of social and economic equality, as a "zealotry" unabashedly vested in the cultural past.

The "furnace" motif is reduced to stuff of far less gravity elsewhere. Poloznev Sr. remonstrates that besides "crude physical strength" his son should also honor "God's spirit and the sacred fire" (*sviatoi ogon'*), a fire that "had been acquired over thousands of years by the best people [that is, the nobility]." With this temporal sweep Chekhov symbolically groups Poloznev with the Babylonian elite (sixth century B.C.). Misail's father exclaims, " 'All of the Poloznevs have preserved this sacred fire just so that you can put it out!' " (9:193). That this "sacred fire" has already been reduced to the pettiness of social custom in the universe of Poloznev Sr. is clear from his blueprints, which are always drawn beginning with the hall and living room "just as in the old days young ladies from the institutes could dance only from the stove" (*pechka*) (9:198). A further detail diminishes talk of "sacred fire" in this pedestrian world: watching his father and sister from the street after he has exiled himself from home, Misail notes that they left the room and "the light [*ogon'*, or 'fire'] went out" (9:240). By radically rejecting the values of his father, Misail tries to kindle values such as those associated with the resurrectional fire that preserved the three youths unharmed.

Misail's encounter with the town governor, who asks him to relocate to a town where his noble origins will not besmirch his father's reputation, seems also to hint at the Book of Daniel. Walking to the interview from an early morning visit at the slaughterhouse (the "three sheds" and bloody horror of which remotely echo Christ's trial of convictions), Misail's mental state is that of one "going to fight a bear with a bear-spear [*s rogatinoi*] on someone's orders" (9:234). Similarly, Daniel was sent to the lions' pit to defend his convictions (Daniel 6:1–24). Daniel's prophetic vision, recounted just after the episode in the lions' pit, refers to a bear who utters the cryptic words: "Arise and devour much flesh" (*"esh' miasa mnogo"* means, literally, "eat a lot of meat") (Daniel 7:5). Critics have long identified the governor's query to Misail during their interview—"Are you a vegetarian?"—as part of Chekhov's gloss on Tolstoyism. Might it also be a sign that Misail's confrontation with authorities over his convictions falls in the shadow of these biblical images?

To return to the *Furnace Drama*, performance thematics linger persistently in the background of "My Life" through the motif of theater and role-playing. They find almost literal expression in the amateur theater run by the Azhogin family. The root of the Azhogin surname is *zhëg*, or "burn." Mme Azhogin (and Chekhov repeats this detail a number of times) burns three candles in order to combat superstition, a paltry gesture of absurd (and, we find out later, hypocritical) convictions placed beside the "furnace" story. The theater is regarded in a religious light by the townspeople. Poloznev

Sr. opines that the amateur theatricals are deflecting young people from religion, and Redka, the housepainter who apprentices Misail, regards the stage "with a pious expression" (9:201; 9:264). The site of patently mediocre productions earns Misail's praise as "the cathedral of the muses" (9:264). As with Poloznev's "sacred fire," the local theater as holy shrine must be understood sarcastically. In this theatrical setting Misail initially becomes attracted to Maria Viktorovna, and their final encounter before the dissolution of their marriage also takes place here.

Misail displays an awareness, at least in the hindsight of his narration, of the theatrical nature of his relationship with Maria Viktorovna. On the first evening at the Dolzhikovs, after witnessing her antics and impersonations, he calls her an "excellent comic actress" (9:229). (That evening Blagovo, too, demonstrates some "real acting.") Maria Viktorovna accuses Misail of "not yet having acclimated to your new role" when he refuses to wear his painter's frock to dinner (9:236). When she arrives at Dubechnia dressed as a simple woman, Misail thinks "this was a talented actress playing a small-time bourgeoise (*meshchanochka*)" (9:242). Dolzhikov calls Misail and Maria Viktorovna's union a "comedy" (9:250). In his final despair at Maria Viktorovna's withdrawn affection, Misail recognizes "that my role here in Dubechnia had been played out to the end" (9:261).

These images of superficial, theatrical behavior intimate a discrepancy betwen the sacred paradigm of the *Furnace Drama* and the substance of Misail's relationship with Maria Viktorovna. This would be nothing more than a general observation but for a subtly Chekhovian move: Blagovo returns from Petersburg "a week before Christmas" and soon thereafter brings Misail to Maria Viktorovna's house; thus the first visit between the two roughly correlates with 17 December, or the date when the *Furnace Drama* was performed. As it turns out, the Book of Daniel is linked to Marian texts; indeed, it is probably best known to Orthodoxy through Mary. First, the Mother of God fulfills Daniel's prophetic reading of Nebuchadnezzar's dream (Dan. 2): She is the "Uncut Mountain" who sends the "Rock Uncut by Hand [Christ]" to obliterate pagan empires and found an everlasting kingdom (see Fig. 5). Second, New Testament theology embellishes the *Furnace Drama* with the legend that Christ extinguished the fire in Nebuchadnezzar's furnace with dew, prefiguring his birth from the Most Holy Mary. Liturgical verse hails as miraculous the way that both the youths and the Virgin withstand holy fire (a typical line reads: "The Old Testament youth, surrounded by a flame that doesn't consume, prefigured the locked womb of the Maiden who gave birth supernaturally").[5] If he adheres to a set of social convictions that he himself seems to hold up to the religious feats of his forebear (Misail of the *Furnace Drama*), Misail Poloznev's romance also seems to be prompted by religious texts, as it is characterized by all-out veneration of Maria Viktorovna.

MISAIL, MASHA, AND "MARIOLATRY"

Misail's love affair with Maria Viktorovna represents a detour from his ideological agenda insofar as she, while performing the role of social innovator, never
renounces her bourgeois tastes and views. Their coupling (and her trajectory,
in particular) brings to mind the thousands of American young people who
turned to rural life in the 1970s as a means to critique upper-middle-class
privilege, but whose upbringing came home to roost as they returned to
cities and professional callings. This plane of social characterization is difficult
to miss in Chekhov's story. Less obvious is the plane of religious allusion,
sparingly sketched in, that helps illuminate the very different conclusions
the two reach from their experiment in rusticity. Maria Viktorovna, who has
been mistaken for a woman of "spiritual elegance and beauty" and for a sort
of feminist heroine lucky enough to escape to the symbolic New World,[6]
in fact remains unconsciously beholden to redundant cultural patterns of
thinking that Chekhov seems to relate ironically to Orthodoxy. Thus, she is
placed contiguous to signs of the Mother of God, but mirrors a negative
reflection of the enduring values associated therewith through her transitory
passions and rootlessness. On the other hand, Misail's allegiance to cultural
patterns—on which, as we have seen, he seems almost to consciously model
his convictions—leads him to an adoration of Maria Viktorovna modeled on
Marian veneration. His absolutely realistic assessment of their differences,
however, and his ability to love her differences notwithstanding, means that
he is able to use the religious prototype to find real value for his life.

Maria Viktorovna and Misail become intrigued with one another during
the Christmas holidays in the course of a series of evenings that follow their
initial social visit before Christmas. "On the first day of Christmas we dined
at Maria Viktorovna's, then we went there almost every day throughout the
holidays" (9:231). The Christmas setting is accompanied by a Marian motif in
a number of Chekhov stories (see comments on "A Liberal Fellow," "On the
Road," and "A Woman's Kingdom").[7] In the Christmas tale "The Cobbler and
the Evil Spirit" ("Sapozhnik i nechistaia sila," 1888) the cobbler's wife is named
Maria. Misail and Masha's romance, born at Christmas, does not turn into an
eternal love, but rather ends the next year near Christmas time. The romance
is threaded along with a series of pictorial and iconographic images. Ironically,
actual icons accompany the development of Maria Viktorovna's ephemeral
passion for Misail and the pastoral experiment, while Misail imagines Maria
Viktorovna in profane images that end up holding eternal value for him.

The couple's courtship takes place as Maria Viktorovna watches Misail
work on an iconostasis in the local church, where he is part of a team of
workmen who are plastering the wall in preparation for painting and gilding.
The workmen stand on scaffolding high above the sanctuary in front of the

iconostasis. Maria Viktorovna is taken by Misail's outward appearance, by his dark hands and workman's clothing, by his comradely interactions with the crew. This idealized "iconographic" image of Misail that so pleases her abounds in disjunctive detail: Misail works on the framework around icons, not with the holy images themselves; the laborers at work "stood or sat motionlessly, like statues" (9:226)—a phrase that recalls the ban on statuary in Orthodoxy as a remnant of pagan idolatry. If an icon displays the extraordinary (and spiritual), Maria Viktorovna valorizes Misail's ordinariness (and physical presence). She harbors a dubious "miraculous image" of her future husband in his state of *oproshchenie* (simplification), a fashionable word that Chekhov borrows from Tolstoy's vocabulary.

For his part, Misail's romantic attraction to Maria Viktorovna—or Masha, as she soon becomes known—is accompanied by a series of secular images. When he meets her for the first time, having come to their home to petition Dolzhikov for a job, he immediately notices the bourgeois opulence of the drawing room: "There were expensive carpets, enormous easy chairs, bronzes, paintings, gold and plush frames; in the photographs, which were strewn about the walls, sat very beautiful women with intelligent, splendid faces posing freely" (9:203). These paintings and photographs (like the secular "Marian" images discussed in several of Chekhov's early stories) resonate as something of an iconographic sign. Rapid and colorless photographic reproductions are clearly the opposite in all respects of the sacred images that traditionally adorned the Russian home.[8] They signal Misail's visual infatuation with Maria Viktorovna, at whom he gazes ceaselessly during rehearsals and performances in the Azhogin theater (the "cathedral of the muses"), and of whom he fantasizes in pictorial terms: "My sinful imagination immediately began to draw for me marvelous [*chudnye*], seductive pictures" (9:240). Misail's Mariolatrous projections are colored by the erotic, further distancing her from a Madonna. When they do marry, the wedding takes place "just after St. Thomas' week" (9:243), the celebration of a saint known as a doubter. She comes quickly to doubt their bond, but he remains faithful to the end.

The iconographic motif is articulated by the (implied) appearance of an icon of the Mother of God in "My Life." Maria Viktorovna puts into motion her plan to build a village school in nearby Kurilovka after she and Misail are married and have moved to the Dubechnia estate. She encounters the obstinacy, duplicity, greed and drunkenness of the very peasants she has set out to help and becomes quickly disillusioned. Her enthusiasm turns to passionate hatred as she realizes that her act of "benevolence" has failed to bring about the immediate transformation she had counted on. Her last act as rural philanthropist sees Maria Viktorovna attending the dedication of the new school, where the village peasants bring forth icons and sing the troparion to the feast of the Kazan Mother of God, "O, Zealous Intercessor" (*Zastupnitsa userdnaia*) (9:260). The icon they carry up to Masha (by emphatic implication the Kazan icon) most obviously comments ironically on Maria Viktorovna's "zealous intercession" in the peasants' affairs, an intercession regarded by them with ill-will as interference and imposition.

The citation from the troparion, another of Chekhov's far-reaching details, points to other meanings associated with the 22 October holiday, too. The kontakion to the feast calls the Kazan Virgin "Swift Helper" (*Skoraia Pomoshchnitsa*),[9] a satiric reflection on Maria Viktorovna's wish for a rapid solution to social and economic problems that had plagued the Russian countryside for centuries. The Kazan Mother of God is a miracle-working icon explicitly associated with military victories.[10] Dolzhikova's patronymic, Maria *Viktor*ovna, speaks to a propensity for conquests. (Such, ultimately, is her affair with Misail.) Her martial approach to transforming peasant society, forceful imposition of her plans on an unwilling army of peasants, results in a fiasco of misunderstanding. The school is built, but no social or moral change is effected. The peasants enact their rituals of gratefulness, presenting her with the icon, bread, and salt, but this traditional rite borders on the hypocritical given their thoroughly antagonistic behavior toward their "benefactress" during the construction of the school. Proximity of Masha to an icon of the Mother of God, then, marks the culmination of her false agrarian "miracle."

A broader significance to the image of the icon can be located in a conversation Masha has with Misail just before the dedication ceremony. Reasoning that their efforts in the country have been useless, she lights upon a new project that holds promise of instant success. Interestingly, it involves secular images alone: "Dear, dear art!" (Her wanting talent in regard to art was suggested earlier, when the portraits she drew of Misail and Blagovo both came out the same.) Maria Viktorovna proclaims: "Here other means of combat are needed—strong, bold, swift means! If you really want to be useful, get out of your confined circle of habitual activity and try to act immediately on the masses! Loud, energetic sermonizing is needed above all" (9:259). The underlying proclivity that feeds this new plan resembles her former zeal for miraculously changing the peasantry. And, indeed, the plea for spreading this "gospel" is couched in the religious expressions common to late nineteenth-century political discourse. Chekhov was aware of the attraction of such tropes to the Russian mind and saw the frightening potential for these "new religions" to gain ground precisely because they are so thoroughly anchored in the familiar cultural contours of the past. Masha appears to reject the imperfection of the past ("other means of combat are needed"), but continues figuratively to spin her wheels. She still imagines acting as a "Swift Helper." Ultimately, Maria Viktorovna attaches herself to the secular images of worldly art; at the story's end, she and her father travel to America to visit an exhibition.

She initially renders profane the sacred image, and now views the profane in a sacred mode.

Before Masha leaves Dubechnia forever, a final pictorial image marks the termination of the romance with Misail. It functions as the apotheosis of the iconographic motif. This is an illustration of a dress that Masha admires in a magazine, and that Misail then regards with an almost religious dedication: "Looking with tenderness at the dress, admiring this gray spot only because she liked it, I continued lovingly: —Marvelous [*chudnoe*], charming dress! Beautiful, incredible Masha! My dear Masha! And tears dropped onto the picture" (9:261). Earlier in the story, Maria Viktorovna welcomed Misail into her home wearing a gray dress (9:227–28). Like the black-and-white photographs in the Dolzhikov drawing room, the colorless gray connotes an absence of heightened value. This icon of fashion or "gray spot," a dress devoid of a human body, turns out to be the object of Misail's veneration. He himself endows the picture with meaning, in keeping with the custom of iconographic veneration, just as he infuses his secular social ordeal with Christian dimensions in order to create a life of value.

Maria Viktorovna ultimately accedes to her paternal legacy, the power of which Chekhov underscores by the striking dearth of mothers in the provincial town. (Mothers of the major protagonists have died; even the former Poloznev nurse, Karpovna, is not a biological mother, but has adopted her son. Misail angrily declaims to his father, "Your houses are accursed nests in which mothers and daughters are sentenced to death and children are tormented . . . My poor mother!" [9:279].) The symbolic locus of paternal authority in the story is the secular, printed word. Poloznev Sr. treats newspapers with sanctity, binding them in biannual volumes and forbidding anyone to touch them. In the earlier chapters, Maria Viktorovna is depicted reading newspapers several times. More consequentially, Viktor Dolzhikov, who constantly sends and receives telegrams (the word reduced to expendable signals), binds his daughter to himself through them.[11] He tells Misail that when Maria Viktorovna first "left him" to become an opera singer, "I searched for her for two months and, my good man, on telegrams alone I spent a thousand rubles" (9:250). Telegrams were often used as billets-doux; earlier Dolzhikov and his daughter go out for a troika ride at night together, an activity with distinct romantic overtones. Maria Viktorovna has taken the place of her deceased mother in the home and the relationship between father and daughter appears to foster an erotic attachment.[12]

True to her father's style, Maria Viktorovna sends a letter from Petersburg asking Misail to dissolve their marriage by telegram ("telegraph your willingness to rectify our joint error, to remove this one stone from my wings" [9:271]). Her father is to manage the divorce proceedings. Maria Viktorovna's language continues to echo sacred text. She speaks in her letter of a new fervor for singing, which has become "my mooring [*pristan'*], my cell." In the service to the Kazan icon, the kontakion opens, "Let us float into this quiet and welcoming mooring" (*pristanishche*).[13] Far from anchoring her far-flung passions, Maria Viktorovna is setting off across the ocean for America. This is not exile to a symbolic Dostoevskian America of moral degeneracy, but a Chekhovian escape metaphor. Her destination has little to it of comforting refuge. The song Maria Viktorovna sings in the Azhogin theater just before leaving the provincial town is telling in this respect. Chekhov indicates only the first line of the Polonsky poem, "Why do I love you, O luminious night?" It ends, "Perhaps because peace for me is remote!"

It should be clear that the entire complex of associations with the Marian Kazan icon does not function as censure of Maria Viktorovna for failing to conform to the character-type recommended by the cultural image (tender, compassionate, forgiving). However, a general notion of enduring value can be abstracted from the religious image. As a final sign of disaffiliation from any values that might be "useful" to the social progress of Russia (one of the story's cardinal themes), Chekhov positions Maria Viktorovna by the second pole of the Marian paradigm, the "fallen woman." "May you be happy," writes Maria Viktorovna, "and may God bless you. Forgive me, sinning woman that I am." The allusion is more than a clichéd apology ("sinner that I am") because the image is reinforced through repetition: "I thank God that such a bad woman as am I has no children" (9:272).[14] It is important that these are among her last words in the story, and that they issue from Maria Viktorovna herself, not from Misail. Although rhetorical and delivered in passing, this admission of sinfulness and barrenness, the two principles differentiating the harlot from the virgin, conforms to the dominant paradigm and gives a final touch to the opposition between Maria Viktorovna's life and a life of genuine (although not necessarily spiritual) worth, an opposition established throughout the story.

Maria Viktorovna tells Misail in the letter that she has commissioned a new ring, bearing the inscription in Hebrew, "Everything passes"—a paraphrase from Ecclesiastes. Maria Viktorovna's gusto for new experiences guides her migrating passions, which means that everything does pass in her life. Yet the shape of her convictions is still determined by the language and modes of perception inherited from her culture's past. In this sense, everything does not pass; Maria Viktorovna's patterns of thinking remain unconsciously redundant. The choice of an inscription from the Old Testament itself intimates the unconscious roots of her thinking, while the quotation from King David would seem to confirm Maria Viktorovna's bond with the patriarchs.

The value of a culturally scripted life looks quite different in "My Life" than it does in "The Teacher of Literature," something suggested by Misail's reaction to the ring. Unlike Nikitin, Misail never abandons his attachment to Maria. (Although he is consciously aware of the impossibility, he still hopes that Masha might return by Christmas, as if a rebirth of their love were possible.) Misail takes in stride the deviation from his ethical route that his idolization of Maria Viktorovna entails because of a broader conviction that is expressed in the words that he would have inscribed on a ring, were he to order one: "Nothing passes" (9:279). In contrast to the town patriarchs, who embrace the authority of the ephemeral word (newspapers, telegrams), this motto emblematizes Misail's apprehension of his textual heritage. Earlier he questions why the sixty thousand people in his town read Scripture, pray, and read books and magazines: "What use have they made of all that has been written and said up until now if the psychic darkness and aversion to freedom of one hundred or three hundred years ago still governs them?" (9:269). Misail makes "use" of Scripture, books, and magazines: he extracts the values of a rebellion in the name of articulated convictions from the Book of Daniel and grafts onto that contemporary ideas, constructing a life that has meaning for him (his job as a building contractor is not mere coincidence). He also makes "use" of iconography; he sanctifies what is objectively a profane image of woman through an attitude of belief. His deep affection for Masha—even as he realizes how entirely dissimilar their natures are—produces the value of emotional depth. In other words, as much of a maverick as he is, and as ridiculous a figure as he cuts in the town, Misail makes peace with the deeper cultural currents that influence his life. This, too, is repetition ("nothing passes"), but it is repetition with a degree of consciousness. We must acknowledge our cultural heritage, Chekhov is saying, and while there is no one prescription for coming to terms with it (certainly no one would claim that Misail is a quintessential hero for Chekhov, nor his love for Maria Viktorovna a paragon), the act of acknowledgment is the only thing that can free us to make decisions about how we live.

BLAGOVO

Doctor Blagovo is often identified with Maria Viktorovna because of their similar "escapes" from the provincial town to Europe at the story's end. Blagovo, who married young and has three children, is pursuing his medical career in Saint Petersburg. He frequently visits his native town, where he socializes with Maria Viktorovna and Misail, expounding at length on Social Darwinism, and where he becomes involved with Misail's sister, Kleopatra. The affinities between Blagovo and Maria Viktorovna are many. Early in the story, for instance, Blagovo is serving in the military, something that aligns him with the aggressive military nature of Maria Viktorovna. (Blagovo's name—Vladimir—corresponds, too, with the "Order of Vladimir" that the governor, a former military general, wears around his neck.) Despite their liberal social theorizing, both belong to the "power elite" ready to defend the privileges of the status quo. The elemental unity between the two concerns their patterns of thinking.

Chekhov seems to suggest that Blagovo's philosophy, like that of Maria Viktorovna, rehearses the paradigms of Orthodox thought. The actual ideas that Blagovo propounds, of course, have nothing to do with religion. Blagovo espouses a doctrine of rationalism and positivism akin to the philosophy of Ernest Renan, whose works were banned in Russian translation by the censor for their "extreme materialistic and atheistic views."[15] Blagovo's theories of social well-being, however, although clearly reflecting popular forward-thinking ideas of the day, are expressed in a manner that corresponds to certain Christian tenets. Such undercurrents can be found in many progressive ideologies, especially the social utopias of modern times. Chekhov was one of the first to recognize this.

The central notion preached by Blagovo concerns the "secret X awaiting man in the distant future" (9:221,252). This secular dream duplicates in essence the promise of Christian eschatology. Blagovo's prescription for reaching the X involves the metaphor of a staircase or ladder. He says: "I'm walking up the ladder known as progress, civilization, culture; I walk and walk, not knowing exactly whence I go, but, truly, life is worth living only for the sake of this marvelous [*chudesnaia*] ladder" (9:221). The "ladder" is a familiar trope of positivism. It also, as already noted, recalls the biblical legend of Jacob's heavenly (and miraculous [*chudesnaia*]) ladder, viewed by church exegetes as a prefiguration of Mary. The possibility that Blagovo's secular adaptation of the ladder may figure as a parody of the scriptural ladder could not be put forth without further context, but Chekhov does implicate Blagovo in the Marian scheme. Twice he uses the Virgin's name as a conversational emphatic. "Holy Mother, what air!" utters the doctor as he arrives at Dubechnia (9:212). Later, visiting Misail at Karpovna's, Blagovo announces, "Most Pure Mother, is it ever hot!" (9:219). These exclamations might easily be translated "Good Heavens!" The point is that Chekhov chose these expressions over scores of others. The profane manner in which they are delivered sheds an ironic light on the association between Blagovo and claims on abiding truths.

Significantly, Blagovo's surname is related to the holiday of *Blagoveshchenie*, or the Annunciation. The "Blagaia vest'" (Good News) delivered by Gabriel to the Virgin Mary is echoed in Blagovo's long address to Maria Viktorovna and Misail in which he maintains that knowledge gained through science will guarantee "the happiness of humankind in the future" (9:230). Blagovo's prophecy of humanity's future well-being, like his ladder of uncertain destination, functions as a displacement of the prophecies (and the unshakable ladder) of Christian faith. His pronouncements turn into a parody because he is a dilettante, dabbling in philosophical concepts, whose hypocritical behavior in his personal life discredits him. Blagovo promotes the goals of positivism as if they were solid and worthwhile, yet his convictions amount to an admission of aimlessness. He is a sham bearer of the "Good News."

Blagovo reiterates a litany concerning Russia throughout the story: "Cultural life has not yet begun here" (9:230). While he is referring to elite, intellectual culture, the comment can be read as an inversion of his relationship to religious culture, just as Maria Viktorovna's claim that "everything passes" belies her own mode of thinking. Although himself unaware, Blagovo has assimilated an "advanced" set of ideas in such a way as to render them an empty repetition of patterns of Christian belief. At every turn, Chekhov seems to be saying, the nearly indiscernible guide wires of an Orthodox religious heritage prompt the worldly convictions and behavior of these characters. Thus while Blagovo pontificates on the absence of culture in Russia, Chekhov insists that culture runs deep, even when we fail to notice it.

"KLEOPATRA OF EGYPT"

The original 1896 publication of "My Life" includes several passages later deleted by the author. One of these describes a momentary revery in which Misail pictures himself and his sister Kleopatra on the town's market square: "and then it is as if I am walking with my sister through the market square, and the railroad workers and shopkeepers, taking her for *a loose woman*, whistle contemptuously and throw something at us" (my emphasis).[16] A related remark in the final edition appears at an entirely different point in the narration as a characterization of the railroad workers: "they ate, drank, swore, and escorted each loose woman who passed with a penetrating whistle" (9:206). This rearrangement of text, divulged by the availability of two drafts of the story, provides a splendid example of Chekhov's effort to disperse semantically related material throughout a text. It is as if the first draft drew too obvious a picture. The original version situates the presenting factor of Kleopatra's life unambiguously: she bears a child out of wedlock, and is therefore regarded by society as a woman fallen into sin.

Kleopatra's name establishes this potentiality from the outset. Whether in reference to Roman history, to Plutarch, Virgil, and Horace, to Shakespeare's interpretation of the story, or to Pushkin, the name has but one referent: the archetypal femme fatale and "loose woman," Cleopatra, Queen of Egypt. The allusion is especially conspicuous in the Russian milieu, where the name is a rarity. Needless to say, Kleopatra enacts an awkward parody of the femme fatale. Another reference draws our attention as well. In chapter 17 she appears at the Azhogin theater rehearsal dressed gaudily, causing someone to remark sarcastically, "Cleopatra of Egypt" (*Egipetskaia*) (9:266). To the ear conditioned by Orthodoxy, the modifier "Egyptian" fits the context doubly because of the association with Mary of Egypt (*Egipetskaia*).

Chekhov's Kleopatra bears the mark of the Mary of Egypt figure. Her breakdown on the stage during her first theater rehearsal, where she sinks to her knees and begins to sob, is a public confession, a sacrament displaced to, and misplaced in, the fraudulent "cathedral of the muses." This scene echoes in reverse a scene in Saint Mary of Egypt's *Vita*. There the repentant woman falls to her knees before an icon of the Virgin among crowds entering the Jerusalem cathedral, acknowledges her wrongdoing, and vows to serve the Lord. Whereas Mary of Egypt ascends from the depths of sin to sainthood, the results in Kleopatra's case are quite the opposite. The ensuing revelation that she is pregnant and the general horror at the shame and scandal Kleopatra has caused clearly establish her as a fallen woman in society's eyes.

The father of Kleopatra's child is Blagovo, a surname, as noted, that evokes the Annunciation to the Virgin that she is with child (as will be Kleopatra, thanks to Blagovo's attentions). As in the case of Maria Viktorovna, Kleopatra refracts characteristics of both the Mother of God and the "sinful woman." Unlike her sister-in-law, who remains under the roof of the "mental architecture" derived from the Christian paradigm, Kleopatra comes to ignore the two roles, replacing them with an artless acceptance of what life puts before her. Although unanalytical and unconscious, this response does mean that Kleopatra is able to live by her own reckonings.

Kleopatra, like Maria Viktorovna, bridges the void left by her deceased mother in her father's life. She fills the capacity of housekeeper and female companion to her hypocritical father. Poloznev Sr. allows Kleopatra to walk arm-in-arm with no one but himself. On a symbolic plane, her behavior and gestures bear a sketchy resemblance to the Christian virgin/mother. Kleopatra's name means "glory of the father" (Greek, *kleos* and *pater*), and her filial obedience in the story's early chapters echoes the paramount characteristic of the Virgin, whose subjugation to the Father's will earned her everlasting praise. The quintessence of the Virgin's role is to intercede with the Father on the part of sinners. We first encounter Kleopatra in a slight reversal of this role, interceding with the son on the part of the father, who hopes he will accept a new job.[17] Her gesture toward Misail duplicates the eternal gesture of intercession on the part of Mary toward the adult Christ, familiar from the *Deisus* of all iconostases: she is weeping and extending her hands toward him. Kleopatra, still fully under the influence of her moralistic, bombastic father, performs these acts of supplication in her culturally shaped female role as intercessor and peacemaker. Her pleas come "in the name of our deceased mother" (9:200). Later, Kleopatra petitions him anew: "In the name of our mother I beseech you: Reform yourself!" (9:219).

Before her sexual "fall," the epithets accompanying Kleopatra speak of her tenderness, compassion, and aggrieved expression. For Misail's wedding to Maria Viktorovna, she dresses in white, an allusion to her state of virginal innocence under her father's care.

> During the wedding ceremony, she cried quietly from tenderness and joy. The expression on her face was motherly, infinitely kind . . . and looking at her during our wedding, I understood that for her there was nothing in the world loftier than love, earthly love, and that she dreamt of it secretly and timidly, but constantly and passionately. (9:243)

Orthodox dogma considers the Virgin Mary an exemplar of earthly love in a spiritual sense. Kleopatra's understanding of love is exclusively earthly. She adores a man whose positivistic creed has no room for spiritual value.

The setting for the drama of Kleopatra's passion introduces a further Christian context: it is in the Dubechnia garden by an apple tree that Kleopatra confesses her love. Kleopatra appears in the garden wearing black, the same color as the dress she later wears during the fatal theater rehearsal where her pregnancy is revealed. She paces back and forth, staring at the ground, but starts at the sound of an apple falling from the tree. When Misail approaches, Kleopatra openly admits her great (and forbidden) love for Blagovo. Blagovo then appears in his silk shirt and high boots, and Misail realizes that they had arranged to meet next to the apple tree. Their garb reveals discrepant understandings: she dresses according to an underlying religious apprehension of her position (she has already succumbed to the serpent's temptation), while for Blagovo the situation is purely romantic.

This Edenic theme would seem to be remote from the Marian context, but it is actually a consistent extension thereof. According to Byzantine exegetes, the advent of Mary in the New Testament cancels the sins of the past and Eve is forgiven her transgression. A prominent eulogistic epithet bestowed on the Mother of God is "The New Eve." Kleopatra, a new version of the New Eve, rejects the traditional female role of imitating the virtuous Virgin and interprets the role of disgraced woman in an original way.

Whereas Maria Viktorovna moves from rebellion to reconciliation with her father, Kleopatra moves in the opposite direction. Just before her collapse at the Azhogins she says to Misail: "I despise my past, I feel ashamed of it, and I now look upon our father as my enemy" (9:265). Kleopatra does not feel the shame expected of a female sexual trangressor, but is ashamed instead of her past, when she believed in her father and behaved according to the socially sanctioned prototype of the virginal woman. Nor does Kleopatra conform to expectations born of the other Mary, Saint Mary of Egypt. When she says to Misail, "Did you know? At the Azhogins' I've been assigned a role" (9:266), we can understand it as more than a bit part in amateur theatricals. She has been assigned the role of the fallen woman, but she refuses to consider her behavior unseemly, and far from repenting, remains pleased with her circumstances until the end.

In fact, Kleopatra's last words in the story conflate both poles of the Marian paradigm. She says, "When I lived at home, I had no idea what happiness was, but now I wouldn't change places with a queen" (*s korolevoi*) (9:273). There is no place now in Kleopatra's life for either label, Virgin Mary, Queen of Heaven, or Cleopatra, Queen-Whore of Egypt. Misail's consistent comments that his sister has come to learn about freedom most obviously concern rejection of their father's world; in a symbolic reading, however, Kleopatra's freedom has something to do, as well, with her ability to respond to these models for her life in an original way.

Ironically, at the story's end when Misail comes to his father's house in order to inform him of Kleopatra's impending death, Aksinia, the Poloznev cook, recommends the Mother of God as the solution to the siblings' problems. Her traditional formula nicely caps the Marian context in the story for its complete incongruity with the exigencies of the Poloznev children's lives: "She said . . . that if my sister and I were to bow low to our father and ask him nicely, then maybe he would forgive us; that we should have a church service sung in praise of the Queen of Heaven" (9:276). Aksinia promotes this archetypal queen (with whom Kleopatra would now not trade places) in an innocent defense of the patriarchal order which is all she has known.

The birth of Kleopatra's child creates some final twists in expectations spawned by the Marian mode. First, Chekhov hints that Kleopatra and Misail, whose departure from the Azhogins "looked something like flight" (*begstvo*) (2:268) and who, at Christmastide, are asked to move from Karpovna's because of the shame of Kleopatra's pregnancy, represent an inverted version of the Holy Family (deprived of accommodations in Bethlehem, the Family later embarked on the flight [*begstvo*] to Egypt). Second, if Maria Viktorovna thanks God that such a bad woman as she has no children, Kleopatra gives birth to a child out of wedlock. Her child is a daughter, although she anticipated a son. The fact that she expected a son is important: she is never entirely divorced from the Marian paradigm; it illuminates her life throughout the story. She is not a radical dissenter bent on willfully breaking away from oppressive cultural prototypes, but an individual yielding to life and attempting to exist on her own terms.

Kleopatra possesses none of the admirable qualities associated with a "real" heroine (if such can be said to exist in Chekhov). Like Misail, albeit in different ways, she is a social misfit, and many of her actions and words appear foolish. She believes to the end, for instance, in Blagovo's worthiness. Yet Kleopatra's quiet movements carry with them a certain importance in Chekhovian terms. She lives in the shadow of the popular paradigm of the Virgin and whore, yet manages gradually and clumsily to shape her own destiny by rebelling against her father and conceiving a naive, passionate affection for an undeserving married man. Unlike Maria Viktorovna, who tries to mold her cultural legacy to new purposes by espousing new dogmas— dogmas unconsciously grounded in terms of the past, but that intend to alter tradition radically and miraculously—Kleopatra takes some unstable steps toward creating something new for herself. Her death at the end of the story demonstrates conclusively that she plays no directive ideological role (such symbolism, in any case, was foreign to Chekhov). Yet she does manage to respond freshly to the models of religious culture.

Chekhov was to write "Peasants" immediately following the publication of "My Life." The stories were published together by Suvorin in a separate volume that underwent seven printings from 1897 to 1898. Oddly enough, given this pairing, it is really the two of these works in tandem that best manifest Chekhov's understanding of the power of religious paradigms in popular life and, in particular, most fully illustrate the range and richness of Chekhov's interest in the ramifications of a culture captivated by Marian images.

If in "Peasants" Chekhov paints a bleak picture of Russian village life, its companion-piece may offer an even more frightening picture of Russia precisely because it portrays a milieu that should have the sophistication to better recognize or acknowledge the cultural wellsprings from which its patterns of cognition derive. Instead, the "forward-thinking" elite fails to disengage from tautological modes of discourse and forms of thinking that the individual repeats, like Blagovo on his ladder, "not knowing exactly whence I go," but believing that "truly, life is worth living only for the sake of this marvelous ladder." As long as such cognitive patterns remain in force, Chekhov suggests, there is little hope that the basic structures of Russian culture might ever yield greater freedom for independent individuals. The alternative offered by Misail, who discovers value in assimilating cultural patterns to create personal satisfaction, provides one example of a creative response to the problem. It is not held up as a prescription for others. That would mean positing yet another ideological framework.

In his quest to urge an introspective, civic culture upon Russia, in which responsibility for self might be a cornerstone, Chekhov ran up against a culture of orthodoxies that, I have argued, he understands as deriving from Orthodoxy. His "Marian" stories of the 1890s suggest that there is more than one solution to this enormous dilemma, and that the process must begin with an individual's challenging the premises upon which the culture operates. This is Masha in "Peasant Women" arguing for her right to love whom she will; this is Nikitin in "The Teacher of Literature" overcoming his delusions about Maria Shelestova; and this is Misail in "My Life," coping uniquely with inherited cultural material. As tragic as the fates of some are, and as unstable the autonomy of others, these forms of individual self-determination represent a freedom, in Chekhov's book, far less sensational, far more amorphous, and, ultimately, far more momentous than the freedom blithely tendered by Orthodox/orthodox blueprints.

Final Remarks

—Oh, Mother Intercessor!
—These Bolsheviks will do us in!
—A. Blok, "The Twelve" (1918)

You're being brought to an interrogation—you
pray to the Mother of God. . . . Later I was often
at pains to figure out: Why the Mother of God?
Not God, and not even Christ, but the Heavenly
Mother?
—A. Terts, *Good Night* (1984)

"What shall I do with your tender name, Maria?
What shall I do with your sorrowful heart, Maria?
What shall I do with your lifeless life, Maria?
I love you, and I hate you, Maria."
—L. Kiselev, "Mary Magdalene" (1968)

ANTON CHEKHOV lived to see in the twentieth century.
Plagued by declining health, he published only four stories in the final five
years before his death in 1904. In Chekhov's penultimate story, "The Bishop"
("Arkhierei," 1902), a final note sounds on the Marian theme. The story is
about an ailing middle-aged bishop who knows that he is about to die and
questions the meaning of his calling. In the course of performing the liturgies
through Passion Week, the bishop comes to realize that he is isolated and
lonely. His mother, Maria Timofeevna, whom he has not seen in years, arrives
on Palm Sunday. "Heavenly Queen, *matushka*!" she exclaims, looking him
over during their first interview. Dazzled by her son's rank, she avoids his
company, but simply and gaily chats with the deacon outside his door. The
lofty bishop craves his mother's affection. As he lies on his deathbed on Easter
Day, mentally disencumbering himself of his diocese and fantasizing life as
an ordinary man, his mother Maria comes to him, but when her love for him
finally pours forth, it is over an unconscious body. This pietà configuration
moves as close to the Paschal "plot" as Chekhov comes: here is Mary, the
aggrieved mother, on the day of Christ's Resurrection, weeping and embracing
her dead son. Chekhov does not, of course, stoop to facile synonymy; to the

143

end, the Marian figure appears in a situation shot through with ironies. Not only has living contact between mother and son failed, but the world soon *forgets* the bishop; when out fetching her cow, the bishop's mother says timidly that she had a son who was a bishop, but many of the village women disbelieve her words. With this final twist, it is almost as if Chekhov meant to bring to closure his orchestration of the Marian theme.

Chekhov died in Germany, where he had gone with his wife Olga Knipper, ostensibly for treatment of the tuberculosis that was clearly destined to end his life. At the time of his death Chekhov already enjoyed broad renown as an ingenious innovator in the arena of drama, a reputation that only grew with the passing of the century. His prose, broadly popular in his lifetime and up to the present day, has been subject overall to more conservative evaluations, assessments that duly note his genius but much less often esteem the profound innovations he brought to literature. In particular, the tendency to read Chekhov as a realist whose chief accomplishment was to reflect nineteenth-century Russian life "in a mirror" hampered the discovery of the symbolic dimensions of religious imagery in his work for close to a century. This prospect sat in front of readers who saw Chekhov's holidays, hymns, and Christian idioms as a faithful rendering of Russian life, but who were often unequipped with the knowledge of religious texts and/or an appreciation of the complex nuances in his prose requisite to recognizing the author's fuller agenda. In the cases when Orthodox critics brought their knowledge to bear on Chekhov's prose, they chose to debate the status of the author's own spirituality rather than to follow his clues toward a story's inner life.

In this book I have entered two discussions. The first concerns the nature of Chekhov's poetics. The arguments presented here depend in large part on attention to the cumulative meanings of unobtrusive details. This approach, theorized in the work of Savely Senderovich, rests on the conviction that, as in poetry, few of Chekhov's words are random. The interpretations posited here depend largely on the yield of apparently casual references to the Annunciation and Dormition, to liturgical phrases from Scripture or the acathist to the Mother of God, to iconography, and to legends and poems about the "sinful" Marys. Reading in this manner, the symbolic plane of a story may be accessed best through what appear at first to be its most peculiar lexical traits. For example, two characters named Gabriel in "A Dreadful Night," a horse named Count Nulin in "The Teacher of Literature," and the name Misail in "My Life" turn out to be important textual signals.

The second discussion concerns interpretations of the religious context in Chekhov's works. I have argued that Chekhov "deconstructs" those cultural myths about women that are based on the Christian models of the Virgin Mary and Mary of Egypt / Mary Magdalene. In accordance with Chekhov's keen eye for the subtleties of culture, this is achieved with a delicate touch.

144

He recognizes that the ideals and ideologies that humans embrace, a prime example of which is the Orthodox creed, rarely operate straightforwardly. In the course of his career Chekhov brings endless imagination to bear on the potential functions of the Marian paradigm in human lives, exhibiting the numerous ways that received cultural material can be imprinted on the individual consciousness. These range from the comic "acathist" speech of Maria Petrovna's buffoonish husband in "Tears the World Doesn't See" to Matvei Savvich's violently abusive "harlot" slander that leads to Mashenka's death in "Peasant Women." Each fresh "take" reveals insights into the suppleness of language and the psychology behind our appropriation of inherited cultural material.

Clearly work on the religious idiom in Chekhov does not figure as an exclusive key to understanding his prose. It does, however, throw light on the broader question of how Chekhov views the human search for meaning, or, more precisely, on how he understands the ways that humans construct meaning. For Chekhov in general, as I. N. Sukhikh has eloquently worded it, an ideological or philosophical system "cannot serve as a concrete orientation point in life, an absolute 'norm' upon which each individual can rely in his spiritual quest" because "life turns out to be 'wiser' and more complex than any of these systems of explanation."[1] Chekhov saw the breakdown of an ideological system at the point where interpretation and adaptation of text dislodge the authoritarian word. And because one of the most powerful authoritarian languages that his society knew was that of the church, the study of Russian religious culture proves particularly fruitful. Orthodoxy as a cultural identity meant a great deal to Chekhov; "Ortho/doxy" (correct/belief) had little place in his affections.

The prominence of the Orthodox/orthodox mind-set in Russian culture means that the Marian images were bound to hold a continuing appeal long after Chekhov treated their reception in late nineteenth-century life. What lay ahead of Chekhov in the twentieth century has nothing directly to do, of course, with interpretation of his work. Nonetheless, a gesture toward the future of the Marian theme in Russian letters may be of some interest, for it helps to confirm the novelty of Chekhov's vision. Imagery of the Marian Madonna and harlot in the twentieth century, as in pre-Chekhovian literature, appears in extremely varied forms and fulfills vastly discrepant functions, from the aesthetic to the political. Like most of their forebears, however, most twentieth-century writers tuned their Marian images to the Christian prototypes, even if not promoting the affiliated religious ideals. In other words, *association* in one form or another again predominates. The brief survey that follows charts this trend in the broadest outline, and nothing more.

Imagery of the Mother of God far outweighs allusions to the "sinful" Marys in this century. In his 1929 book, *The Mother of God in Russian*

145

Literature, Boris Kisin catalogues an impressive inventory of early twentieth-century poems by the well-known Bunin, Esenin, Kliuev, and Sologub, and the lesser-known A. Kusikov, I. Novikov, Anna Regatt and L. Stolitsa, poems bearing titles such as "The Flight to Egypt" (Bunin) and "The Mother of God" (Stolitsa) that valorize the Mother of God in her folk incarnations as the keeper of the fields and minister to all human ills.[2] Kisin notes a number of passages in Gorky that relay folk belief in the Mother of God (the same could be done for Remizov), and points in this same vein to Kuprin's story "The Garden of the Most Pure Virgin."

The twentieth-century Virgin is harnessed to political purpose as well. The shielding Mother of God is called on in patriotic verse by Khlebnikov, Bely and Akhmatova when World War I breaks out; during the war the Virgin appears on the cover of *The Russian Pilgrim* (1916) as succor to the Russian troops. In Pilniak's "The Third Capital" the Mother of God is committed to counterrevolutionary agitation.[3] Later in the century, in his lament "Ave Maria" (1969), Aleksandr Galich splices a tale of Soviet interrogation and exile with the image of a drained and heckled Madonna walking through Judea.

During the decades of the Silver Age, the image of the Mother of God also inspired avant-garde artists, who reclaimed features of Marian iconography, something we witness in Natalia Goncharova's *Mother of God* (1905–7), Marc Chagall's *The Holy Family* (1909), Vasnetsov's *Mother of God* (1914), and Petrov-Vodkin's *The Mother of God, Tenderness for Evil Hearts* (1914–15).[4] The thrust toward the religious image in literature and art certainly reflects the era's intellectual interest in folklore and in theology (Viacheslav Ivanov repeatedly deployed the motif of the Mother of God in his poetry).[5] But evocation of the Virgin seems also to have offered a comforting cultural handhold in turbulent political times.

The Virgin visits the lyrics of Blok, Akhmatova, and Tsvetaeva in more complex literary capacities. Blok considered writing a thesis on "The Miracle-Working Icons of the Mother of God."[6] Although the Orthodox image contributed to his idea of the Beautiful Lady, it is the Western Mary of Italian church frescoes whom he reveres in poems from the cycle *Italian Verses.* Gerald Pirog argues that Blok turns to the image of the Virgin in an attempt to bridge the gap between the act of artistic creation in modernity and the act of creating in the Renaissance, when the artist experienced "a way of living in the world that made the sacred and profane inseparable."[7] When Blok died in 1921, his burial (on 28 July) was commemorated by Anna Akhmatova in the requiem poem "Today is the Nameday of the Smolensk Virgin":

> We brought to the Smolensk Intercessor,
> To the Most Holy Mother of God,
> In our arms in a silver coffin

> Our sun, extinguished in torment,—
> Aleksandr, the pure swan.

Decades later the Virgin and Magdalene at the Crucifixion appear in Akhmatova's *Requiem*. As Susan Amert has suggested in relationship to Akhmatova's evocation of the "veil/shroud" (*pokrov*) in the poem, the Virgin's image here, too, assumes metapoetic meaning: "*Requiem* commemorates the 'velikie skorbi'/'great sorrows' of the Russian land, but it is the poet who plays the role of intercessor for Russia by fashioning a metaphorical burial shroud for it, a shroud that will preserve and sanctify, ensuring Russia's future resurrection."[8] Tsvetaeva favors a different Marian feast day, proclaiming in one poem: "The Annunciation is my favorite holiday!" ("On Annunciation Day," 1916). In regard to another Tsvetaeva poem, "Annunciation Eve," Sibelan Forrester suggests that "the Immaculate Conception has been an image of great power for women writers, linking as it does womb and word; in Tsvetaeva's poetry it proves to be a crucial metaphor for the poetic process."[9] Evocations of the Mother of God in the poetry of Blok, Akhmatova, and Tsvetaeva, then, while tethered to a host of received meanings, represent highly sophisticated metapoetic functions.

The twentieth century, divorced from direct exposure to Orthodox teachings, seems to have virtually forgotten Mary of Egypt. (An exception is Aleksei Remizov, who published his stylized folk narrative "Mary of Egypt" in 1910.) Mary Magdalene, on the other hand, remained popular. If in *Requiem* Akhmatova depicts Magdalene as the Orthodox myrrophore, the Western church's sinful/repentant Magdalene captures the interest of others. Tsvetaeva's triptych "Magdalene" (1923) is built on the tale from Luke's Gospel account of the sinful woman washing Christ's feet in oil and drying them with her long, loose hair. This is also a central image of Pasternak's poem "Magdalene," the fictional composition of his novel's protagonist, Yurii Zhivago. Some of Pasternak's most cherished ideas in *Doctor Zhivago* (1957) are expressed in relationship to the full Marian paradigm: the power of nature, birthing, and poetic inspiration are linked to a series of images of the Mother of God conveyed by holidays, iconography, and Marian prayers; the Magdalene poem refers back both to the Lara/Komarovsky liaison and to three passages in the novel in which Magdalene's presence at the entombment and Resurrection figure as a confirmation of life in the face of death—and, too, reflect on the poetic process.[10] Pasternak's revisionist Christianity expands freely on the canonized meanings of the Marian figures. Finally, in poetically clumsy, but culturally telling, verse, Leonid Kiselev's "Mary Magdalene" (see his epigraph to this chapter) bemoans the spiritually destitute Brezhnev years.[11]

In poetry there is little attention to the name Maria, but it enjoys some modest reverberations in the century's prose. Such is the name of

147

Zhivago's mother, Maria Nikolaevna, who is affiliated with the Mother of God, and passes the name on to Zhivago's first daughter. Two heroines with related names, Margarita in Bulgakov's *The Master and Margarita* and Matryona in Solzhenitsyn's "Matryona's Home," possess qualities that have led to association with the prototypical compassionate mother.[12] A most interesting Marian move, however, belongs to Nabokov. His first novel, *Mashenka* (1926, translated as *Mary*), seems to play with two very different possible outcomes for the novel's highly anticipated event, a meeting between Mashenka and the protagonist Ganin, who imagines that he will be seeing his first love again after many years. She could resemble the icon-like "feminine image" of Mashenka that he retains from his childhood—or the meeting could be a trick. As Dostoevsky does in "Polzunkov," Nabokov introduces the date of 1 April (Mary of Egypt's feast *and* April Fools' Day). A calendar leaf bearing the date marks the room in the Berlin boardinghouse where Mashenka's husband Alfyorov resides. This ambivalent sign suggests that Ganin's final decision to flee from the imminent meeting with Mashenka is not, as some critics have seen it, a decision to cut his ties with Mother (Maria) Russia.[13] Rather, it suggests a trick of memory (a cardinal theme in early Nabokov): Mashenka's arrival cannot but herald a woman fallen from memory's grace. In fact, it is possible that she is not even the woman Ganin thinks she is. The ending refuses to commit to any certainties, and in this, as in the dissociative spirit of the Marian cue, the novel breathes a Chekhovian sensibility.

If Nabokov writes from "outside" the Russian Christian tradition, most of these twentieth-century writers stand "inside" to the extent that they draw on its images as part of a normative cultural code. Their evocations and metaphors illustrate the heartiness of the set features associated with the Marian figures and testify to the tenacity of cultural habit. Perhaps what is most remarkable is that a nineteenth-century Russian author was able to step outside the paradigm, examine its premises, and explore its effects.

The powerful imprint of Christian thinking on secular life in Russia may in some respects be a unique product of the country's history. Rich medieval traditions, a predominantly peasant population, and the prolonged alliance between church and state created a peculiarly hardy foundation for Christian modes of thinking. The Russian culture that reproduced itself in the twentieth century was, and continues to be, anchored in many ways in this historical legacy. One need not search far to find evidence of social and psychological patterns derived from religious culture throughout twentieth-century Russia, ranging from the political arena to the cultural values reproduced in everyday discourse in the private sphere.[14] Of course, the Orthodox religion itself has resurged in the post-Soviet era, bringing with it renewed demands that cultural orthodoxies be privileged—and bringing, too, a mass of publications and organizations devoted to the Mother of God. In this sense, Chekhov's insights about the psychological force of the patterns of religious culture were also foresight.

A final inversion sees out the Marian theme at the end of Chekhov's life. Katherine T. O'Connor has read the author's death as a sort of scripted text that reverberates back in time through his letters and fiction and forward in time to the return of his remains from Germany to Moscow.[15] In this vein, one more event deserves mention, an event redolent of Chekhovian humor and irony given his sophisticated and shrewd treatment of the Christian Marian figures. Not long after Chekhov's last breath, Olga Knipper sought out a church in the Black Forest resort town of Badenweiler that might resemble an Orthodox Church in order to honor her husband in the Russian tradition. Knipper had Chekhov's body laid out in the small, local Catholic Marienkirche, which was filled with garish Marian statuary and dedicated to Our Lady.

Appendix

I supply here a reference to the Russian titles and year of publication of Chekhov stories related to the Marian theme.

1. Twenty stories are considered individually in relationship to the Marian theme. They are listed chronologically by year of publication; also supplied is their place of principal discussion in this book.

English Title	Russian Title	Date	Chapter
"Sinner from Toledo"	"Greshnik iz Toledo"	1881	2
"The Lady"	"Barynia"	1882	3
"The Grateful One"	"Blagodarnyi"	1883	2
"The Dowry"	"Pridanoe"	1883	2
"The Swedish Match"	"Shvedskaia spichka"	1883	2
"In the Autumn"	"Osen'iu"	1883	2
"The Stationmaster"	"Nachal'nik stantsii"	1883	2
"Maria Ivanovna"	"Mar'ia Ivanovna"	1884	2
"Tears the World Doesn't See"	"Nevidimye miru slezy"	1884	2
"The Uproar"	"Perepolokh"	1886	2
"The Requiem"	"Panikhida"	1886	3
"A Dreadful Night"	"Nedobraia noch'"	1886	2
"During Passion Week"	"Na strastnoi nedele"	1887	2
"An Attack of Nerves"	"Pripadok"	1888	3
"Peasant Women"	"Baby"	1891	4
"A Woman's Kingdom"	"Bab'e tsarstvo"	1894	5
"The Teacher of Literature"	"Uchitel' slovesnosti"	1894	5
"My Life"	"Moia zhizn'"	1896	6
"Peasants"	"Muzhiki"	1897	4
"The Bishop"	"Arkhierei"	1902	Final Remarks

2. Fifteen stories reflect some element, however small, of the Marian motif. They are listed chronologically by year of publication.

English Title	Russian Title	Date	Chapter
"The Correspondent"	"Korrespondent"	1882	2
"Incident with a Classics Scholar"	"Sluchai s klassikom"	1883	2
"A Liberal Fellow"	"Liberal'nyi dushka"	1884	5
"Grief"	"Gore"	1885	2, note 21; 5
"On Holy Night"	"Sviatoiu noch'iu"	1886	1
"Trouble"	"Beda"	1886	2
"On the Road"	"Na puti"	1886	2
"A Meeting"	"Vstrecha"	1887	1 and 6
"The Nameday Party"	"Imeniny"	1888	5, note 17
"The Cobbler and the Devil"	"Sapozhnik i nechistaia sila"	1888	6
"The Duel"	"Duèl'"	1891	3
"Fear"	"Strakh"	1892	5, note 20
"Three Years"	"Tri goda"	1895	2
"In the Ravine"	"V ovrage"	1900	1
"At Christmastide"	"Na sviatkakh"	1900	1

Notes

INTRODUCTION

1. Aleksandr Pavlovich Chekhov, "Iz detskikh let A. P. Chekhova," in *A. P. Chekhov v vospominaniiakh sovremennikov*, ed. N. I. Gitovich and I. V. Fedorova (Moscow: Gos. izd. khudozhestvennoi literatury, 1960), 39, 63–74; Mikhail Chekhov, *Vokrug Chekhova* (Moscow: Moskovskii rabochii, 1960), 33. The story "Choirboys" (1884) offers a taste of the rehearsal regimen familiar to Pavel Egorovich's sons.

2. The play was written for Suvorin as a private joke. According to John Racin, this gave Chekhov "the freedom to display, in his imagination, at least, the power of the church ritual that so shaped the sensibilities of nineteenth-century Russians." "Chekhov's Use of Church Ritual in 'Tatiana Repina,'" in *Drama and Religion*, ed. James Redmon (Cambridge: Cambridge University Press, 1983), 16.

3. The line belongs to the first antiphon of the Orthodox liturgy of Saint John Chrysostom. Letter to N. A. Khlopov, 13 February 1888 (*Letters*, 2:200).

4. A recent study of the work of William Carlos Williams shows how such a cohesive symbolic system can function (the virgin in his verse stands for imagination and art, the whore for the vulgar world full of wisdom, truth and life). Audrey Rodgers, *Virgin and Whore: The Image of Women in the Poetry of William Carlos Williams* (Jefferson, N.C.: McFarland, 1987).

5. Marina Warner's book on the Catholic Marian cult borrows its title from a medieval verse. *Alone of All Her Sex: The Myth and the Cult of the Virgin Mary* (New York: Vintage Books, 1983); Julia Kristeva, "*Stabat Mater*," in *The Kristeva Reader*, ed. Toril Moi (New York: Columbia University Press, 1986), 163.

6. Savely Senderovich, *Chekhov s glazu na glaz* (Saint Petersburg: Izd. "Dmitrii Bulanin," 1994). See also earlier versions of this study: "Chudo Georgiia o zmie: Istoriia oderzhimosti Chekhova odnim obrazom," *Russian Language Journal* 39 (1985): 135–225; "Anton Chekhov and St. George

the Dragonslayer," in *Anton Chekhov Rediscovered,* ed. Savely Senderovich and Munir Sendich (East Lansing, Mich.: Russian Language Journal, 1987), 167–87.

7. Of course it can, and has, been argued that the language of the Bible per se is not authoritarian. Walter Reed, for instance, reads the Bible from the point of view of Bakhtinian dialogism, demonstrating that it admits a struggle between many competing voices. However, scriptural language has been so effectively harnessed to the aims of authoritarian institutions that it rarely concedes to a plurality of meaning in its cultural manifestations. See Walter Reed, *Dialogues of the Word: The Bible as Literature According to Bakhtin* (New York: Oxford University Press, 1993).

8. M. M. Bakhtin, *The Dialogic Imagination,* trans. Caryl Emerson and Michael Holquist (Austin: University of Texas Press, 1981), 69.

9. Barthes points out that the language of the image embraces not only the utterances it emits, but also the totality of utterances it receives. *Image-Music-Text* (New York: Hill and Wang, 1977), 46–47.

10. Letters to I. L. Leontev (Shcheglov), 9 March 1892, and to A. S. Suvorin, 7 May 1889 (*Letters* 5:20, 3:1).

11. Predictably, claims of Chekhov's atheistic leanings were common coinage in the Soviet era. E. I. Morozov writes: "Chekhov thought that [religion] maims people spiritually and morally, places heavy shackles on their reason and emotions, paralyzing their will." "Kritika A. P. Chekhovym religioznoi morali," in *Sbornik statei i materialov,* ed. L. P. Gromov (Rostov: Rostovskoe knizhnoe izd., 1969), 13.

12. See Katherine Tiernan O'Connor, "Chekhov on Chekhov: His Epistolary Self-Criticism," in *New Studies in Russian Language and Literature,* ed. A. L. Crone and C. V. Chvany (Columbus, Ohio: Slavica, 1986), 239–45. Chekhov's letters occupy a place not far from the fiction as literary documents. See Marena Senderovich's "Chekhov's Name Drama," in *Reading Chekhov's Text,* ed. R. L. Jackson (Evanston: Northwestern University Press, 1993), 31–48.

13. The theologian Sergei Bulgakov reads the words of Likharev in "On the Road" and Masha in *Three Sisters* concerning the search for faith as moral edicts issuing "from Chekhov's own lips." "Chekhov kak myslitel'," Parts 1 and 2. *Novyi put'* 10:32–54 (1904); 11:138–52 (1904). See also M. Stepanov, "Religiia A. P. Chekhova," in *Religiia russkikh pisatelei* 1 (1913): 3–58. Boris Zaitsev, who ascribes an unconscious religious faith to Chekhov, sees Lipa ("In the Ravine") as an incarnation of "the Virgin-Mother." *Chekhov: Literaturnaia biografiia* (New York: Izd. imeni Chekhova, 1945), 200.

14. A. Izmailov, *Chekhov: Biograficheskii nabrosok* (Moscow, 1916), 555.

15. D. S. Merezhkovskii, *Chekhov i Gor'kii* (Saint Petersburg: 1906,

reprint, Letchworth Herts: Prideaux, 1975), 49. Later in the century M. Kurdiumov joins Merezhkovsky in condemning Chekhov for his lack of religious convictions. *Serdtse smiatennoe* (Paris, 1934).

16. Simon Karlinsky, *Anton Chekhov's Life and Thought* (Berkeley and Los Angeles: University of California Press, 1975), 14.

17. Letter to A. S. Suvorin, 18 November 1891 (*Letters*, 4:296). The comment comes in the course of a polemical exchange about Vladimir Solovyov, whom Suvorin castigated in his paper *Novoe vremia* for "daring to call himself Orthodox."

18. A. S. Sobennikov considers Chekhov's philosophical outlook on religion to be of greater significance. "A. P. Chekhov i D. S. Merezhkovskii: K probleme religioznogo simvola," in *Chekhovskie chteniia v Ialte* (Moscow: Gosudarstvennaia ordena Lenina biblioteka SSSR imeni Lenina, 1990), 88. See also Sobennikov, "Bibleiskii obraz v proze A. P. Chekhova," in *O poètike A. P. Chekhova*, ed. A. S. Sobennikov (Irkutsk: Izd. Irkutskogo universiteta, 1993), 23–38; " 'Pravda' i 'spravedlivost' " v aksiologii Chekhova," in *Chekhoviana: Melikhovskie trudy i dni,* ed. V. Ia. Lakshin et al. (Moscow: "Nauka," 1995), 27–34.

19. R. L. Jackson, "Perspectives on Chekhov," in *Chekhov: A Collection of Critical Essays*, ed. R. L. Jackson (Englewood Cliffs, N.J.: Prentice-Hall, 1967), 11.

20. See Robert Louis Jackson, "Dostoevsky in Chekhov's Garden of Eden: 'Because of Little Apples,' " in *Dialogues with Dostoevsky: The Overwhelming Questions* (Stanford: Stanford University Press, 1993), 83–103; "Chekhov's 'A Woman's Kingdom': A Drama of Character and Fate," *Russian Language Journal* 39 (1985): 1–11; " 'If I Forget Thee, O Jerusalem': An Essay on Chekhov's *Rothschild's Fiddle*," in *Anton Chekhov Rediscovered*, 35–49; "Chekhov's 'The Student,' " in *Reading Chekhov's Text*, 127–33; "Kontsovka rasskaza 'Toska': Ironiia ili pafos?" *Russian Literature* 40, no. 3 (1996): 355–61.

21. S. Senderovich, *Chekhov s glazu na glaz*, 85–138.

22. Savely Senderovich, "Anton Chekhov and St. George the Dragon-slayer," in *Anton Chekhov Rediscovered*, 184.

23. Although there is an overlap between the Georgian and Marian contexts (see Chapter 2), the complex of meaning associated with the Marian figures functions differently in Chekhov's prose from the components of the Saint George legend. In particular, the legend of the dragonslayer is plot-centered. It involves two or three "actors" with distinct attributes and roles. The Mother of God, although "activated" through apocryphal tales, is essentially a static iconographic figure toward whom gestures are made. Saint Mary of Egypt, also a lone figure to whom only one distinctive attribute belongs (harlotry), stands for a single virtue: repentance. Thus narrative motifs

tend to be curtailed in favor of gestures or descriptive qualities when the Marian motif is operative.

24. R. L. Jackson, introduction to *Reading Chekhov's Text,* 2–3; S. Senderovich, "Toward Chekhov's Deeper Reaches," in *Anton Chekhov Rediscovered,* 2–4. Earlier critics, too, discuss poetic aspects of Chekhov's prose.

25. Savely Senderovich, "A Fragment of Semiotic Theory of Poetic Prose (The Chekhovian Type)," *Essays in Poetics* 14, no. 2 (1989): 43–64.

26. Marena Senderovich, "Chekhov's Existential Trilogy," in *Anton Chekhov Rediscovered,* 77–91. See also "The Implicit Semantic Unities in Chekhov's Work of 1886–1889" (Ph.D. diss., New York University, 1981).

27. Laurence Senelick, "Offenbach and Chekhov; or, La Belle Elena," in *Reading Chekhov's Text,* 201–13; Michael Finke, "The Hero's Descent to the Underworld in Chekhov," *Russian Review* 53 (1994): 67–80; Caryl Emerson, "Chekhov and the Annas," in *Life and Text: Essays in Honour of Geir Kjetsaa on the Occasion of His 60th Birthday,* ed. Erik Egeberg, Audun J. Mørch, and Ole Michael Selberg (Oslo: Universitetet i Oslo, 1997).

28. For example, because of the designation Saint Mary *of Egypt,* the adjective "Egyptian" carries special weight in two stories where a "Maria" is depicted adjacent to the "sinful woman" theme. Isolated from this context, the component parts remain unconnected: Chekhov names a man "Mr. Egyptian" for its comic effect in "Surgery" (1884); the "fallen woman" serves as a trope for the doctor's view of nature in "The Enemies" (1887).

29. These studies bring to light much valuable material indisputably coded to Orthodox sources. See George Pahomov, "Chekhov's 'The Grasshopper': A Secular Saint's Life," *Slavic and East European Journal* 37, no. 1 (1993): 33–45; and "Religious Motifs in Chekhov's 'Muzhiki,'" *Zapiski russkoi akademicheskoi gruppy v SSHA* 25 (1992–93): 111–19; Willa Chamberlain Axelrod, "Passage from Great Saturday to Easter Day in 'Holy Night,'" in *Reading Chekhov's Text,* 96–102; "The Biblical and Theological Context of Moral Reform in 'The Duel,'" *Russian Literature* 35, no. 2 (1994): 129–52; Alexandar Mihailovic, "Eschatology and Entombment in 'Ionych,'" in *Reading Chekhov's Text,* 103–14; Maxim Shrayer, "Christmas and Paschal Motifs in 'V rozhdestvenskuiu noch',"" *Russian Literature* 35, no. 2 (1994): 243–59.

30. Roman Jakobson, *Puškin and His Sculptural Myth* (The Hague: Mouton, 1975), 40.

31. Savely Senderovich, *Chekhov s glazu na glaz,* 137.

32. See Mironov, "Razlichnye fazisy v razvitii zhenshchin v proizvedeniiakh Chekhova," and Cheshikhin, "Kabotinki i vliublennye zhenschiny u Chekhova," in *Anton Pavlovich Chekhov. Ego zhizn' i sochineniia,* ed. D. Pokrovskii (Moscow, 1907), 409–20; 423–29.

33. Sophie Laffitte, *Tchekov* (Paris: Librairie Hachette, 1963), 198.

34. Virginia Llewellyn Smith, *Anton Chekhov and the Lady with the Dog* (London: Oxford University Press, 1973). Several other studies essen-

tially concur with Smith's condemnatory view of Chekhov's depictions of women. See Toby Clyman, "Čexov's Victimized Women," *Russian Language Journal* 28, no. 100 (1974): 26–31; Elena Nevzgliadova, "S zhenshchin u nego inoi spros," *Avrora* 1 (1985): 127–30; O. A. Petrova, "Problemy zhenskoi èmansipatsii v khudozhestvennoi traktovke Chekhova," in *Tvorchestvo A. P. Chekhova* (Rostov-na-Donu: RGPI, 1986), 3–13; Tatyana Mamonova, *Russian Women's Studies: Essays on Sexism in Soviet Culture* (New York: Pergamon, 1989), 46–54.

35. Beverly Hahn in *Chekhov: A Study of the Major Stories and Plays* (Cambridge: Cambridge University Press, 1977); Carolina De Maegd-Soëp, *Chekhov and Women: Women in the Life and Work of Chekhov* (Columbus, Ohio: Slavica, 1987).

36. Barbara Heldt, *Terrible Perfection: Women and Russian Literature* (Bloomington: Indiana University Press, 1987), 49.

37. For works treating the question of Chekhov's sexuality, see C. De Maegd-Soëp, *Chekhov and Women,* 82–100; Helena Tolstoy, "From Susanna to Sarra: Chekhov in 1886–1887," *Slavic Review* 50, no. 3 (1991): 590–600; Michael Finke, " 'At Sea': A Psychoanalytic Approach to Chekhov's First Signed Work," in *Reading Chekhov's Text,* 49–60; and S. Senderovich, *Chekhov s glazu na glaz,* 114–24.

38. Marena Senderovich, "Chekhov's 'Kashtanka': Metamorphoses of Memory in the Labyrinth of Time (A Structural-Phenomenological Essay)" and "Chekhov's Existential Trilogy," in *Anton Chekhov Rediscovered,* 63–91.

39. See the volume of proceedings from the Second International Symposium held in Badenweiler, Germany, in 1994: V. B. Kataev, R.-D. Kluge, and R. Nohejl, eds., *Anton P. Chechov: Philosophische und religioese Dimensionen im Leben und im Werk* (Munich: Otto Sagner, 1997). For representative publications, see preceding notes 6, 18, 20, and 29.

CHAPTER 1

1. Michael Carroll, *The Cult of the Virgin Mary: Psychological Origins* (Princeton: Princeton University Press, 1986), 20.

2. For some recent studies of Mary's status in the Western tradition, see Marina Warner, *Alone of All Her Sex: The Myth and the Cult of the Virgin Mary* (New York: Vintage Books, 1983); Nicholas Perry and Loreto Echeverría, *Under the Heel of Mary* (New York: Routledge, 1988); Sandra L. Zimdars-Swartz, *Encountering Mary* (Princeton: Princeton University Press, 1991); Jaroslav Pelikan, *Mary Through the Centuries: Her Place in the History of Culture* (New Haven: Yale University Press, 1996).

3. Carroll, *Cult of the Virgin Mary,* 19.

4. Sergei N. Bulgakov, *Kupina neopalimaia* (Paris, 1927).

5. D. Samarin, "Bogoroditsa v russkom pravoslavii" (*Russkaia mysl'*,

1918); N. Berdiaev, "Dusha Rossii" (1915), cited in Boris Kisin, *Bogoroditsa v russkoi literature* (Moscow: Ateist, 1929), 19; P. S. Bulgakov, *L'Orthodoxie* (Paris, 1932), 164–65.

6. D. J. Strottman, "Quelques aperçus historiques sur le culte marial en Russie," *Irénikon* 32 (1959): 195.

7. N. Losskii, *Dostoevskii i ego khristianskoe miroponimanie* (New York: Izd. imeni Chekhova, 1953), 167.

8. See *Molitvy Bozhiei Materi* (San Francisco: Blagoslovenie Bogoroditse-Vladimirskago Zhenskago Monastyria), 6, 9; S. V. Bulgakov, ed. *Nastol'naia kniga dlia sviashchenno-tserkovnosluzhitelei* (Khar'kov, 1900), 317; Ieromonakh Serafim, "Khavalebnoe imia v chest' Bogomateri," *Dushepoleznoe chtenie* 4, no. 2 (June 1885): 225.

9. A. I. Kirpichnikov, *Uspenie Bogoroditsy v legende i iskusstve* (Odessa: 1888), 8.

10. A. N. Veselovskii, "Opyty po istorii khristianskoi legendy," *Zhurnal Ministerstva Narodnago Prosviashcheniia* 184, no. 1 (April 1876): 342; G. Fedotov, *Stikhi dukhovnye* (Moscow: "Progress," 1991), 129.

11. George P. Fedotov, *The Russian Religious Mind* (Belmont, Mass.: Nordland, 1975), 1:40.

12. See *Skazaniia o zemnoi zhizni Presviatoi Bogoroditsy* (Moscow, 1904) and *The Life of the Virgin Mary, the Theotokos* (Buena Vista, Colo.: Holy Apostles Convent, 1989).

13. *Izbrannyia slova sviatykh ottsev v chest' i slavu Presviatoi Bogoroditsy* (Moscow, 1896).

14. Z. M. Korotkova, *Bogorodichnye prazdniki* (Moscow: Izd. politicheskoi literatury, 1968), 56; P. Florenskii, *Stolp i utverzhdenie istiny* (Berlin, 1929), 369–70.

15. Natalia Sheffer, *Russkaia pravoslavnaia ikona* (Washington, D.C., 1967), 58.

16. Strottman, "Quelques aperçus," 189; A. F. Nekrylova, ed., *Kruglyi god* (Moscow: "Pravda," 1991), 143.

17. See V. V. Kargalov, *Pokrov* (Moscow: Izd. politicheskoi literatury, 1975).

18. A. P. Kuzicheva and E. M. Sakharova, eds., *Melikhovskii letopisets: Dnevnik Pavla Egorovicha Chekhova* (Moscow: "Nauka," 1995), 79, 87, 197.

19. Letters to A. S. Suvorin, 1 April 1890 and 11 March 1892 (*Letters,* 4:53, 5:22).

20. Fedotov, *Russian Religious Mind,* 1:54.

21. Aleksei Popov, *Pravoslavnye Russkie Akafisty, izdannye s blagosloveniia Sviateishago Sinoda* (Kazan, 1903).

22. T. N. Mikhel'son, who claims that no subsequent acathists "surpassed the original in artistic expression," reviews the literature on the debate about

the origins of this acathist. "Zhivopisnyi tsikl Ferapontova monastyria na temu Akafista," *Trudy Otdela Drevnerusskoi Literatury* 22 (1966): 144–45.

23. Bouyer notes that some parts of the Catholic liturgy are translations of Byzantine troparions. "Le culte de Marie dans la liturgie byzantine," *Maison-Dieu* 38 (1954): 83.

24. Chekhov knew Kondakov from his years in Yalta and they corresponded from 1900 to 1902. Kondakov writes to Chekhov about his continuing projects to preserve icons and protect them from his archenemy, the Holy Synod. N. I. Gitovich, ed., "Pis'ma N. P. Kondakova k A. P. Chekhovu," *Izvestiia Akademii nauk SSSR: Otdelenie literatury i iazyka* 19, no. 1 (1960): 32–40.

25. L. F. Soloshchenko and Iu. S. Prokoshina, eds. *Golubinaia kniga. Russkie narodnye dukhovnye stikhi XI–XIX vekov* (Moscow: Moskovskii rabochii, 1991), 259.

26. For a full explication of the treatment of the Mother of God in medieval texts, see Andreas Ebbinghaus, *Die altrussischen Marienikonen-Legenden* (Berlin: Otto Harrassowitz, 1990).

27. Joanna Hubbs writes, "The transformation of the *Theotokos* into the powerful *Bogoroditsa* appears to have begun with the first stages of Christianization [of Russia]. Hoping to entice converts by prominently displaying the image of Mary and proclaiming her attributes, the missionaries of the new faith found that in time Mary resembled less the subservient divinity of the male Christian religion than the pagan goddess whose worship she had been created to supersede." *Mother Russia: The Feminine Myth in Russian Culture* (Bloomington: Indiana University Press, 1988), 101.

28. Strottman, "Quelques aperçus," 182.

29. A. E. Gruzinskii, ed., *Pesni sobrannyia P. N. Rybnikovym* (Moscow: "Sotrudnik shkol," 1910), 3:47, 64, 66, 98; Aleksandr Mozharovskii, "Svadebnye pesni kazanskoi gubernii," *Etnograficheskoe obozrenie* 1–2 (1907): 87–115; I. Sakharov, *Pesni russkago naroda* (Saint Petersburg, 1838), 1–32, 78–80, 101–36, 149–51.

30. A. V. Khanilo, "Ikony i kresty A. P. Chekhova i ego blizkikh v ialtinskom muzee." Conference paper (paper presented at the Second International Symposium, "A. P. Chekhov—Religious and Philosophical Dimensions in His Life and Work," Badenweiler, Germany, October 1994).

31. Ibid.

32. See A. P. Kuzicheva, *"Vash A. Chekhov"* (Moscow: "Iskona," 1994), 68, 118, 201.

33. Letter to Liza Mizinova, 7 August 1892 (*Letters*, 5:103). Chekhov's correspondence with Liza Mizinova in 1892 also includes something of a flirtatious play on the Marian theme. On 25 March—the feast day of the

Annunciation—he writes Mizinova that Masha invites her to Melikhovo during *Passion* Week (my emphasis), and signs the letter, "Masha's brother."

34. Zoia Maslenikova, *Portret Borisa Pasternaka* (Moscow: Sovetskaia Rossia, 1990), 72–73.

35. See Warner, *Alone of All Her Sex,* 224–35; and esp. Susan Haskins, *Mary Magdalen: Myth and Metaphor* (New York: Harcourt, Brace, 1993), 3–32.

36. Haskins points out that the seven devils may have referred to madness or to other ills. When a man is possessed with devils (Luke 8:26–39), he is never suspected of sexual misconduct. *Mary Magdalen,* 15, 16.

37. Some regard the fossilization of Magdalene the harlot as a very late development. Elaine Pagels finds that the Mary Magdalene of the Gnostic Gospels occupied the powerful position of Christ's favored disciple. *The Gnostic Gospels* (New York: Random House, 1979), 62–67; Larissa Taylor contends that the Mary Magdalene of medieval issue enjoyed a broad range of representations and that only in the sixteenth century was she boxed into the role of sinful woman. "The Three Faces of Magdalene: Changing Images in the Renaissance," unpublished paper.

38. See André Paléologue, "Maria Madeleine dans la tradition byzantine," in *Marie Madeleine dans la mystique, les arts et les lettres* (Paris: Beauchesne, 1989), 163–71.

39. *Polnyi pravoslavnyi bogoslovskii èntsiklopedicheskii slovar'* (London: Variorum Reprints, 1971), 2:1555.

40. For an account of the Western texts and literature on Saint Mary of Egypt, see Benedicta Ward, S.L.G., *Harlots of the Desert* (Kalamazoo, Mich.: Cistercian Publications, 1987), 26–56. Maria Aegyptiaca makes an appearance as one of the holy anchorites at the end of Part 2 of Goethe's *Faust.*

41. Haskins, *Mary Magdalen,* 111.

42. Warner, *Alone of All Her Sex,* 234.

43. Arkhimandrit Panteleimon, ed., *Zhitiia sviatykh na russkom iazyke izlozhennyia po rukovodstvu Chet' ikh-minei sv. Dmitriia Rostovskago* (Moscow, 1902–11), 8:13.

44. Nekrylova, *Kruglyi god,* 147–48.

45. "Pro Mariiu Egipetskuiu," *Golubinaia kniga,* 163–64.

46. The National Library in Saint Petersburg has the most complete holdings of *lubok* reproductions. The collections of V. I. Dal', A. V. Olsufev, and M. P. Pogodin include a number of eighteenth-century *lubok* prints entitled *The Life of Saint Mary of Egypt,* as well as versions from the 1820s and 1830s, from 1860, 1879, 1894, and 1912.

47. Aleksei Makarenko, *Sibirskii narodnyi kalendar'* (Saint Petersburg, 1913), 67.

48. Letters to Maria Kiseleva, 29 March 1886 and 25 March 1888 (*Letters*, 1:220, 2:217).

49. See "Detstvo," in M. Gorky, *Polnoe sobranie sochinenii* (Moscow: "Nauka," 1972), 15:56–57.

50. Haskins, *Mary Magdalen*, 392.

51. Margaret R. Miles, *Image as Insight: Visual Understanding in Western Christianity and Secular Culture* (Boston: Beacon, 1985), 81.

52. The Abalatskaia-Znamenskaia icon belongs to a monastery in the former Tobol diocese. *Skazaniia o zemnoi zhizni*, 273.

53. Changes that ensued in the wake of the seventeenth century schism in the Russian Orthodox Church, one cause of which was the question of names, led to a subsequent lack of differentiation. B. A. Uspenskii, *Iz istorii russkikh kanonicheskikh imen* (Moscow: Izd. Moskovskogo universiteta, 1969), 39–40.

54. Andrzej Dudek, "Poeticheskaia Mariologiia Viacheslava Ivanova," *Studia Litteraria Polono-Slavica* 1 (1993): 41. See also A. Dudek, "Z badań nad rosyjską literaturą religijną. Motyw Matki Boskiej w poezji XIX wieku," in *Z badań nad dawną i nową literaturą rosyjską*, ed. K. Prusa, (Rzeszów, 1991), 105–46.

55. *K. N. Batiushkov: Sochineniia* (Moscow and Leningrad: Academia, 1934), 564.

56. R. Sorenson, "Puškin's *Gavriiliada:* From Style to Meaning," *Russian Language Journal* 35, no. 120 (1981): 59–73.

57. Gerald Pirog, *Blok's* Italianskie stikhi: *Confrontation and Disillusionment* (Columbus, Ohio: Slavica, 1983), 54.

58. Joe Andrews, *Women in Russian Literature, 1780–1863* (London: Macmillan, 1988), 32; Stephanie Sandler, *Distant Pleasures: Alexander Pushkin and the Writing of Exile* (Stanford: Stanford University Press, 1989), 176.

59. See the notes to *Poltava* in A. S. Pushkin, *Polnoe sobranie sochinenii v desiati tomakh* (Leningrad: "Nauka," 1977), 4:422–23, and Yu. M. Lotman, "Posviashchenie 'Poltavy,'" in *Pushkin* (Saint Petersburg: "Iskusstvo-SPB," 1995), 253–65.

60. V. N. Suzi, "Bogorodichnye motivy v peizazhnoi lirike F. Tiutcheva," in *Evangel'skii tekst v russkoi literature XVIII–XX vekov*, ed. V. Zakharov (Petrozavodsk: Izd. Petrozavodskogo universiteta, 1994), 170–78.

61. *Maria* appeared in Shevchenko's collection *Kobzar'*, parts of which Chekhov first read in 1887 and which he reports purchasing in 1894. See *Letters*, 2:105–6, 5:318. For more on the poem, see Kevin Windle, "Shevchenko's Narrative Poem *Maria* in Three Russian Translations: A Comparative Study," *Australian Slavonic and East European Studies* 7, no. 1 (1993): 25–47.

62. See George Siegel, "The Fallen Woman in Nineteenth-Century

Russian Literature," *Harvard Slavic Studies* 5 (1970): 81–107; and Olga Matich, "A Typology of Fallen Women in Nineteenth-Century Russian Literature," in *American Contributions to the Ninth International Congress of Slavists,* ed. P. Debreczeny (Columbus, Ohio: Slavica, 1983), 2:325–43.

63. These poems were brought to my attention by Margaret Ziolkowski, *Hagiography and Modern Russian Literature* (Princeton: Princeton University Press, 1988), 73–78. The texts of the poems appear as follows: Ivan S. Aksakov, *Stikhotvoreniia i poèmy* (Leningrad: Sovetskii pisatel', 1960), 143–50; *Sochineniia B. N. Almazova* (Moscow, 1892), 1:405–28; *Sobranie sochinenii v stikhakh Elisavety Shakhovoi* (Saint Petersburg, 1911), 210–58. Shakhova's poem is not dated; she lived from 1822 to 1899 and wrote actively in the second half of the century.

64. Christian images in *Taras Bulba* have recently been remarked upon by Gavriel Shapiro, *Nikolai Gogol and the Baroque Cultural Heritage* (University Park: Pennsylvania State University Press, 1993), 168–69, 211–12; and by Robert A. Maguire, *Exploring Gogol* (Stanford: Stanford University Press, 1994), 275–80.

65. Simon Karlinsky remarks that the absence of names for the female characters "stands in significant contrast to the full names of dozens of incidental male characters cited in the story." *The Sexual Labyrinth of Nikolai Gogol* (Cambridge: Harvard University Press, 1976), 84.

66. Jane Costlow writes of the "proximity of passion and civilization" in *Fathers and Children,* suggesting that ultimately Turgenev "endorses the deceptions of culture as necessary." This symbolic Marian custody represents an example of how the Kirsanov household has tamed sexuality. *Worlds Within Worlds: The Novels of Ivan Turgenev* (Princeton: Princeton University Press, 1990), 107.

67. Al'bert Opul'skii, *Zhitiia sviatykh v tvorchestve russkikh pisatelei XIX veka* (East Lansing, Mich.: Russian Language Journal, 1986), 172–77.

68. Robert Louis Jackson, *Dostoevsky's Quest for Form: A Study of His Philosophy of Art* (New Haven: Yale University Press, 1966), 48, 57–60.

69. The emblematic differences between Martha and Mary (the active and the contemplative) suggest that Dunya might be considered something of a Martha in her practical, no-nonsense approach to life. She is uncomfortably thrown together with Martha Petrovna, whose own busybody activities parody a Martha-like stance, and whose genuflection to Our Lady after recognizing Dunya's innocence in the matter with her husband is of doubtful sincerity. Raskolnikov mentally remarks to Dunya, "but after all you're not Martha Petrovna."

70. David M. Bethea, *The Shape of Apocalypse in Modern Russian Fiction* (Princeton: Princeton University Press, 1989), 83.

71. Michael C. Finke, *Metapoesis: The Russian Tradition from Pushkin to Chekhov* (Durham: Duke University Press, 1995), 81.

72. Jackson, *Quest for Form,* 59.

73. Susanne Fusso, "Maidens in Childbirth: The Sistine Madonna in Dostoevskii's *Devils,*" *Slavic Review* 54, no. 2 (1995): 271.

74. Nina Pelikan Straus, *Dostoevsky and the Woman Question* (New York: St. Martin's, 1994), 93.

75. Nina Pelikan Straus, *Dostoevsky and the Woman Question,* 153–54.

76. Marie Sémon, *Les femmes dans l'oeuvre de Léon Tolstoï* (Paris: Institut d'études Slaves, 1984), 263–64.

77. Isaiah Berlin, *Russian Thinkers* (New York: Penguin, 1979), 22–24.

78. P. A. Sergeenko, *Tolstoi i ego sovremenniki* (Moscow, 1911), 228.

79. Marina Warner, *Alone of All Her Sex,* 235.

CHAPTER 2

1. See, for instance, A. P. Chudakov, *Poètika Chekhova* (Moscow: "Nauka," 1971), 10–60; Pëtr Bitsilli, "From Chekhonte to Chekhov," in *Twentieth-Century Russian Literary Criticism,* ed. Victor Erlich (New Haven: Yale University Press, 1975), 212–18; I. N. Sukhikh, *Problemy poètiki A. P. Chekhova* (Leningrad: Izd. Leningradskogo universiteta, 1987), 35–67.

2. I comment in one way or another on eighteen stories from 1881 to 1886 in which the name "Maria" resonates symbolically. Full-fledged characters bearing the name appear in seven other very short stories without a Marian context. The name is assigned to unequivocally minor characters in seven more stories from this period.

3. S. G. Bocharov, *Poètika Pushkina* (Moscow, 1974), 84.

4. The phrase "all things Seen and Unseen" appears several times in Chekhov's first published story, "A Letter to a Learned Neighbor" (1881). The "Letter" is a jesting study of how religious and scientific idioms can be "translated" idiosyncratically into a disjointed view of the world.

5. *Blazhennye molebny* (Moscow: "Bogorodichnyi tsentr," 1991), 9.

6. Chekhov's notes are from M. Zabylin's *Russkii narod: Ego obychai, obriady, predaniia, sueveriia i poeziia* (Moscow, 1880).

7. Savely Senderovich, "Chudo Georgiia o zmie: Istoriia oderzhimosti Chekhova odnim obrazom," *Russian Language Journal* 39 (1985): 196–97.

8. Savely Senderovich, *Chekhov s glazu na glaz* (Saint Petersburg: Izd. "Dmitrii Bulanin," 1994), 32–42.

9. The boy seems to ascribe to the unknown lady a Madonna-like pose. He first notes that "The Mother of God and Christ's favorite disciple, *depicted in profile* [on the icon], silently gaze at the unbearable suffering and do not notice my presence," and he later remarks of the lady that "she

was visibly agitated, waited tensely, and *one of her cheeks* glowed feverishly from agitation" (6:142; my emphasis). The boy seems to conflate the two images mentally, and in the process, transports the holy figure into the field of eroticism.

10. An element of the mytheme of Saint George the Dragonslayer appears in "In the Autumn." Savely Senderovich describes the Marian component in the apocryphal version of the Georgian legend: a church is dedicated to the Virgin and Saint George after the warrior has defeated the serpent (*zmei*) and saved/wed the maiden. Here, the peasant-narrator calls Maria Egorovna (Egor is a derivative of Georgii) a "snake" (*zmeia*) for the feigned affection with which she showers Semen Sergeich before their wedding. Thus, the hero marries the "serpent," not the innocent maiden, and she brings about his ruin. Stories in which components of both the Marian and Georgian legends are present in one way or another include "The Green Spit," "The Correspondent," "The Lady," "Late-blooming Flowers," "The Dowry," "The Requiem," "On the Road," "The Nameday Party," "An Attack of Nerves," and "Peasants." See Savely Senderovich, *Chekhov s glazu na glaz*, 89–90 (and analyses of individual stories).

11. In Chekhov's cariacature of marriage, "The Wedding Season," published in 1881, the bride is named Maria Vlasevna (3:449). Senderovich finds a pun in the subtitle of "The Dowry": "The History of (a) Mania" plays on the women's fixation with a dowry and on the name Maria, or Mania. *Chekhov s glazu na glaz*, 160–61.

12. In Chekhov's "Three Years" (1895), Yulia Sergeevna begs the Mother-Intercessor for advice about marrying Laptev (9:23).

13. L. Ouspensky and V. Lossky, *The Meaning of Icons* (Olten, Switzerland: Urs Graf, 1956), 196.

14. D. S. Likhachev, *Poèziia sadov* (Leningrad: "Nauka," 1982), 43.

15. D. E. Kozhanchikov, ed. *Pesni sobrannye P. N. Rybnikovym* (Saint Peterburg, 1867), 4:260.

16. In an 1882 issue of *Moskva* (40:325), a journal in which Chekhov's stories were being published that year, a large double-paged illustration of Flavitsky's painting was reproduced.

17. Virginia Woolf, "The Russian Point of View," in *Collected Essays* (London: Hogarth, 1966), 1:240–41.

18. A folk verse reads, "O, Mother of God, / Swift Helper, / Warmhearted Intercessor! / Intercede, save and protect / This house of the Lord / From burning by fire, / From flooding by water!" Boris Kisin, *Bogoroditsa v russkoi literature* (Ateist, 1929), 7–8.

19. Letter to I. L. Leontev (Scheglov), 9 March 1892 (*Letters*, 5:20).

20. Might Chekhov have been punning later, too, when he depicts Gavrila posing on the way to the fire "as if the fate of Kreshchenskoe depended on him" (5:388)? Note the stated absence of a river in the burning

village of Kreshchenskoe; the central symbol of the Epiphany or Baptism, *Kreschchen'e,* is the river in which Christ is baptized.

21. Contrast between the sacred and the pagan also characterizes the protagonist in the story "Grief" (1885). The alcoholic craftsman, whose own cruel behavior causes the untimely death of his wife Matryona (a name close to "Mary"), calls out as he transports her to the hospital in a snowstorm, "Most Holy Mother, toward what wood demon *(leshii)* am I headed?" (4:233).

22. S. Senderovich, *Chekhov s glazu na glaz,* 73–74.

23. P. N. Tolstoguzov, "Skazka i skazochnost' v tvorchestve A. P. Chekhova 1880-kh godov" (Ph.D. diss., Leningradskii ordena trudovogo krasnogo znameni gosudarstvennyi pedagogicheskii institut imeni A. I. Gertsena, 1988), 96–100.

CHAPTER 3

1. Cathy Popkin calls into question Chekhov's Sakhalin project as a "scientific" ethnographic undertaking in "Chekhov as Ethnographer: Epistemological Crisis on Sakhalin Island," *Slavic Review* 51, no. 1 (1992): 36–51.

2. Gary Saul Morson discusses the "absolute word" in "Tolstoy's Absolute Language," in *Bakhtin: Essays and Dialogues on His Work,* ed. G. S. Morson (Chicago: University of Chicago Press, 1986), 123.

3. Clifford Geertz, "Religion as a Cultural System," in *Interpretation of Cultures* (New York: Basic Books, 1973), 123.

4. Letter to A. S. Suvorin, 30 May 1888 (*Letters* 2:280).

5. M. P. Gromov first identified link between the plots of these two stories (1:588). All of the citations from M. Beloborodov's story "Gremiachevskie luga" are taken from *Moskva,* Parts 1 and 2, 24:179–80 (1882); 25:200–91 (1882).

6. Victor Shklovskii, "A. P. Chekhov," in *Anton Čexov as a Master of Story-Writing,* ed. and trans. Leo Hulanicki and David Savignac (The Hague: Mouton, 1976), 59.

7. Not all critics have managed to distinguish the complexity of Chekhov's early writings from the standardized production of less talented popular writers. M. Smolkin's ill-fated attempt to attribute some Beloborodov stories to Chekhov's pen is thoroughly discredited by N. Gitovich. "Chekhov ili Beloborodov?" *Voprosy literatury* 12 (1959): 143–46.

8. A widespread Russian folk saying quotes a girl's plea: "Holiday-*Pokrov,* cover the earth with snow, and me with a fiancé." V. V. Kargalov, *Pokrov* (Moscow: Izd. politicheskoi literatury, 1975), 31.

9. Thomas Winner identifies "The Lady" as "primarily a traditional treatment of the problem of the conflict between peasant values and those of the decadent aristocracy." *Chekhov and His Prose* (New York: Holt, Rinehart and Winston, 1966), 18; V. L. Smith comments on the power afforded

Strelkova via serfdom to act on her sexual impulses, in *Anton Chekhov and the Lady with the Dog* (London: Oxford University Press, 1973), 32; Donald Rayfield calls the story a "melodrama in which the authorial devices are embarrassingly naive." *Chekhov: The Evolution of His Art* (New York: Harper and Row, 1975), 21–22.

10. Laurence Senelick, "Offenbach and Chekhov; or, La Belle Elena," in *Reading Chekhov's Text*, ed. R. L. Jackson (Evanston: Northwestern University Press, 1993), 201–13. Blatant female desire, in fact, frightened Chekhov, and it may be quite unconsciously that he assigned Strelkova attributes belonging to the Saint George mytheme, the erotic potential of which Savely Senderovich delineates in his discussion of the Christian legend's personal and subjective significance in Chekhov's life; *Chekhov s glazu na glaz* (Saint Petersburg: Izd. "Dmitrii Bulanin," 1994), 114–26. Strelkova's patronymic is *Egor*ovna (based on a derivative of "George"), while her surname is related to "arrow" (*strela*), which recalls the lance used to slay the serpent. The phallic connotations are displaced, in this case, onto a female sexual "warrior."

11. R. L. Jackson illustrates the significance of the fortune-telling theme (and its opposition to Christian values) in the life of Anna Akimovna, another wealthy Chekhovian landlady. "Chekhov's 'A Woman's Fate': A Drama of Character and Fate," *Russian Language Journal* 39 (1985): 1–11.

12. See R. L. Jackson's suggestion that the relationship between the two brothers in "The Lady" reflects the theme of Cain and Abel. "Chekhov's Garden of Eden, or, The Fall of the Russian Adam and Eve: 'Because of Little Apples,'" *Slavica Hierosolymitana* 4 (1979), 75.

13. Michael Finke, "The Hero's Descent to the Underworld in Chekhov," *Russian Review* 53 (1994): 67–80.

14. Much later in Russian letters, Solzhenitsyn would have this hymn sung at the wake of Matryona, his contemporary ideal of Mother Russia, in the story "Matryona's Home."

15. Julia Kristeva, "*Stabat Mater,*" in *The Kristeva Reader*, ed. Toril Moi (New York: Columbia University Press, 1986), 161.

16. Boris Uspensky, *The Semiotics of the Russian Icon* (Lisse: Peter de Ridder, 1976), 9.

17. Lynne Pearce, *Women/Image/Text: Readings in Pre-Raphaelite Art and Literature* (Toronto: University of Toronto Press, 1991), 38.

18. These analyses of Christian imagery in "Peasants" sit uncomfortably because Chekhov's biblical allusions are viewed as an authorial message of religious truth. See George Pahomov, "Religious Motifs in Chekhov's 'Muzhiki,'" *Zapiski russkoi akademicheskoi gruppy v SSHA* 25 (1992–93): 111–19; and Willa Axelrod, "Russian Orthodoxy in the Life and Fiction of A. P. Chekhov" (Ph.D. diss., Yale University, 1991), 203–43.

19. L. M. O'Toole, *Structure, Style and Interpretation in the Russian Short Story* (New Haven: Yale University Press, 1982), 215–16.

20. In contrast, no ambiguity accompanies the eternal value with which the onlookers vest the icon of the Smolensk Mother of God before the battle of Borodino in Tolstoy's *War and Peace,* an illustration of the characteristic differences between Chekhov's and Tolstoy's realism.

21. Moscow and its maternal qualities come to light elsewhere in the story, but always in an ironic light. When his infirmity rouses ill will in the family, Nikolai yearns for a glimpse of Moscow: " 'If only I would dream about her, dear mother!' " Nikolai calls Moscow *matushka,* the title used to address the icon. He valorizes the city that in fact represents for him a lowly service position in a hotel. Olga speaks of Moscow's "forty-times-forty" churches. In Zhukovo there are forty houses (*sorok dvoróv* rhymes with *sorok sorokóv*). The analogy is ironic, but there is a relationship in the symbolic realm: If Moscow is perceived as maternal, Zhukovo—named after General Zhukov— derives from a legacy of paternal, military-spirited authoritarianism.

22. See Savely Senderovich's brief remarks on the motif of silence in the first chapter of "Peasants." "Chekhov and Impressionism: An Attempt at a Systematic Approach to the Problem," in *Chekhov's Art of Writing,* ed. P. Debreczeny and T. Eekman (Columbus, Ohio: Slavica, 1977), 149–50.

23. It is true that Olga's self-identification as "Vladimirskaia" (from Vladimir) replicates the name of a celebrated Marian icon. But it is unwarranted to view her as a stand-in for the Virgin, a "representation of Mary, mother of Christ and all humanity" who ends the story by "showing the peasants the road to Moscow, the way to renewed life." Willa Axelrod, "Russian Orthodoxy," 237, 239–40, 242.

24. O'Toole, *Structure, Style and Interpretation,* 216.

25. Fedotov cites this verse from Bessonov's collection, *Stikhi dukhovnye: Russkaia narodnaia vera po dukhovnym stikham* (Moscow: "Progress," 1991), 133.

26. Chekhov jokingly calls on this image in "Holiday Giving" (1883), where the narrator advises anyone who can't borrow money for holiday expenses to "take his family and run off to Egypt" (3:214).

27. Boris Uspenskii details the enormous popularity of the cult of Saint Nicholas in Russia. *Filologicheskie razyskaniia v oblasti slavianskikh drevnostei* (Moscow: Izd. Moskovskogo universiteta, 1982).

28. G. Fedotov, *Stikhi dukhovnye,* 114.

29. See Senderovich's reading of "The Requiem," in *Chekhov s glazu na glaz,* 177–86.

30. Senderovich, *Chekhov s glazu na glaz,* 184.

31. Maria Fedorovna clearly belongs to the field of Chekhov's inverted Marian images for her insistent appropriation of the mother role. She says to Nadezhda Fedorovna, "for one minute let me be your mother" and "I will be as frank as a mother with you." The latter feels "as if her mother had actually been resurrected and stood before her." Maria Fedorovna's harsh and

egotistical moral verdicts, derived from biblical exhortations against female sin, make her a dubious model of Marian forgiveness.

32. V. B. Kataev recognizes that Vasiliev's ready formula proves insufficient in light of the complex situation. *Proza Chekhova: problemy interpretatsii* (Moscow: Izd. Moskovskogo universiteta, 1979), 78–84.

33. Marena Senderovich, "The Symbolic Structure of Chekhov's Story 'An Attack of Nerves,'" in *Chekhov's Art of Writing,* ed. Paul Debreczeny (Columbus, Ohio: Slavica, 1977), 26.

34. M. L. Semanova reviews this link. "Rasskaz o 'cheloveke garshinskoi zakvaski,'" in *Chekhov i ego vremia,* ed. L. D. Opul'skaia (Moscow: "Nauka," 1977), 62–84.

35. Piskarev in Gogol's "Nevsky Prospekt" colorfully fantasizes his deliverance of, and marriage to, a Petersburg prostitute. Levin's brother Nikolai in *Anna Karenina* lives with a prostitute (named Maria) he has rescued from a brothel. Nekrasov's poem "When from the darkness of erring ways" recounts the rehabilitation of a prostitute. Nikolai Ogarev's third marriage was to a London prostitute, an act meant to demonstrate his liberal convictions.

CHAPTER 4

1. D. Magarschak, *Chekhov* (London: Faber and Faber, 1952), 236.

2. V. V. Rozanov, *Sochineniia* (Moscow: "Sovetskaia Rossia," 1990), 416, 417.

3. M. M. Bakhtin, *The Dialogic Imagination,* trans. Caryl Emerson and Michael Holquist (Austin: University of Texas Press, 1981), 69.

4. Simon Karlinsky, ed., *Anton Chekhov's Life and Thought* (Berkeley and Los Angeles: University of California Press, 1975), 14.

5. Cathy Popkin is the first to challenge the assumption of Mashenka's guilt in print. She discusses questions of judgment (legal, ethical, and otherwise) on the part of the characters, author, and reader. "Paying the Price: The Rhetoric of Reckoning in Chekhov's 'Peasant Women,'" *Russian Literature* 35, no. 2 (1994): 203–22.

6. V. L. Smith, *Anton Chekhov and the Lady with the Dog* (New York: Knopf, 1973), 34.

7. These reactions were recorded after an oral reading of "Peasant Women" in a Russian village. Cited in Jeffrey Brooks, "Readers and Reading at the End of the Tsarist Era," in *Literature and Society in Imperial Russia, 1800–1914,* ed. Wm. Mills Todd III (Stanford: Stanford University Press, 1978), 135.

8. Gorbunov-Posadov to Chertkov, 25 February 1893. Cited in A. P. Chekhov, *Polnoe sobranie sochinenii,* 7:687.

9. Popkin, "Paying the Price," 212.

10. "Zhitie i stradanie sv. Velikomuchenitsy Varvary," *Voskresnoe chtenie* 34 (December 1837): 282. Saint Varvara's full *Vita* can be found in Arkhimandrit Panteleimon, ed., *Zhitiia sviatykh na russkom iazyke po rukovodstvu Chet'ikh-minei sv. Dmitriia Rostovskago* (Moscow, 1902–11), 4:75–96.

11. Popkin, "Paying the Price," 215–16.

12. Rozanov, *Sochineniia,* 417.

13. For instance, the Kapluntsev surname, which Mashenka assumes when she marries Vasia, phonetically recalls a set of Russian icons, the Kaplunov icons of the Mother of God. *Blagodeianiia Bogomateri rodu khristianskomu chrez eia sv. ikony* (Saint Petersburg, 1905), 327–28.

14. V. I. Dal', *Tolkovyi slovar'* (Moscow, 1905), 2:546.

15. *Skazaniia o zemnoi zhizni Presviatoi Bogoroditsy* (Moscow, 1861), 16.

16. At one point Matvei Savvich says that Vasia's yard, where Mashenka's tale took place, now houses a candle factory and a creamery. The candle factory manufactures artificial light; the latter, *masloboinia,* or "butter-beating factory," unites the motif of woman's subservient domestication (symbolized by the cow) with the beating Mashenka received for her attempt at self-assertion.

17. Rozanov, *Sochineniia,* 415, 417.

CHAPTER 5

1. Recent examples of fine readings in this vein include Andrew Durkin, "Allusion and Dialogue in 'The Duel,'" and Michael Finke, "At Sea: A Psychoanalytic Approach to Chekhov's First Signed Work," in *Reading Chekhov's Text,* ed. R. L. Jackson (Evanston: Northwestern University Press, 1993), 49–60, 169–78; Robert Louis Jackson, "Dantesque and Dostoevskian Motifs in Čechov's 'In Exile,'" *Russian Literature* 35, no. 2 (1994): 181–93; Svetlana Evdokimova, "The Curse of Rhetoric and the Delusions of Sincerity: Čechov's Story 'Misfortune,'" *Russian Literature* 35, no. 2 (1994): 153–65; Michael Finke, *Metapoesis: The Russian Tradition from Pushkin to Chekhov* (Durham: Duke University Press, 1995), 134–66; Alexander Lehrman, "Literary Etyma in Čechov's *Višnevyj sad*," *Wiener Slawistischer Almanach* 35 (1995): 41–75.

2. V. V. Maiakovskii, "Dva Chekhova," *Polnoe sobranie sochinenii v dvenadtsati tomakh* (Moscow: "Khudozhestvennaia literatura," 1939–49), 1:335–44.

3. Letter to A. S. Suvorin, 12 November 1889 (*Letters* 3:284).

4. L. N. Tolstoy, *Sobranie sochinenii v dvadtsati dvukh tomakh* (Moscow: "Khudozhestvennaia literatura," 1983), 15:339.

5. Letters to A. S. Suvorin, 14 May 1889, 9 June 1889, and 17 February

1890 (*Letters* 3:215, 3:223, 4:21).

6. Thomas Winner remarks briefly on this link in *Chekhov and His Prose* (New York: Holt, Rinehart and Winston, 1966), 176–77.

7. Boris Gasparov's interpretation adds a suggestive dimension to this subtext. He associates the name Natalia with birth (*natal*), and with Pushkin's Maria in *Poltava,* to conclude that Natalia Petrovna "represents (in the most ironic way) the syncretic image of 'Russia' and 'The Mother of God.'" "The Apocalyptic Theme in Pushkin's 'Count Nulin,'" in *Text and Context: Essays to Honor Nils Äke Nilsson,* ed. P. A. Jensen et al. (Stockholm: Almquist and Wiksell International, 1987), 19.

8. Discourse in the provincial town barely transcends the communicative power of a dog's repetitive utterance. Varya's pronouncements, linguistic sallies against unwitting assailants, are each followed by Mushka's confirmatory growl. Only one litany graces the speech of Shelestov senior, who endlessly repeats, "It's *loutishness!*" (*Eto khamstvo*). Ippolit Ippolitych, Nikitin's fellow teacher at the gymnasium, recapitulates only "that which everyone had already known for a long time" (8:318). The tautology of his name (ironically derived from Hippolytus, tragic hero of Euripides and Racine) is echoed even in death: Ippolit Ippolitych *Ryzh*itskii, with his red beard (*s ryzheiu borodkoi*), dies from an inflammation of the head, (*rozha golovy*).

9. Nikitin is later linked with these latter animals. "To coo" in Russian, *stonat'*, means also to "moan, groan." Dissatisfied with the opinions of others about literature, Nikitin starts pacing the room with a groan (*ston*), reflecting his inability to use language in a rationally persuasive manner. For a different interpretation, see W. W. Rowe, who regards Nikitin's groaning as a sympathetic authorial indication of the trapped status he shares with the caged birds. *Patterns in Russian Literature II: Notes on Classics* (Ann Arbor: Ardis, 1988), 12.

10. Karl Kramer, *The Chameleon and the Dream* (The Hague: Mouton, 1970), 167.

11. Letter to A. S. Suvorin, 11 September 1888 (*Letters,* 2:327).

12. Marena Senderovich, "The Symbolic Structure of Chekhov's Story 'An Attack of Nerves,'" in *Chekhov's Art of Writing,* ed. Paul Debreczeny and Thomas Eekman (Columbus, Ohio: Slavica, 1977), 26.

13. Marena Senderovich, "Chekhov's Existential Trilogy," in *Anton Chekhov Rediscovered,* ed. R. L. Jackson (East Lansing, Mich.: Russian Language Journal, 1987), 82.

14. Senderovich charts these displacements in many of the thirty-two stories he analyzes in *Chekhov s glazu na glaz,* 141–265.

15. Robert Louis Jackson suggests that the polarized domains of the house function symbolically in "A Woman's Kingdom" to reveal the character of Anna Akimovna, who prefers the fate-ruled "pagan" world and dependent

status of the "downstairs" to the challenge of forging a responsible life in the "upstairs" chambers—an opposition played out with reference to the Paschal episode in the Garden of Gethsemane. We might add a note relevant to the Marian theme: "red-haired Masha" recalls Magdalene's mythical red hair, and it is she who tries to waken Anna Akimovna on Christmas morning *three* times, perhaps a further pointer to the irrelevance of Christian values in the mistress's life. R. L. Jackson, "Chekhov's 'A Woman's Kingdom': A Drama of Character and Fate," *Russian Language Journal* 39 (1985): 1–11.

16. Her worst enemy, Spiridonova claims, was hypocritical enough to take up with an old man—the Joseph theme strings through the story—yet to demand that visitors genuflect while she sang the troparion to the Dormition, "In Birth-giving Thou didst preserve Thy virginity" (8:292).

17. In this regard, something of a Marian context can be found in "The Nameday Party" (1888). When Olga Mikhailovna goes into labor, the servant Maria helps open drawers in her bedroom, while another servant sends orders to the priest to open the Heavenly Gates in observance of the belief that opened receptacles will facilitate a safe birth (as modeled by the Virgin). A hint of dissociation with the feminine birth-giving powers of the Virgin comes earlier in the story, incidentally, when Olga Mikhailovna puts on her most hypocritical show as enthusiastic hostess by pretending to protest the departure of one of her unwanted guests, Maria Grigorevna.

18. See Z. S. Papernyi, *Zapisnye knizhki Chekhova* (Moscow: Sovetskii pisatel', 1976), 115–16; L. M. Tsilevich, *Siuzhet chekhovskogo rasskaza* (Riga: "Zvaigzne," 1976), 121–23; A. P Chudakov, *Poètika Chekhova* (Moscow: "Nauka," 1971), 152–53.

19. John Baggley, *Doors of Perception* (Crestwood, N.Y.: St. Vladimir's Seminary Press, 1988), 128; A. S. Lewis, trans., *Apocrypha Syriaca: The Protoevangelium Jacobi and Transitus Mariae* (London: C. J. Clay and Sons, 1902), 5; N. Pokrovskii, *Blagoveshchenie Presv. Bogoroditsy v pamiatnikakh ikonografii* (Saint Petersburg, 1891), 20, 30.

20. Chekhov seems to scramble the idea of Romantic annunciation, too, in the story "Fear" (Strakh) (1892). The story describes a warped love triangle: Dmitry Petrovich loves his wife Maria Sergeevna and is intent on an intimate friendship with the narrator; Maria Sergeevna is in love with the narrator; and the narrator loves neither, but enters a brief liaison with Maria Sergeevna. The large role assigned a ne'er-do-well drunk named Gavrila (Gabriel) and Maria Sergeevna's remark to the narrator—"Raduites'" ("Rejoice"; Gabriel's key utterance in the Bible and the Marian acathist)— tip us off to the "Annunciation" thematics (8:128). In the story, a series of "annunciations" misfire: Dmitry Petrovich confides in detail to the narrator about his wife's indifference toward him; the narrator feels himself in a "blessed state" next to the wretched Gavrila because he is now free to make

advances on Maria Sergeevna (8:137); finally, Maria Sergeevna's profession of "big and serious love" for the narrator is spurned, although he enjoys her sexual favors for a night.

21. This detail was of enough importance to Chekhov that he informed Nemirovich-Danchenko in a letter that the actor assigned the role must have a bass voice. Letter to Vl. I. Nemirovich-Danchenko, 2 November 1903 (*Letters*, 11:294). For an interpretation of this, and other A. K. Tolstoy texts in Chekhov's play, see Alexander Lehrman, "Literary Etyma."

22. D. S. Likhachev, *Poètika drevnerusskoi literatury* (Moscow: "Nauka," 1979), 163.

23. There is a possible echo here, too, of A. K. Tolstoy's sinful woman, who, certain of her sexual conquest, casts a provocative challenge to her interlocutors: "Let your teacher appear, / He will not trouble my eyes!" Manya similarly refuses to be disconcerted by the teacher Nikitin's persistent attention to her eyes.

24. On the back of a note written by Maria Pavlovna Chekhova sometime in the early 1890s, in which she excuses herself from an excursion due to illness, Chekhov penned in a prankish lampoon: "My doctor brother . . . forbids me to go to the Kremlin tomorrow because of a sore throat. . . . I don't know if my brother is right, but I can't bring myself to disobey him. I'm very sorry that Lidia Ustakhievna [Mizinova] and I won't be coming to your dairy today to milk cows. Affectionately Yours, Mashka-the-Rascal" (18:32).

25. *Skazaniia o chudotvornykh ikonakh Bozhiei Materi imenuemoi "Mlekopitatel'nitsa"* (Odessa, 1900).

26. "Kanon na Blagoveshchenie Prechistoi Bogoroditsy v novom perevode na tserkovnoslavianskii iazyk." *Dushepoleznoe chtenie* (March 1883): 287.

27. Robert L. Jackson, "Chekhov's *Seagull:* The Empty Well, the Dry Lake, and the Cold Cave," in *Chekhov: A Collection of Critical Essays*, ed. Robert Louis Jackson (Englewood Cliffs, N.J.: Prentice Hall, 1967), 99–111.

28. Avreliia Groman to A. P. Chekhov, 16 February 1899, Gosudarstvennaia biblioteka imeni Lenina, Otdel rukopisei, Fond 331, 41:33.

29. Cited in A. P. Chekhov, *Polnoe sobranie sochinenii*, 8:512.

CHAPTER 6

1. Elaine Pagels, in an interview by David Remnick about her book *The Origins of Satan. New Yorker* (3 April 1995): 58.

2. Northrop Frye, *The Great Code: The Bible and Literature* (New York: Harcourt Brace Jovanovich, 1982), xviii.

3. On Ecclesiastes in Chekhov see M. Kurdiumov, *Serdtse smiatennoe* (Paris: YMCA, 1934), 38; E. A. Polotskaia, *A. P. Chekhov: Dvizhenie*

khudozhestvennoi mysli (Moscow: Sovetskii pisatel', 1979), 58–62; and N. V. Kapustin, "O bibleiskikh tsitatakh i reministentsiiakh v proze Chekhova," in *Chekhoviana: Chekhov v kul'ture XX veka,* ed. V. Lakshin (Moscow: "Nauka," 1993), 17–26.

4. Chekhov originally planned a different title for the story. He writes to his editor: "I telegraphed you the title of the story: 'My Life.' But it seems to me a repulsive title, especially the word 'my.' Wouldn't 'In the 1890s' be better? For the first time in my life I'm having difficulty with a title" (*Letters,* 6:179).

5. *Skazaniia o zemnoi zhizni Presviatoi Bogoroditsy* (Moscow, 1904), 34.

6. The opinions, respectively, of A. P. Skaftymov, *Stat'i o russkoi literature* (Moscow, 1958), 309, and V. L. Smith, *Anton Chekhov and the Lady with the Dog* (London: Oxford University Press, 1973), 79. Other critics assess Maria Viktorovna more soberly.

7. Maxim Shrayer finds a Marian motif in "On Christmas Night." "Christmas and Paschal Motifs in 'V rozhdestvenskuiu noch','" *Russian Literature* 35, no. 2 (1994): 243–59.

8. Maxim Gorky recounts an anecdote in which Chekhov baits a "modern-thinking" young lawyer, who praises the gramophone, with the words: "I can't stand gramophones. . . . They speak and sing, feeling nothing. Everything comes out as a caricature, dead. . . . And do you like photography?" M. Gor'kii, *Polnoe sobranie sochinenii* (Moscow: "Nauka," 1968), 6:50.

9. *Velikii sbornik* (Jordanville, N.Y.: Sviato-Troitskii Monastyr', 1951), part 2, book 1, 127,129.

10. The autumnal feast of the Kazan Mother of God honors the Russian victory over the Poles in 1612, when the icon is credited with the salvation of the Russian land. Fedotov discusses the general phenomenon of "the military dignity of Mary" in the Russian Middle Ages and the important role of icons therein. *The Russian Religious Mind* (Belmont, Mass.: Nordland, 1975), 1:296–98.

11. A "hidden resemblance" between Dolzhikov and his daughter has been remarked upon by A. P. Kuzicheva in her social/moral interpretation of the story. " 'Udivitel'naia povest' ('Moia zhizn')," in *V tvorcheskoi laboratorii Chekhova,* ed. L. D. Opul'skaia et al. (Moscow: "Nauka," 1974), 272–73.

12. While the epithet is never called upon in the story, we might note that Mary is known as the Bride of God the Father (Tone One of Matinal Lauds to the feast of the Entrance of the Virgin into the Temple). A Lenten acathist states: "The finger of the Father, the Holy Spirit, inscribes the Word on the Virgin book, the womb of Mary." Olga Dunlop, trans., *The Living God* (Crestwood, N.Y.: St. Vladimir's Seminary Press, 1989), 2:248.

13. Mary in the major acathist, too, is a "mooring in the navigation of

life's seas" and "prepares a mooring for souls." The citation is from *Velikii sbornik,* part 2, book 1, 129.

14. Reading backward, one can locate several seeds of the image of the "sinful woman." The courtship and move to Dubechnia take place in late March and early April, a chronology referred to four times, and one that corresponds to the Annunciation (25 March) and Saint Mary of Egypt's feast day (1 April). During their final, dreadful night at Dubechnia, Masha appears for the first time "with her hair let down" (9:262), a cultural sign, by now familiar, of the "fallen woman."

15. Chekhov writes from Vienna in the spring of 1891 that the bookstores are full of Russian books. He cites the translation of Renan, adding, "It's strange that you can read everything and speak about anything you want here" (*Letters,* 4:200, 460). Skaftymov discusses the sources of Blagovo's philosophy, noting that all manner of popular brochures, newspapers, and journals published pieces about Social Darwinism, Spencer's organic theory of society, and the cult of science during the last decades of the nineteenth century. *Stat'i,* 307–8.

16. A. Chekhov, "Moia zhizn'," *Niva: Ezhemesiachnyia literaturnyia prilozheniia* 12 (December 1896): 735.

17. Kleopatra, in fact, fails to fulfill the real function of "intercessor." When he is receiving a beating from their father, Misail notes her brief entrance, but she turns away from the scene "not saying one word in my defense" (9:196). The faithful often hail the Virgin expressly for her defense against injustices.

FINAL REMARKS

1. I. N. Sukhikh, *Problemy poètiki A. P. Chekhova* (Leningrad: Izd. Leningradskogo universiteta, 1987), 157.

2. Boris Kisin, *Bogoroditsa v russkoi literature* (Moscow: "Ateist," 1929), 25–33.

3. Ibid., 35–40.

4. Several of these painters worked repeatedly with the motif. Goncharova's many virgins include *Virgin with Icicles* (1905), *Flight to Egypt* (1908–9), and *In Church* (1909–11). Petrov-Vodkin painted a whole series of secular madonnas.

5. See Andrzej Dudek, "Poeticheskaia mariologiia Viacheslava Ivanova," *Studia Litteraria Polono-Slavica* 1 (1993): 41–51.

6. Avril Pyman, *The Life of Aleksandr Blok* (New York: Oxford University Press, 1979), 1:160.

7. Gerald Pirog, *Aleksandr Blok's* Italianskie stikhi: *Confrontation and*

Disillusionment (Columbus, Ohio: Slavica, 1983), 122.

8. Susan Amert, *In a Shattered Mirror: The Later Poetry of Anna Akhmatova* (Stanford: Stanford University Press, 1992), 53.

9. Sibelan Forrester, "Bells and Cupolas: The Formative Role of the Female Body in Marina Tsvetaeva's Poetry," *Slavic Review* 51, no. 2 (1992): 235. For more on the name "Maria" in Tsvetaeva's poetry, see Sibelan Forrester, "Not Quite in the Name of the Lord: A Biblical Subtext in Marina Cvetaeva's Opus," *Slavic and East European Journal* 40, no. 2 (1996): 278–96.

10. In his explication of the crucial role of the Georgian myth in *Doctor Zhivago*, Savely Senderovich speaks of the need to "reread and rethink" the novel through the cycle of poems at the end. Such an endeavor regarding the Marian imagery has yet to be undertaken. *Georgii Pobedonosets v russkoi kul'ture* (New York: Peter Lang, 1994), 305.

11. "Mariia-Magdalina" appeared in *Ogonek* 45 (November, 1991): 12.

12. Edward Erickson writes of Margarita that "in her efforts to secure the release and rehabilitation of the Master, she parallels the mediatorial aspect of the Virgin Mary." "The Satanic Incarnation: Parody in Bulgakov's *The Master and Margarita*," *Russian Review* 33 (1994), 31; see also R. L. Jackson, " 'Matryona's Home': The Making of a Russian Icon," in *Solzhenitsyn*, ed. K. Feuer (Englewood Cliffs, N.J.: Prentice Hall, 1976), 60–70.

13. See Andrew Field, *Nabokov: His Life in Art* (Boston: Little, Brown, 1967), 128; Leona Toker, *Nabokov: The Mystery of Literary Structures* (Ithaca: Cornell University Press, 1989), 39.

14. Aspects of iconography, iconoclasm, confession, communion, and eschatological and apocalyptic belief have played roles in Soviet-era political life, something most eloquently documented by Richard Stites. See *Revolutionary Dreams: Utopian Vision and Experimental Life in the Russian Revolution* (New York: Oxford University Press, 1989). Nancy Ries considers underlying religio-cultural configurations in Russian verbal expression in her ethnography of discourse genres in contemporary Russian society: *Russian Talk: Culture and Conversation During Perestroika* (Ithaca: Cornell University Press, 1997).

15. Katherine Tiernan O'Connor, "Chekhov's Death: His Textual Past Recaptured," in *Studies in Poetics. Commemorative Volume: Krystyna Pomorska, 1928–1986,* ed. E. S. Pankrotov (Columbus, Ohio: Slavica, 1994), 39–50.

Selected Bibliography

LITERARY CRITICISM

Axelrod, Willa Chamberlain. "The Biblical and Theological Context of Moral Reform in 'The Duel.'" *Russian Literature* 35, no. 2 (1994): 129–52.

———. "Passage from Great Saturday to Easter Day in 'Holy Night.'" In Jackson, ed., *Reading Chekhov's Text,* 96–102.

———. "Russian Orthodoxy in the Life and Fiction of A. P. Chekhov." Ph.D. diss., Yale University, 1991.

Bakhtin, M. M. *The Dialogic Imagination.* Translated by Caryl Emerson and Michael Holquist. Austin: University of Texas Press, 1981.

Barthes, Roland. *Image-Music-Text.* Translated by Stephen Heath. New York: Hill and Wang, 1977.

Bethea, David M. *The Shape of Apocalypse in Modern Russian Fiction.* Princeton: Princeton University Press, 1989.

Bocharov, S. G. *Poètika Pushkina.* Moscow, 1974.

Bulgakov, S. "Chekhov kak myslitel'." Parts 1 and 2. *Novvi put'* 10 (1904): 32–54; 11 (1904): 138–52.

Chudakov, A. P. *Poètika Chekhova.* Moscow: "Nauka," 1971.

Clayton, J. Douglas, ed. *Chekhov Then and Now: The Reception of Chekhov in World Culture.* New York: Peter Lang, 1997.

Clyman, Toby, ed. *A Chekhov Companion.* Westport, Conn.: Greenwood, 1985.

Debreczeny, Paul, ed. *Chekhov's Art of Writing.* Columbus, Ohio: Slavica, 1977.

De Maegd-Soëp, Carolina. *Chekhov and Women: Women in the Life and Work of Chekhov.* Columbus, Ohio: Slavica, 1987.

Dudek, Andrzej. "Poeticheskaia mariologiia Viacheslava Ivanova." *Studia Litteraria Polono-Slavica* 1 (1993): 41–51.

———. "Z badań nad rosyjską literaturą religijną. Motyw Matki Boskiej w poezji XIX wieku." In *Z badań nad dawną i nową literaturą rosyjską,* edited by K. Prusa, 105–46. Rzeszów, 1991.

Finke, Michael. " 'At Sea': A Psychoanalytic Approach to Chekhov's First Signed Work." In Jackson, ed., *Reading Chekhov's Text,* 49–60.

———. "The Hero's Descent to the Underworld in Chekhov." *Russian Review* 53 (1994): 67–80.

———. *Metapoesis: The Russian Tradition from Pushkin to Chekhov.* Durham: Duke University Press, 1995.

Forrester, Sibelan. "Bells and Cupolas: The Formative Role of the Female Body in Marina Tsvetaeva's Poetry." *Slavic Review* 51, no. 2 (1992): 232–46.

———. "Not Quite the Name of the Lord: A Biblical Subtext in Marina Cvetaeva's Opus." *Slavic and East European Journal* 40, no. 2 (1996): 278–96.

Fusso, Susanne. "Maidens in Childbirth: The Sistine Madonna in Dostoevskii's Devils." *Slavic Review* 45, no. 2 (1994): 261–75.

Frye, Northrop. *The Great Code: The Bible and Literature.* New York: Harcourt Brace Jovanovich, 1982.

Hahn, Beverly. *Chekhov: A Study of the Major Stories and Plays.* Cambridge: Cambridge University Press, 1977.

Heldt, Barbara. *Terrible Perfection: Women and Russian Literature.* Bloomington: Indiana University Press, 1987.

Hulanicki, Leo, and David Savignac, eds. and trans. *Anton Čexov as a Master of Story-Writing.* The Hague: Mouton, 1976.

Izmailov, A. *Chekhov: Biograficheskii nabrosok.* Moscow, 1916.

Jackson, Robert Louis. " 'The Betrothed': Chekhov's Last Testament." In Senderovich and Sendich, eds., *Anton Chekhov Rediscovered,* 51–62.

———. "Chekhov's 'A Woman's Kingdom': A Drama of Character and Fate." *Russian Language Journal* 39 (1985): 1–11.

———. "Chekhov's Garden, or, The Fall of the Russian Adam and Eve: 'Because of Little Apples.' " *Slavica Hierosolymitana* 4 (1979): 70–79.

———. "Chekhov's 'The Student.' " In his *Reading Chekhov's Text,* 127–33.

———. "Dantesque and Dostoevskian Motifs in Chekhov's 'In Exile.' " *Russian Literature* 35, no. 2 (1994): 181–93.

———. *Dialogues with Dostoevsky: The Overwhelming Questions.* Stanford: Stanford University Press, 1993.

———. " 'If I Forget Thee, O Jerusalem': An Essay on Chekhov's Rothschild's Fiddle." In Senderovich and Sendich, eds., *Anton Chekhov Rediscovered,* 35–49.

———. "Kontsovka rasskaza 'Toska': Ironiia ili pafos?" *Russian Literature* 40, no. 3 (1996): 355–61.

———, ed. *Chekhov: A Collection of Critical Essays.* Englewood Cliffs, N.J.: Prentice Hall, 1967.

————, ed. *Reading Chekhov's Text*. Evanston: Northwestern University Press, 1993.

Jakobson, Roman. *Puškin and His Sculptural Myth*. The Hague: Mouton, 1975.

Kapustin, N. V. "O bibleiskikh tsitatakh i reministentsiiakh v proze Chekhova." In Lakshin et al., eds., *Chekhoviana: Chekhov v kul'ture XX veka*, 17–26.

Karlinsky, Simon, ed. *Anton Chekhov's Life and Thought*. Berkeley and Los Angeles: University of California Press, 1975.

Kataev, V. B. *Proza Chekhova: problemy interpretatsii*. Moscow: Izd. Moskovskogo universiteta, 1979.

Kataev, V. B., R.-D. Kluge, and R. Nohejl eds. *Anton P. Chechov: Philosophische und religioese Dimensionen im Leben und im Werk*. Munich: Otto Sagner, 1997.

Kramer, Karl D. *The Chameleon and the Dream*. The Hague: Mouton, 1970.

Kurdiumov, M. *Serdtse smiatennoe*. Paris, 1934.

Kuzicheva, A. P. *"Vash A. Chekhov."* Moscow: "Iskona," 1994.

Kuzicheva, A. P., and E. M. Sakharova, eds. *Melikhovskii letopisets: Dnevnik Pavla Egorovicha Chekhova*. Moscow: "Nauka," 1995.

Laffitte, Sophie. *Tchekhov*. Paris: Librairie Hachette, 1963.

Lakshin, V. Ia., et al., eds. *Chekhoviana*. Moscow: "Nauka," 1990.

————. *Chekhoviana: Chekhov v kul'ture XX veka*. Moscow: "Nauka," 1993.

————. *Chekhoviana: Melikhovskie trudy i dni*. Moscow: "Nauka," 1995.

Lehrman, Alexander. "Literary Etyma in Čechov's *Višnevyj sad*." *Wiener Slawistischer Almanach* 35 (1995): 41–75.

Likhachev, D. S. *Poètika drevnerusskoi literatury*. Moscow: "Nauka," 1979.

————. *Poèziia sadov*. Leningrad: "Nauka," 1982.

Linkov, V. Ia. *Skeptitsizm i vera Chekhova*. Moscow: Izd. Moskovskogo universiteta, 1995.

Losskii, N. *Dostoevskii i ego khristianskoe miroponimanie*. New York: Izd. imeni Chekhova, 1953.

Matich, Olga. "A Typology of Fallen Women in Nineteenth-Century Russian Literature." In *American Contributions to the Ninth International Congress of Slavists*, edited by P. Debreczeny, 2:325–43. Columbus, Ohio: Slavica, 1983.

Mel'nikova, V. E., ed. *Chekhovskie chteniia v Ialte*. Moscow: Gos. bib. SSSR imeni V. I. Lenina, 1990.

Merezhkovskii, D. S. *Chekhov i Gor'kii*. 1906. Reprint, Letchworth Herts: Prideaux, 1975.

Mihailovic, Alexandar. "Eschatology and Entombment in 'Ionych.'" In Jackson, ed., *Reading Chekhov's Text*, 103–14.

Moi, Toril, ed. *The Kristeva Reader*. New York: Columbia University Press, 1986.

179

Morson, Gary Saul, ed. *Bakhtin: Essays and Dialogues on His Work.* Chicago: University of Chicago Press, 1986.

O'Connor, Katherine Tiernan. "Chekhov's Death: His Textual Past Recaptured." In *Studies in Poetics: Commemorative Volume Krystyna Pomorska (1928–1986),* edited by E. Semeka-Pankratov, 39–50. Columbus, Ohio: Slavica, 1995.

———. "Chekhov on Chekhov: His Epistolary Self-Criticism." In *New Studies in Russian Language and Literature,* edited by A. L. Crone and C. V. Chvany, 239–45. Columbus, Ohio: Slavica, 1986.

Opul'skaia, L. D., et al., eds. *V tvorcheskoi laboratorii Chekhova.* Moscow: "Nauka," 1974.

Opul'skii, Al'bert. *Zhitiia sviatykh v tvorchestve russkikh pisatelei XIX veka.* East Lansing, Mich.: Russian Language Journal, 1986.

O'Toole, L. M. *Structure, Style, and Interpretation in the Russian Short Story.* New Haven: Yale University Press, 1982.

Pahomov, George. "Chekhov's 'The Grasshopper': A Secular Saint's Life." *Slavic and East European Journal* 37, no. 1 (1993): 33–45.

———. "Religious Motifs in Chekhov's 'Muzhiki.'" *Zapiski russkoi akademicheskoi gruppy v SSHA* 25 (1992–93): 111–19.

Pearce, Lynne. *Women/Image/Text: Readings in Pre-Raphaelite Art and Literature.* Toronto: University of Toronto Press, 1991.

Pelikan, Jaroslav. *Mary through the Centuries: Her Place in the History of Culture.* New Haven: Yale University Press, 1996.

Pirog, Gerald. *Aleksandr Blok's* Italianskie stikhi: *Confrontation and Disillusionment.* Columbus, Ohio: Slavica, 1983.

Polotskaia, E. A. *A. P. Chekhov: Dvizhenie khudozhestvennoi mysli.* Moscow: "Sovietskii pisatel'," 1979.

Popkin, Cathy. "Chekhov as Ethnographer: Epistemological Crisis on Sakhalin Island." *Slavic Review* 51, no. 1 (1992): 36–51.

———. "Paying the Price: The Rhetoric of Reckoning in Chekhov's 'Peasant Women.'" *Russian Literature* 35, no. 2 (1994): 203–22.

———. *The Pragmatics of Insignificance.* Stanford: Stanford University Press, 1993.

Racin, John. "Chekhov's Use of Church Ritual in 'Tatyana Repina.'" In *Drama and Religion,* edited by James Redmon, 1–19. Cambridge: Cambridge University Press, 1983.

Reed, Walter. *Dialogues of the Word: The Bible as Literature According to Bakhtin.* New York: Oxford University Press, 1993.

Rodgers, Audrey T. *Virgin and Whore: The Image of Women in the Poetry of William Carlos Williams.* Jefferson, N.C.: McFarland, 1987.

Sémon, Maria. *Les femmes dans l'oeuvre de Léon Tolstoï.* Paris: Institut d'études Slaves, 1984.

Senderovich, Marena. "Chekhov's Existential Trilogy." In Senderovich and Sendich, eds., *Anton Chekhov Rediscovered*, 77–91.

———. "Chekhov's Name Drama." In Jackson, ed., *Reading Chekhov's Text* 31–48.

———. "'Kashtanka' Chekhova: Metamorfozy pamiati v labirinte vremeni." *Russian Language Journal* 39 (1985): 121–33.

———. "The Implicit Semantic Unities in Chekhov's Work of 1886–1889." Ph.D. diss., New York University, 1981.

———. "The Symbolic Structure of Chekhov's Story 'An Attack of Nerves.'" In Debreczeny, ed., *Chekhov's Art of Writing*, 11–26.

Senderovich, Marena, and Savely Senderovich. *Penaty: Issledovaniia po russkoi poèzii*. East Lansing, Mich.: Russian Language Journal, 1990.

Senderovich, Savely. "Anton Chekhov and St. George the Dragonslayer (An Introduction to the Theme)." In Senderovich and Sendich, eds., *Anton Chekhov Rediscovered*, 167–87.

———. "Chekhov and Impressionism: An Attempt at a Systematic Approach to the Problem." In Debreczeny, ed., *Chekhov's Art of Writing*, 134–52.

———. *Chekhov s glazu na glaz*. Saint Petersburg: Izd. "Dmitrii Bulanin," 1994.

———. "Chudo Georgiia o zmie: Istoriia oderzhimosti Chekhova odnim obrazom." *Russian Language Journal* 39 (1985): 135–225.

———. "The End of Carnival in Anton Chekhov." In *Studies in Slavic Literature and Culture in Honor of Zoya Yurieff*, edited by M. Sendich, 293–302. East Lansing, Mich.: Russian Language Journal, 1988.

———. "A Fragment of Semiotic Theory of Poetic Prose (The Chekhovian Type)." *Essays in Poetics* 14, no. 2 (1989): 43–64.

———. *Georgii Pobedonosets v russkoi kul'ture*. New York: Peter Lang, 1994.

———. "K geneticheskoi èidologii 'Doktora Zhivago.' 1: Doktor Zhivago i poèt Chekhov." *Russian Language Journal* 45, no. 150 (1991): 3–16.

———. "K intellektual'noi istorii Rossii u Chekhova: 'Chernyi monakh.'" *Russian Language Journal* 48, nos. 159–61 (1994): 57–77.

———. "Poetics and Meaning in Chekhov's 'On the Road.'" In Senderovich and Sendich, eds., *Anton Chekhov Rediscovered*, 135–66.

———. "The Cherry Orchard: Čechov's Last Testament." *Russian Literature* 35 (1994): 223–42.

Senderovich, Savely, and Munir Sendich, eds. *Anton Chekhov Rediscovered: A Collection of New Studies With a Comprehensive Bibliography*. East Lansing, Mich.: Russian Language Journal, 1987.

Sherlock, Wallace. "The Pastoral Theme in the Short Stories of A. P. Chekhov." Ph.D. diss., Cornell University, 1996.

Shrayer, Maxim. "Christmas and Paschal Motifs in 'V rozhdestvenskuiu noch'.'" *Russian Literature* 35, no. 2 (1994): 243–59.

Siegel, George. "The Fallen Woman in Nineteenth-Century Russian Literature." *Harvard Slavic Studies* 5 (1970): 81–107.

Skaftymov, S. P. *Stat'i o russkoi literature*. Moscow, 1958.

Smith, Virginia Llewellyn. *Anton Chekhov and the Lady with the Dog*. London, 1973.

Sobennikov, A. S. "Bibleiskii obraz v proze A. P. Chekhova." In *O poètike A. P. Chekhova*, edited by A. S. Sobennikov, 23–38. Irkutsk: Izd. Irkutskogo universiteta, 1993.

Sorenson, R. "Puškin's *Gavriiliada:* From Style to Meaning." *Russian Language Journal* 35, no. 120 (1981): 59–73.

Stepanov, M. "Religiia A. P. Chekhova." *Religiia russkikh pisatelei* 1 (1913): 3–58.

Straus, Nina Pelikan. *Dostoevsky and the Woman Question*. New York: St. Martin's, 1994.

Sukhikh, I. N. *Problemy poètiki A. P. Chekhova*. Leningrad: Izd. Leningradskogo universiteta, 1987.

Tolstoguzov, P. N. "Skazka i skazochnost' v tvorchestve A. P. Chekhova 1880-kh godov (Na materiale rozhdestvennykh rasskazov pisatelia)." Ph.D. diss., Leningradskii ordena trudovogo krasnogo znameni gosudarstvennyi pedagogicheskii institut imeni A. I. Gertsena, 1988.

Tolstoy, Helena. "From Susanna to Sarra: Chekhov in 1886–1887." *Slavic Review* 50, no. 3 (1991): 590–600.

Windle, Kevin. "Shevchenko's Narrative Poem *Maria* in Three Russian Translations: A Comparative Study." *Australian Slavonic and East European Studies* 7, no. 1 (1993): 25–47.

Winner, Thomas. *Chekhov and His Prose*. New York: Holt, Rinehart and Winston, 1966.

Zaitsev, Boris. *Chekhov: Literaturnaia biografiia*. New York: Izd. imeni Chekhova, 1954.

Zakharov, V., ed. *Evangel'skii tekst v russkoi literature XVIII–XX vekov*. Petrozavodsk: Izd. Petrozavodskogo universiteta, 1994.

Ziolkowski, Margaret. *Hagiography and Modern Russian Literature*. Princeton: Princeton University Press, 1988.

SOURCES ON RELIGION AND CULTURE

Arkhimandrit, Panteleimon, ed. *Zhitiia sviatykh na russkom iazyke izlozhennyia po rukovodstvu Chet'ikh-minei sv. Dmitriia Rostovskago*. 12 vols. Moscow, 1902–11.

Baggley, John. *Doors of Perception*. Crestwood, N.Y.: St. Vladimir's Seminary Press, 1988.

Bouyer, Louis. "Le culte de Marie dans la liturgie byzantine." *Maison-Dieu* 38 (1954): 79–84.

Bulgakov, S. N. *Kupina neopalimaia*. Paris, 1927.

Bulgakov, S. V., ed. *Nastol'naia kniga dlia sviashchennotserkovno-sluzhitelei*. 1900. Reprint, Graz, Austria, 1965.

Carroll, Michael P. *The Cult of the Virgin Mary: Psychological Origins*. Princeton: Princeton University Press, 1986.

Dal', V. I. *Tolkovyi slovar'*. 4 vols. Moscow, 1905.

Dunlop, Olga, trans. *The Living God*. 2 vols. Crestwood, N.Y.: St. Vladimir's Seminary Press, 1989.

Duperray, Eve, ed. *Marie Madeleine dans la mystique, les arts, et les lettres*. Paris, 1989.

Ebbinghaus, Andreas. *Die altrussischen Marienikonen-Legenden*. Berlin: Otto Harrassowitz, 1990.

Fedotov, G. P. *The Russian Religious Mind, I and II*. Belmont, Mass.: Nordland, 1975.

———. *Stikhi dukhovnye (Russkaia narodnaia vera po dukhovnym stikham)*. Moscow: "Progress," 1991.

Florenskii, P. A. *Stolp i utverzhdenie very*. Berlin, 1929.

Galavaris, George. *The Icon in the Life of the Church*. Leiden: E. J. Brill, 1981.

Geertz, Clifford. *Interpretation of Cultures*. New York: Basic Books, 1973.

Haskins, Susan. *Mary Magdalen: Myth and Metaphor*. New York: Harcourt, Brace, 1994.

Holy Apostles Convent. *The Life of the Virgin Mary, The Theotokos*. Buena Vista, Colo., 1989.

Hubbs, Joanna. *Mother Russia: The Feminine Myth in Russian Culture*. Bloomington: Indiana University Press, 1988.

Izbrannye akafisty i kanony. Saint Petersburg, 1994.

Izbrannye slova sviatykh ottsev v chest' i slavu Presviatoi Bogoroditsy. Moscow, 1896.

Kargalov, V. V. *Pokrov*. Moscow: Izd. politicheskoi literatury, 1975.

Khanilo, A. V. "Ikony i kresty A. P. Chekhova i ego blizkikh v ialtinskom muzee." Paper presented at the Second Badenweiler Symposium, "A. P. Chekhov—Religious and Philosophical Dimensions in His Life and Work," Badenweiler, Germany, October 1994.

Kirpichnikov, A. I. *Uspenie Bogoroditsy v legende i v iskusstve*. Odessa, 1888.

Kisin, Boris. *Bogoroditsa v russkoi literature*. Moscow, 1929.

Kondakov, N. P. *Ikonografiia Bogomateri*. 2 vols. Petrograd, 1914–15.

Korotkova, Z. M. *Bogorodichnye prazdniki*. Moscow: Izd. politicheskoi literatury, 1968.

Kozhanchikov, D. E., ed. *Pesni sobrannye P. N. Rybnikovym.* Saint Petersburg, 1867.

Ledit, Joseph. *Marie dans la Liturgie de Byzance.* Paris: Beauchesne, 1976.

Makarenko, Aleksei. *Sibirskii narodnyi kalendar'.* Saint Petersburg, 1913.

Miles, Margaret R. *Image as Insight: Visual Understanding in Western Christianity and Secular Culture.* Boston: Beacon, 1985.

Nekrylova, A. F., ed. *Kruglyi god: russkii zemledel'cheskii kalendar'.* Moscow: "Pravda," 1990.

Ouspensky, L., and V. Lossky. *The Meaning of Icons.* Olten, Switzerland: URS Graf, 1956.

Pokrovskii, N. *Blagoveshchenie Presv. Bogoroditsy v pamiatnikakh ikonografii.* Saint Petersburg, 1891.

Rozanov, V. V. *Liudi lunnago sveta. Metafizika khristianstva.* Saint Petersburg, 1913.

———. *Sochineniia.* Moscow, 1990.

Saint John of Damascus. *On the Divine Images.* Crestwood, N.Y.: St. Vladimir's Seminary Press, 1980.

Sheffer, Natalia. *Russkaia pravoslavnaia ikona.* Washington, D.C., 1967.

Skazaniia o chudotvornykh ikonakh Bozhiei Materi imenuemoi "Mlekopitatel'nitsa." Odessa, 1900.

Skazaniia o zemnoi zhizni Presviatoi Bogoroditsy. Moscow, 1904.

Snessoreva, S., ed. *Zemnaia zhizn' Presviatoi Bogoroditsy i opisanie sviatykh chudotvornykh ee ikon.* Yaroslavl': Verkhne-Volzhskoe knizhnoe izd., 1994.

Soloshchenko, L. F., and Iu. S. Prokoshina, eds. *Golubinaia kniga. Russkie narodnye dukhovnye stikhi XI–XIX vekov.* Moscow: Moskovskii rabochii, 1991.

Strotmann, D. T. "Quelques aperçus historiques sur le culte marial en Russie." *Irénikon* 32 (1959): 178–202.

Uspenskii, B. A. *Filologicheskie razyskaniia v oblasti slavianskikh drevnostei.* Moscow: Izd. Moskovskogo universiteta, 1982.

———. *Iz istorii russkikh kanonicheskikh imen.* Moscow: Izd. Moskovskogo universiteta, 1969.

———. "Mifologicheskii aspekt russkoi ekspressivnoi frazeologii." Parts 1 and 2. *Studia Slavica Academiae Scientiarum Hungaricae* 29 (1983): 33–69; 33 (1987): 37–76.

———. *The Semiotics of the Russian Icon.* Lisse: Peter de Ridder, 1976.

The Orthodox Prayer Book/Pravoslavnyi molitvoslov. South Canaan, Pa.: St. Tikhon's, 1975.

Velikii sbornik. 5 vols. Jordanville, N.Y., 1951.

Ward, Benedicta, S.L.G. *Harlots of the Desert.* Kalamazoo, Mich.: Cistercian Publications, 1987.

Warner, Marina. *Alone of All Her Sex.* New York: Vintage Books, 1983.

Index

Akhmatova, A. A.: "By the Sea," 117; *Requiem*, 147; "Today Is the Nameday of the Smolensk Virgin," 146
Aksakov, I. S.: "Mary of Egypt," 13, 33–35, 83
Aleksei, Man of God, 27, 38
Almazov, B. N.: "Mary of Egypt," 34, 83
Amert, Susan, 147
Andrews, Joe, 31
Annensky, I. F., 78
Avvakum, 127
Axelrod, W. C., 156n29, 166n18, 167n23

Bakhtin, M. M., 3, 9, 67, 91, 154n7
Baratynsky, E.: "Madonna," 32
Barthes, Roland, 3
Batiushkov, K. N.: "To Masha," 30, 117
Beloborodov, M., 68–70, 73–74, 87, 165n7
Berlin, Isaiah, 42
Blok, A. A., 7, 147; *Italian Verses*, 146; "The Twelve," 143
Bocharov, S. G., 46
Bogoroditsa, see Mary, Virgin
Bouyer, Louis, 21
Bulgakov, M. A.: *The Master and Margarita*, 148
Bulgakov, S. N., 14, 154n13
Bunin, I. A.: "The Flight to Egypt," 146

Carroll, Michael, 14
Chekhov, Aleksandr Pavlovich, 1, 23
Chekhov, Anton Pavlovich: and authoritarian religious discourse, 3, 9–10, 46, 67, 86–87, 91–95, 126, 145; childhood, 1, 23, 42–43,

54, 63; and Christianity, criticism, 4–5, 7, 154nn11, 13–15, 155nn18–22, 156n29, 157n39; correspondence, 3, 7–8, 154nn10, 12, 161n48; 164n19, 172n21, 173n4; dissertation, 21; drama, 1, 6, 57, 89, 119, 144, 154n13, 172n21; ethnographic perspective of, 4–5, 21, 60, 65, 88; functions of iconography in, 19, 55–56, 71, 75–78, 82, 84, 122, 131–33, 135; intentionality, 2, 6–8, 50, 56, 65, 87, 77, 110–11; intertextuality in prose, 3, 52, 59, 68–70, 107, 109–13, 169n1; name "Maria" in prose, 15, 46, 48, 51–52, 54–58, 61, 63, 73, 77, 81, 83, 100, 108, 115, 126, 131, 143, 163n2; 164n11; names/surnames in prose, 5, 48–50, 54, 59, 61–62, 71, 77, 90, 94, 96, 99, 101, 110, 116, 126–29, 137–38; as phenomenologist, 9, 42, 65, 125; play with language ("translation"), 45–47; poetics, 6–7, 21, 42–43, 107, 115, 119, 144; and women, 8–9, 23, 93, 156n34
—Works of (*see also* English and Russian titles of Marian stories, 151–52): "3,000 Foreign Words That Have Entered Russian," 47; "At Christmastide," 21; "An Attack of Nerves," 68, 83, 85–87, 114, 164n10; "The Bishop," 143–44; *The Cherry Orchard*, 119; "Choirboys," 153n1; "The Cobbler and the Evil Spirit," 131; "The Correspondent," 55, 56, 164n10; "The Dowry," 57, 58, 117, 164nn10, 11; "A Dreadful Night," 60, 62–65,

185

116, 144, 164n20; "The Duel," 86, 167n31; "During Passion Week," 55, 59, 96, 163n9; "The Enemies," 156n28; "Failure," 55; *Fatherless*, 89; "Fear," 171n20; "The Grateful One," 52–53; "The Green Spit," 164n10; "Grief," 116, 165n21; "Incident with a Classics Scholar," 65; "In the Autumn," 56–58, 164n10; "The Lady," 10, 68–74, 81, 87, 91, 121, 164n10, 165n9, 166nn10, 12; "Lady with a Dog," 86; "Late-blooming Flowers," 164n10; "A Letter to a Learned Neighbor," 163n4; "A Liberal Fellow," 119, 131; "Love Spurned," 46; "Maria Ivanovna," 7, 58–59; "A Meeting," 19; "Murder," 18; "My Life," 9, 11, 62, 125–42, 144, 173n4, 174n14, 17; "The Nameday Party," 164n10, 171n17; "On Christmas Night," 173n7; "On Holy Night," 20, 48; "On the Open Road," 57; "On the Road," 55, 65, 131, 154n13, 164n10; "O, Women, Women," 96; "Peasants," 7, 10, 19, 68, 74–83, 115, 121, 142, 164n10, 166n18, 167nn21–23; "Peasant Women," 8, 10, 51, 89–105, 107, 121, 126, 142, 145, 168n7, 169nn13, 16; "The Philistines," 108; "The Requiem," 10, 26, 68, 83–85, 87, 126, 164n10, 167n29; *Sakhalin Island*, 67; "The Sinner from Toledo," 50, 51; "The Stationmaster," 53, 54; "The Steppe," 97; "Surgery," 156n28; "The Swedish Match," 51–52, 59, 109; *Tatiana Repina*, 1, 119, 153n2; "The Teacher of Literature," 9–10, 35, 64, 107–24, 135, 142, 144, 170nn7, 8; "Tears the World Doesn't See," 47–50, 145; *Three Sisters*, 154n13; "Three Years," 164n12; "Trouble," 56; "The Uproar," 9, 60–62; "The Wedding Season," 164n11; "Without a Title," 65; "A Woman's Kingdom," 115–16, 131, 170n15
Chekhov, Mikhail Pavlovich, 1
Chekhov, Pavel Egorovich, 1, 19, 23, 43, 54, 153n1
Chekhova, Evgeniia Yakovlevna, 23
Chekhova, Maria Pavlovna, 19, 23, 46, 50, 160n33, 172n24
Chernyshevsky, N. G., 8, 67

Christ, 4, 14–16, 18–19, 22, 31–32, 40, 65, 80–81, 91, 100, 103, 129–30; and myrrophores, 1, 27; and "sinful" women, 24, 35, 72, 119, 147, 160n37; Ascension, 18, 25, 58; depicted on icons, 23, 55, 84, 139; Easter, 18, 143, 170n15; Epiphany (*Kreshchen'e*), 122, 164n20; Last Judgment of, 81, 82, 93
Chudakov, A. P., 163n1
Costlow, Jane, 162n66

Daniel, Book of, 11, 20, 127–30, 135
Danilevsky G. P.: *Princess Tarakanova*, 61
de Maegd-Soëp, Caroline, 8, 157n37
Dostoevsky, F. M., 4, 9, 36–40, 43, 51, 68, 101, 107, 109, 122, 135; *The Adolescent*, 37; *The Brothers Karamazov*, 38; *Crime and Punishment*, 39, 52, 99; *The Devils*, 39, 40; *The Idiot*, 39; "Akulka's Husband," 94, 105; "Polzunkov," 38, 148
Du Bos, Charles, 107
Dudek, Andrzej, 30, 174n5

Ecclesiastes, Book of, 127, 135, 172n3
Emerson, Caryl, 6
Epiphanius the Wise, 28

Fedotov, G. P., 19, 158n11, 167nn25, 28, 173n10
Fet, A. A.: "Ave Maria," 32; "The Fornicatress," 35; "Madonna," 32; "Our Lady of Zion," 32; "Sistine Madonna," 32
Finke, Michael, 6, 39, 71, 157n37, 169n1
Forrester, Sibelan, 147
Frye, Northrop, 125
Fusso, Susanna, 40

Gabriel, Archangel, 18, 30, 63–64, 117–18, 137, 144, 171n20
Galich, A.: "Ave Maria," 146
Garshin, V. M., 87
Geertz, Clifford, 67
Gogol, N. I., 4, 9, 43, 68, 107, 109; "Nevsky Prospect," 168n35; *Taras Bulba*, 36, 37; "Woman in the World," 37
Gorky, A. M., 21, 146, 173n8

Hahn, Beverly, 8
Haskins, Susan, 27, 160nn35, 36, 41
Hebbel, Friedrich: "The Sinful Woman," 35

Index

Heldt, Barbara, 8

Ivanov, V. I., 146
Izmailov, A., 4

Jackson, Robert Louis, 5, 6, 38, 39, 122,
    166nn11, 12, 169n1, 170n15, 175n12
Jacob: prophecy of ladder (Genesis), 20, 64,
    116, 137; and well, 103
Jakobson, Roman, 7
Job, Book of, 109, 126
John, Gospel of, 24, 103
Joyce, James: "The Dead," 122
Judaism, 5, 10, 79, 89, 102, 103, 125, 128;
    Hebrew language, 2, 19, 135

Karamzin, N. M.: "Poor Liza," 32
Karlinsky, Simon, 4, 91, 162n65
Kataev, V. B., 168n32
Kiselev, L.: "Mary Magdalene," 143, 147
Kiseleva, Maria, 21, 161n48
Kisin, Boris, 145–46, 158n5
Klychkov, S.: "The Storyteller of
    Chertukhinsk," 117
Knipper, Olga, 144, 149
Koltsov, A. K.: "The Harvest," 32
Kramer, Karl, 113
Kristeva, Julia, 2, 74
Kuprin, A. I.: "The Garden of the Most
    Pure Virgin," 146
Kuzicheva, A. P., 159n32, 173n11

Lafitte, Sophie, 8
Lay of Igor's Host, 28
Lermontov, M. Yu., 107, 109; "Prayer," 32
Leskov, N. S., 4, 40, 51, 68, 101, 107; "Lady
    Macbeth of the Mtsensk District," 52
Lessing, G. E., 109, 114
Lotman, Yu. M., 31
Luke, Gospel of, 24, 72, 94, 118, 147,
    160n36

Marian Paradigm, see Marys, Christian
Mark, Gospel of, 50
Mary Magdalene (see also Marys, "Sinful"),
    1, 9, 13, 23–27, 33, 65, 86, 123, 144; in
    Dostoevsky, 38–39; in "The Lady," 72;
    in "Peasant Women," 94; in poetry, 143,
    147; in A. K. Tolstoy, 119; in Turgenev,

37; interpretations of, 24, 160n37; in "A
    Woman's Kingdom," 171n15
Mary of Bethany, 24, 39, 162n69
Mary of Egypt (see also Marys, "Sinful"),
    1, 2, 9, 13–14, 23–28, 65, 67, 123, 144,
    155n23, 156n28, 160n40; in "An Attack
    of Nerves," 10, 86; in Dostoevsky, 37–38;
    in "My Life" (echo of), 139–40, 174n14;
    in Nabokov (echo of), 148; in Pasternak,
    124; in "Peasant Women" (echo of), 94;
    in poetry, 29, 33–35; in Remizov, 147;
    in "The Requiem," 10, 83, 85; in "The
    Teacher of Literature" (echo of), 120
Marys, Christian (Marian paradigm), 1,
    6, 9, 11, 14, 28, 36, 42, 60, 68, 144–45;
    in Almazov, 34; in Dostoevsky, 38; in
    "My Life," 135, 140–41; in "Peasant
    Women," 102; in Pushkin, 1, 31; in "The
    Teacher of Literature," 115–16, 123;
    Madonna/whore syndrome, 29
Marys, "Sinful," 23–25, 39, 65, 144–45;
    loose hair, 23, 26, 37, 82, 86, 116, 122,
    147, 174n14; nudity of, 26, 28, 82, 123
Mary, Virgin (Mother of God), 1–2, 9–11,
    27, 102, 144, 149, 155n23, 159nn26, 27,
    164n12; dark blue robe, 55, 58, 117;
    folk verse about, 21–22; Immaculate
    Conception, 14, 18, 147; in "The Bishop,"
    143; in "The Dowry," 58; in "A Dreadful
    Night," 62–65; in "During Passion Week,"
    55, 59, 163n9; in "The Lady," 69–70, 73; in
    liturgical text, 73, 132; in "My Life," 130–
    35, 137, 139–41; in "On the Open Road"
    ("In the Autumn"), 57; in "The Peasants,"
    75–82; in realist prose, 36–42; in "The
    Requiem," 84–85; in "The Teacher of
    Literature," 115–21; in twentieth-century
    letters, 145–48; in "The Uproar," 60–61;
    and milk/nurturance, 81–82, 98, 112, 121,
    123, 144; Orthodox appellations, 15, 28;
    Orthodox vs. Catholic, 13–18; patroness
    of marriage, 22, 39, 41, 53, 56, 58, 69, 115,
    117, 119, 126; prayers to, 13–15, 18, 23,
    34–35, 53, 73, 78, 115; and Romanticism,
    30–32, 52–53, 171n20
    —Acathist to, 2, 19–21, 27, 58, 89,
        144, 158n22, 171n20; in "A Dreadful
        Night," 63–64; in "My Life," 173nn12,
        13; in "Tears the World Doesn't See,"

187

47–49; in "The Teacher of Literature," 117, 121
—Apocrypha concerning, 16, 19, 31, 117, 155n23; "The Dream of the Mother of God," 15, 64; "The Virgin's Travels Through the Torments," 21–22, 64, 75, 81
—Holidays and iconography of, 2, 3, 9–11, 13–19, 21–25, 27–29, 32, 34, 35, 40, 51, 54–59, 75, 139, 144, 146, 158n14, 169n13; Annunciation, 18, 19, 30–31, 47, 62–63, 81, 115–18, 120, 123, 137, 144, 147, 159n33, 171n20, 174n14; Bogolubsky, 15, 54; Burning Bush, 63; "Chairete," 1, 27; Christmas, 18, 65, 115–16, 119, 131, 136, 173n7; Crucifixion, 1, 27, 55; Dormition (Assumption), 14, 18–19, 39, 50, 69, 76, 81–82, 120, 144, 158n9, 171n16; Intercession or Veil (*Pokrov*), 15, 19, 41, 69, 76, 79, 147, 158n17, 165n8; Hodegitria, 17, 84; Kazan Mother of God, 19, 39, 69, 78, 132–33, 135, 173n10; Life-Bearer, 74–78, 82–83; Smolensk Mother of God, 23, 146, 167n20; Uncut Mountain, 64; Vladimir Mother of God, 167n23
Matthew, Gospel of, 24, 80, 89, 93, 104, 116
Mayakovsky, V. V., 7, 78, 107
Merezhkovsky, D. S., 4
Miles, Margaret, 27
Mizinova, Liza, 23, 159n33, 172n24
Mother of God, *see* Mary, Virgin

Nabokov, V. V.: "Mary," 148
Nekrasov, N. A.: "When from the Darkness of Erring Ways," 168n35
Novikov, N. I.: *Letters to Falalei,* 28

O'Connor, Katherine T., 149, 154n12
O'Toole, L. M., 75, 79
Ouspensky, Leonid, 58

Pagels, Elaine, 125, 160n37
Pahomov, George, 156n29, 166n18
Pasternak, B. L.: *Doctor Zhivago,* 24, 147, 148, 175n10
Pearce, Lynne, 75
Pechersky, Andrei, 51–52

Pelikan, Jaroslav, 157n2
Pirog, Gerald, 146, 161n57
Pleshcheev, A. N., 87; "The Sinful Woman," 35
Polezhaev, A. I.: "The Sinful Woman," 35
Polonsky, Ia. P., 135
Polotsky, Simeon, 128
Popkin, Cathy, 96, 98, 165n1, 168n5
Pushkin, A. S., 7, 9, 29–32, 43, 107, 109, 115, 118, 138; "An Acathist to E. N. Karamzina," 48; *Boris Godunov,* 109; *Count Nulin,* 108, 110–13, 123; "Earthly Authority," xiv, 1, 27, 31; *Eugene Onegin,* 46, 109; "Gavriiliada," 30–31, 53; *The Fountain of Bakchisarai,* 31; "Madonna," 31; *Poltava,* 31, 170n7; "A poor knight lived in the world," 31; "You are the Mother of God, there is no doubt," 31

Remizov, A. M., 146
Roman Catholicism, 5, 21, 50, 126; Marian figures in, 9, 13–15, 19, 22, 23, 25, 26, 32, 51, 58, 120, 149, 153n5, 159n23
Rozanov, V. V., 90, 91, 105
Russian Orthodoxy (*see also* Christ; Mary, Virgin), 3, 7, 19, 36, 46, 67–68, 85, 90, 120, 125, 127, 132, 137–38, 142, 145, 148; ascetic ideal, 24, 26; saints, 13, 25, 90, 100–101; liturgy, 19, 73, 77, 153n3; Magdalene in, 24; Marian dogma, 14–18

Saint George, 2, 5, 6, 55, 115, 155n23, 164n10, 166n10
Saint John of Damascus, 16, 35
Saint Mary Magdalene, *see* Mary Magdalene
Saint Mary of Egypt, *see* Mary of Egypt
Saint Nicholas, 23, 81
Saint Sophia (Divine Wisdom), 10, 13, 90, 96, 99, 104
Saint Thomas, 19, 132
Saint Varvara, 10, 13, 90, 96–98, 103–4
Sandler, Stephanie, 31
Sémon, Marie, 41
Senderovich, Marena, 6, 9, 65, 86, 87, 114, 154n12
Senderovich, Savely, 2, 5–7, 55, 83, 115, 144, 157n37, 164nn10, 11, 166n10, 167n22, 175n10
Senelick, Laurence, 6, 71

Index

Shakhova, E.: "The Power of Repentance," 34, 35, 83, 162n63
Shakespeare, William, 107, 138; *The Rape of Lucrece*, 110–13
Shevchenko, T. G.: "Maria," 32–33
Shklovsky, Viktor, 68
Shrayer, Maxim, 156n29, 173n7
Smith, Virginia L., 8, 165n9, 168n6, 173n6
Sobennikov, A. S., 155n16
Solovyov, V. S., 68, 99, 155n16
Solzhenitsyn, A. I.: "Matryona's Home," 148, 166n14
Sorensen, Robert, 30
Stolitsa, L.: "The Mother of God," 146
Straus, Nina Pelikan, 40
Strottman, D. J., 158nn6, 16, 159n28
Sukhikh, I. N., 145, 163n1
Suvorin, A. S., 109, 142; Chekhov correspondence, 154n10, 155n17, 158n19, 165n4, 169nn3, 5, 170n11; *Novoe vremia*, 60, 95, 155n17

Terts, A.: "Good Night," 143
Tiutchev, F. I., 32; "Oh my prophetic soul!" 33
Tolstoguzov, P. N., 65

Tolstoy, A. K., 108; "The Sinful Woman," 11, 35, 118–20, 172n23
Tolstoy, L. N., 4, 9, 11, 29, 36, 37, 40–43, 68, 80, 101, 107, 109, 122, 125, 127, 129, 132; *Anna Karenina*, 6, 37, 40, 78, 95, 168n35; "The Cossacks," 40; "The Death of Ivan Ilych," 123; "Family Happiness," 40; "Father Sergius," 41, 42; *Khadzhi Murat*, 41; "My Life," 127; *The Power of Darkness*, 105; *Resurrection*, 41; *War and Peace*, 41, 167n20
Tsvetaeva, M. I, 146; "Magdalene," 147; "On Annunciation Day," 147
Turgenev, I. S., 9, 36, 43, 107; *Fathers and Children*, 37; *A Nest of Gentry*, 37; *Notes of a Hunter*, 74; "Spring Torrents," 37

Uspenskii, B. A., 18, 166n16, 167n27

Virgin Mary, *see* Mary, Virgin

Warner, Marina, 2, 153n5, 157n2, 160nn35, 42, 163n79
Weber, Max, 4
Woolf, Virginia, 62

Zhukovsky, V, A.: "Mary's Grove," 29